The Trinity's Weak Links Revealed

The Trinity's Weak Links Revealed

A chain is only as strong as it's weakest link

Robert L. George

iUniverse, Inc.
New York Lincoln Shanghai

The Trinity's Weak Links Revealed
A chain is only as strong as it's weakest link

Copyright © 2007 by Robert L. George

All rights reserved. No part of this book may be used or reproduced by any means, graphic, electronic, or mechanical, including photocopying, recording, taping or by any information storage retrieval system without the written permission of the publisher except in the case of brief quotations embodied in critical articles and reviews.

iUniverse books may be ordered through booksellers or by contacting:

iUniverse
2021 Pine Lake Road, Suite 100
Lincoln, NE 68512
www.iuniverse.com
1-800-Authors (1-800-288-4677)

The views expressed in this work are solely those of the author and do not necessarily reflect the views of the publisher, and the publisher hereby disclaims any responsibility for them.

ISBN: 978-0-595-44288-1 (pbk)
ISBN: 978-0-595-88617-3 (ebk)

Printed in the United States of America

This book is dedicated exclusively to my God Jehovah from my "whole heart, soul, mind, and strength," (Mark 12:30). May the words within leave the printed page and adhere themselves into the hearts of those "conscious of their spiritual need," (Matthew 5:3). This will rightfully bring honor and glory to the one and only true God, through his Son, Jesus Christ.

"You are worthy, Jehovah, even our God, to receive the glory and the honor and the power, because you created all things, and because of your will they existed and were created," (Revelation 4:11-*NWT*).

Contents

Acknowledgements xi
Bible abbreviations xiii
Introduction xvii
    Is it easy to identify Jesus Christ? xvii
    A 'trinity' of weak links revealed xxi
    Must rely on scriptures alone xxiii
    Knowledge or accurate knowledge? xxiv
    Questions for meditation xxvi
Part I   Development of the trinity chain 1
    Today's definition of the trinity 2
    The Didache 3
    Apostle's Creed 4
    Nicene Creed 5
    Athanasian Creed 9
    Does your church accept these creeds and trinity doctrine? 13
    The first weak link identified 15
    Is the trinity unique to Christendom? 24
    Bible scholars in Jesus' day vs. scholars of today 25
    Is it a mystery or just plain confusion? 26
    Jesus answers with logic and reason 28
    The 'missing link' 33
    Final thoughts 39
Part II   Who is the only true God?—John 17:3 43
    Titles and personal names 43
    Does God have a personal name? 45
    The importance of a personal name 46

How does Jehovah feel about his name?..48
How did Jesus view his Father's name?...51
No scholarly evidence of removal of divine name? 52
A difference between LORD and Jehovah? 54
Why Jehovah & not Yahweh? 55
Does kyrios ever refer to Jehovah?...62
Great opposition to the Christian Greek Scriptures 68
Hallelujah...70
The Father Jehovah is the only true God 73
Jehovah is Father of Jesus Christ 74
Only one biblical conclusion 75
List of English Bible's containing divine name in NT 78
List of Hebrew Bible's containing divine name in NT 85

PART III   Does Almighty God have a God? 87
Jesus Christ has a God?..87
Jesus Christ is not Almighty God 90
More scriptural proof Jesus has a God 91
How is it then Jesus is a God?..95

Part IV   The conclusion of the matter...101
Which anchor is your 'chain' attached to?..101
Review of weak link one 102
Review of weak link two 110
Review of weak link three 114
The truth will set you free 118
Worship what we know 122

Part V   Extra biblical exegeses—John 1:1 125
Test your belief against the whole Bible 125
Jesus and Paul fully reasoned from the scriptures 126
Definition of 'God'...127
Scrutinizing John 1:1...128
Many Scholars agree Jesus is 'a' god. 132

Is Jesus Christ a false God?		134
Ones correctly called G/god in the Bible		136
The Sahidic Coptic translation of John 1:1c		139
Final thoughts		140
List of translations regarding John 1:1		141
Part VI	Extra biblical exegeses: knowledge—John 17:3	149
	Salvation through literature?	149
	John 17:3 mistranslated?	149
	Christians are witnesses of Jesus & Jehovah	151
Part VII	Extra biblical exegeses: The cross—a Christian symbol?	154
	Spiritually trained mind must lead us	154
	Meaning of the word cross	155
	Origin of the cross	161
	Adoration and worship of the cross	165
	Be determined to worship God in truth	168

Acknowledgements

My first recognition of deep heartfelt gratitude belongs to my self-sacrificing wife Kym, affectionately "Blue Eyes." Her loyal support and never doubting the accomplishing of this book enabled me to persist on. You willingly set aside 'our time' together for me. I indeed truly know how much of a sacrifice it was for you, so does Jehovah. The Bible asks: "A capable wife who can find? Her *value* is far more than that of corals," (Proverbs 31:1). I found this woman and she is you. Kym, you are an invaluable and precious wife. I love you Blue Eyes.

I want to thank my children Amanda, Sara, and Jeremia for their patience and many lessons we have learned together. It is my sincere heartfelt desire for you to always make Jehovah your true Father and Jesus your only leader. Your Dad loves each of you and always will. You are truly a precious gift from God.

It would require another book to include all my family members and friends who have guided me thus far and enabled me to write a book such as this. However, first and foremost is a very special thanks to my parents, Mom and Pop. It must have taken an enormous amount of special love to adopt a boy at the age of eight. But where would I be today without you? May the true God bless all your love and kind acts shown to so many over the years. I love you with all my heart.

Claus and Pauline, thank-you for your love and patience with me. It was you twenty years ago, that taught me the precious truths of God's Word. You will always have a special place in my heart. I love you.

Appreciation and gratefulness are certainly in order for my very superlative friends, the Johnson family. Jehovah has indeed blessed us immensely when he allowed our families to draw closer together. Jehovah says: "There exists a friend sticking closer than a brother," (Proverbs 18:24). You have without a doubt proven this proverbial saying true. From my heart to yours, I love you.

Also my good friend, Jay Baugniet, deserves special thanks. You helped to open my 'spiritual ears' to hear God's written Word as an orchestra, not just a one-man band. Hearing God's Word in stereo has given me more zeal and love of truth than I ever thought possible. My relationship with Jehovah and his Son Jesus has been made firmer and has drawn me closer than I ever imagined. Thank-you.

I most assuredly cannot forget the influence of one very humble, loyal and faithful servant of Jehovah; my mother-in-law, "Mama Girl." Your being a part of our family has helped me to understand so much better how it is to be self-sacrificing. You are an example to all of us. I love you.

It is always a little nerve racking to speak from your heart concerning what you have found to be truth, especially towards family and friends. It is even harder to divulge one's inner feelings through a book for the world to see. However, a special thanks to my Uncle who advised me in my teen years these wise words: 'You cannot please everyone.' I would perhaps like to add: 'if you try to please everyone all the time, you will never be happy any of the time.' Why? Because trying to please man is the end result of already possessing fear of man. I have learned from this little phrase through life and from study of God's word the Bible whom we should be pleasing and having reverential fear of. "The conclusion of the matter, everything having been heard, is: Fear the [true] God and keep his commandments. For this is the whole [obligation] of man," (Ecclesiastes 12:13). I thank Jehovah for all my family and friends.

Bible abbreviations

ALT	- Analytical Literal Translation, Gary Zeolla, second edition	2005
ASV	- American Standard Version	1901
AT	- American Translation, Smith, Goodspeed	1940
CEV	- Contemporary English Version	1995
CPV	- Cotton Patch Version, Clarence Jordan	1969
DBW	- The Emphatic Diaglott, Benjamin Wilson	1942
DSS	- The Dead Sea Scrolls, Abegg Jr., Flint, Ulrich	1999
EB	- Emphasized Bible, J.B. Rotherham	1994
ENT	- Extreme New Testament, Tommy Tenney	2001
FF	- Ferrar Fenton	1903
FPE	- Five Pauline Epistles, W.G. Rutherford	1984
GHCM	- The Gospel of John, G.H.C. MacGregor	1928
GNB	- Good News Bible	1977
GWN	- God's Word to the Nations	1995
HBJS	- Holy Bible, Julia E. Smith, 1876, reprint edition	2000
HCSB	- Holman Christian Standard Bible	2004
ISV	- International Standard Version	1999
JB	- Jerusalem Bible	1968
JBP	- J.B. Philips, The NT in Modern English	1972
JD	- John N. Darby	1998
JGA	- NT Everyday American English, Julian G. Anderson	1992
JWCW	- The NT Letters, J. W. C. Wand, 1947	1947
KI	- The Kingdom Interlinear Translation of the Greek Scriptures	1995
KJV	- King James Version,	1972
KL	- The New Testament, Kleist and Lilly	1952
LCNTV	- A Literal And Consistent NT Version, Donald A. Nash	1998
LD	- Living Destiny, Marley Cole	1987
LDB	- The Last Days NT	1999
LXX	- Septuagint Version, Charles Thomson, 1808, reprint	1954
LXX2	- Septuagint Version, Sir Lancelot C.L. Brenton, reprint	2001
MKJV	- Modern King James Version, Jay P. Green Sr.	1998
MNT	- Helen B. Montgomery NT	1924
NAB	- New American Bible	1995

NASB	-New American Standard Bible	2002
NBAV	-New Berkley Authorized Version	1998
NCV	-The Devotional Bible, New Century Version, Max Lucado	2003
NEB	-New English Bible	1972
NIV	-New International Version	1995
NIVI	-The New International Version Greek Interlinear	1976
NJB	-New Jerusalem Bible	1999
NKJVI	-The New King James Version Greek Interlinear	1994
NLT	-New Living Translation	2000
NMB	-The New Millennium Bible, A Rendition, George A. Wallace	2004
NRSV	-New Revised Standard Version	1989
NS	-The NT, Nathaniel Scarlett, reprint	1992
NSB	-New Simplified Bible, Jim Madsen	2005
NWT	-New World Translation reference edition	1984
PTM	-Psalms, The Message, Eugene H. Peterson	1994
RAK	-The Old Testament In English, Ronald A. Knox	1949
RJC	-Richard J. Clifford, A Commentary	1999
RL	-The NT, A New Translation, Richard Lattimore	1998
RSV	-Revised Standard Version	1952
RVNT	-Revised Version NT	1881
TA	-The Apocalypse, Willis Barnestone	2000
TAB	-The Amplified Bible	1987
TB	-The Book	1971
TBJ	-The Book of Jeremiah, N. L. Brown	1921
TBLE	-The Bible in Living English, Steven T. Byington	1972
TCNT	-The 20th Century New Testament, Revised Edition	1904
TCVNT	-The Coptic Version NT, 2/3 century, reprint Horner	1911
TFG	-The Five Gospels, Robert W. Funk, Roy W. Hoover	1993
TGOJ	-The Genius of John, A Critical Commentary, Peter F. Ellis	1984
TINT	-The Inclusive NT	1994
TLB	-The Living Bible, Tyndale publishers	1988
TM	-The Message, Eugene H. Peterson	1993
TMB	-The Millennium Bible, William Edward Biederwolf	1964
TNIV	-Today's New International Version NT	2001
TNTBW	-The New Testament, Charles B. Williams	1950
TP	-The Psalms, Samuel Terrien	1952
TPNT	-The Pioneer's New Testament, Ruth P. Martin	2002
TS	-The Scriptures	2002
TST	-The NT from 26 Translations	1967

TUNT	-The Unvarnished NT, Andy Gaus	1991
VC	-21st Century New Testament, Vivian Capel	2000
WB	-The NT Vol. II, A New Translation by William Barclay	1969
WEY	-The NT in Modern Speech, Richard Francis Weymouth	1903
WFB	-The NT in the Language of Today, W. F. Beck	1964
YLT	-Young's Literal Translation of the Bible, Revised Ed.	1907

All Scriptures are quoted from the 1901 American Standard Version, unless otherwise stated with one of the abbreviations above. NT refers to New Testament.

Introduction

Is it easy to identify Jesus Christ?

In the year 33CE during the Jewish month of Nisan 14—March/April—Jesus Christ had just completed a covenant between his eleven, remaining disciples, and himself, in a quiet, upper room in Jerusalem. Although Jesus and his disciples had celebrated the annual Passover for the previous three years, Jesus was fully aware that the symbolic, foreshadowed Passover lamb was to be special this year. The weight of fulfilling the prophecies regarding the Messiah had to be accomplished—perfectly.[1] Jesus knew of the sacrificial death that was to be offered, not only on behalf of the world's undeserved benefit, but to honor his Father in the heavens.[2] This year, Jesus Christ was to be the sacrificial lamb. The apostle Paul confirms this when he states: "… For Christ is for us the Passover Lamb, sacrificed for our deliverance."[3] Still, this kindhearted and compassionate one—Jesus Christ—says: "I have looked forward to celebrating this Passover with you with all my heart before my ordeal begins."[4] Prior to all twelve leaving that upper chamber to head towards the garden of Gethsemane—which would forever change their ordinary lives—Jesus offers this selfless prayer on his disciples' behalf: "Father, the hour has come. Glorify Your Son … This is eternal life: that they may know You, the only true God, and the One You have sent—Jesus Christ."[5] Can you visualize a more severe, emotionally stimulating, and heart-rending event for the Son of God? Hebrews 5:7 reads: "In the days of his flesh, with bitter cries and weeping Jesus offered up prayers and supplications to Him who was able to save him out of death; and he was heard because of his devout submission."[6]

The only successful perfect man to have ever walked this earth was the long awaited for messiah, Jesus Christ. His influence, motivating words, loving deeds, and sacrifice have touched the lives of countless individuals—and changed the world forever. Even if for this reason only, it would be in our greatest interest to come to know whom this Jesus really is. There have been—and still are—many

---

1   Compare Genesis 3:15; Isaiah 53:7; John 1:29; 1 Corinthians 5:7; 1 Peter 1:19; Revelation 5:12
2   John 17:5
3   1 Corinthians 5:7, *WB*
4   Luke 22:15, *TFG*
5   John 17:1, 3; *HCSB*
6   *MNT*

ideas as to the identity of Jesus Christ. Was Jesus just a man? Was he Almighty God? Is Jesus the 'second person' of a triune deity? Most importantly, is Jesus Christ the revealed Jehovah from the Hebrew Scriptures? "What, then, is the dividing line between the Christian faith and that which is pseudo-Christian or openly non-Christian? The line must be drawn based on the identity of the person and work of Jesus Christ, for it is his person on whom the Church is built."[7] The answers will only be revealed for us in God's written word, the Bible.

Anyone professing to be a Christian has no problem identifying who Jesus Christ is—or do they? For instance, we need to ask ourselves a couple of questions with reference to the above quoted scripture of John 17:3. Who is Jesus praying to?

Who is the Father that Jesus calls the only true God? Who did the disciples at once think about when Jesus was offering up this prayer? In regards to the first question, Trinitarians would answer "the first person of the Godhead." Non-Trinitarians think this to be simply illogical since Jesus is obviously not praying to himself, especially on the night of his sacrificial death. The second question at hand is not that straightforward, if you believe in the doctrine of the trinity. Most of Christendom is taught to believe and accept this so-called fact by faith: Jesus Christ is Almighty God.

If this is indeed truth, then why is there a need for Jesus to call the father the only true God? Again I ask, who is the father mentioned in John 17:3? I also ask once more: did Jesus' disciples imagine him to be praying to the 'first person' of a triune God? As true Christians, the answer to these questions is vital. Our whole faith and life as Christians is based on the identity of knowing the "Living God," and worshipping him on his stipulations. "But Jehovah is the true God; he is the living God."[8] Interestingly, Jesus asked his disciples who the Son of Man is. Simon Peter replied: "You are the Messiah, the Son of the living God."[9] An obviously vital observation then is no one can be saved without knowing intimately and the exact identity of the only living God and his Son.

Jesus' words couldn't be any more straightforward when he said it means our everlasting life to know him (Jesus) and his Father. Regrettably, most of Christendom has actually superseded and usurped the Father with all their devotion and attention on his Son Jesus Christ. Please, don't misunderstand what I am saying here. Scriptures reveal that Jesus Christ is our Savior, Lord, King, Redeemer, et cetera. We are, as well, to honor the Son as we honor the Father. I

---

7   Beisner, *God in Three Persons*, p. 19
8   Daniel 6:26, *TBJ*
9   Matthew 16:13–17, *NAB*

personally accept as true, Jesus to be all these and so much more, as well as my reigning King right now in the heavens.

The Bible teaches clearly, without accepting Jesus Christ and obeying him continually, salvation is impossible.[10] Still, notice Jesus' words more directly. What means everlasting life? Knowing Jesus, but also knowing the Father. We need to have an intimate relationship with each. I am sure most of us have this relationship with Christ, but are we honestly able to say we have a personal relationship with the Father—the one Jesus speaks of as the only true God? So really then, who is the Father?

You may have noticed as well there is a bit of curiosity regarding a subject not mentioned in this verse. There is a 'missing link,' if you will. Why isn't it necessary to have knowledge of the Holy Spirit for everlasting life? The author believes the scriptural answers to these questions reveal weak links to this trinity doctrine, which Christendom demands all need to believe if all are to be saved. This book will investigate and answer these questions to verify which 'chain' the links of this trinity doctrine really belong. Are these links from God's inspired written word the Bible, or from uninspired fallible men?

Today, there are numerous books, magazine articles, and public debates still being brought to our attention concerning the doctrine of the trinity. There doesn't seem to be a more debated subject amongst religious circles today—let alone Trinitarians—than the trinity doctrine. I have read most books and listened intently to many public debates on this subject. I have also been involved in countless discussions with sincere individuals in my ministry for over seventeen years. However, I have noticed there seems to be a trend of repetitiveness in regards to the use of certain scriptural 'proof' texts used by sincere individuals to try and prove the trinity. These generally involve John 1:1; 8:58; 20:28 and so on. I have also noticed as of late more and more theologians, scholars and laity alike are comparing Jehovah[11] of the Hebrew Scriptures with Jesus Christ as being one in the same. This issue seems to be on the increase amongst those who call themselves Evangelical Christians. I personally have no problems with the beliefs that people choose albeit my heartfelt desire is for all to have and attain the correct 'one' faith taught in the Bible.[12] However, the choice remains with the individual and remains their choice alone.

Just as well, I most assuredly never doubt the sincerity of anyone's love for God and Christ. I realize it is their decision and is ultimately between them and God.

---

10 John 3:16, 36
11 The importance of this name will be discussed later on
12 Cf. Ephesians 4:5

Romans 14:11, 12 clearly states: "It is written, "As I live," saith Jehovah, "not a knee but shall bow to me; not a tongue but shall confess to God." Each one of us shall answer to God for his actions."[13]

Nonetheless, it should be noted that if anyone claims to be Christian, works or deeds should be in company with his professed faith. Our works or deeds prove our faith. The Bible does not teach the popular albeit erroneous belief today that one must earn salvation through physical works. Rather, our works or deeds represent our conduct and actions towards others while professing to represent the living God. "Wasn't our ancestor Abraham "made right with God by works" when he placed his son Isaac on the sacrificial alter? Isn't it obvious that faith and works are yoked partners, that faith expresses itself in works? That the works are "works of faith"? The full meaning of "believe" in the Scripture sentence, "Abraham believed God and was set right with God," includes his action. It's that mesh of believing and acting that got Abraham named "God's friend." Is it not evident that a person is made right with God not by a barren faith but by faith fruitful in works? ... the very moment you separate body and spirit, you end up with a corpse. Separate faith and works and you get the same thing: a corpse."[14]

You simply cannot earn salvation. It is the undeserved kindness or grace of God in our fully obeying him through his Son. "The point is, if we benefit by a favor from God that we don't deserve, we can't claim that we earned it by working for it. Otherwise the promise that our salvation is by God's grace doesn't really mean that it's "by God's grace." Because if our salvation is obtained by working for it, it's no longer a gift from God. In that case the word work wouldn't really mean work either."[15]

On the other hand, when any doctrine claims to be based on God's word we need to examine it and make sure it is in complete harmony with the rest of God's word, the Bible. In fact, God encourages us to do this. This would have to include, for genuinely sincere Bible students, an in-depth study to clarify whether or not the trinity is a true or false doctrine. This would especially apply to this trinity doctrine since Christendom demands all to believe in the trinity in order for all to be saved. They claim it to be "the central doctrine of the Christian religion."[16] Therefore, an investigation to verify truth must be had. Otherwise, we would be blindly following fallible men. Jesus candidly remarks: "when a blind

---

13 *FPE*, cf. Galatians 6:5
14 James 2:21–26, *TM*
15 Romans 11:6, *LDB*, see also John 3:16, 36
16 *The Catholic Encyclopedia*, 1912, Vol. XV, p. 47

person leads another who is blind, both will fall into a pit."[17] Please notice the following scriptures.

"But God has given us the revelation of these things through his Spirit, for the Spirit explores everything, even the depths of God," "Put anything that contradicts to the test," and finally "Continue to prove all things until you can approve them."[18] The point God is making is summed up at 1 John 4:1[19] "My dear friends, don't believe everything you hear. Carefully weigh and examine what people tell you. Not everyone who talks about God comes from God. There are a lot of lying preachers loose in the world."

What's more, God has given each and everyone of us the power of reason and expects us to use it. The Bible clearly states at Isaiah 1:18: "Come now, let us reason together, saith Jehovah." There are countless scriptures that show Jesus and his followers reasoning with their audience using the scriptures. Jesus Christ himself always referred back to his audience with the words "It is written," "Is it not written?" and "Did you never read this scripture?" and finally "What is written in the law? What do you read?"[20] The apostle Paul continued this way of teaching, thus imitating and following in the footsteps of Jesus.[21] Those who listened to Jesus and his disciples searched the scriptures as the sincere Beroeans of the first century did. For Acts 17:11 says of them: "Now these were more noble than those in Thessalonica, in that they received the word with all readiness of mind, examining the scriptures daily, whether these things were so." As Christians today, we would be most sensible and shrewd to imitate them.

A 'trinity' of weak links revealed

With sound scriptural reasoning I accept as true, there to be several explicit areas that make up weak links in the trinity chain. They are:

- Progressive development of the trinity
- The Bible's answer to who is the only true God; John 17:3
- Does the Almighty God—which Jesus is claimed to be—have a God?

---

17 Matthew 15:14, *LDB*, compare Isaiah 9:16; Luke 6:39
18 1 Corinthians 2:10 *TST*; Philippians 1:10 *VC*; 1 Thessalonians 5:21 *TNTBW*; respectively
19 *TM*
20 Matthew 4:1–10, Mark 11:17, Mark 12:10, Luke 10:26 respectively
21 Cf. Acts 17:2, 3; 18:19; 1 Peter 2:21

Keep in mind this theme, which is declared throughout this book: A chain is only as strong as its weakest link. Why choose this theme throughout the pages of this book? Chains are often thought of as being unbreakable, indestructible, imperishable, solid, everlasting, and permanent because of the strength placed into them. However, no matter what diameter a chain may seem to be; it will always have a weak link to cause its breaking point. Why? Because it is manmade. Anything made by man is imperfect. In the same manner, the trinity doctrine—a so-called unbreakable chain—is thought of as being impossible to break. The author believes that every link of this trinity chain is a weak link. Why? It will soon be revealed—which is my goal and purpose for this book—this so-called unbreakable trinity chain is manmade—not a divinely inspired revelation from God. However, we are going to explore only a 'trinity' of these frail links in depth. Whereas these might be discussed in debates and books, they are so very often glossed over, (especially by Trinitarians), as non-essential. I consider this to be deft work by Trinitarians to obfuscate the subject at hand. It is the author's view that taking into consideration these three areas alone is enough to confirm the impotence of the trinity chain.

Hence, there is a need to keep searching for God's wisdom in this matter. God states at Proverbs 2:3–6 "If you appeal to intelligence, and lift up your voice to reason; If you seek her as silver, and search for her as for hidden treasures-Then you will understand reverence for the LORD [Jehovah], And will discover the knowledge of God; For the LORD [Jehovah] gives wisdom, Out of his mouth come knowledge and reason."[22] This scripture brings to light the very importance of using God's word and nothing else to base our beliefs on. Wisdom comes only from God, for he is the revealer of all things. Anything else is subject to imperfect man-made logic. "For all have sinned, and all fall short of God's glorious ideal," says Romans 3:23.[23] It is God's word that is inspired, not man that inspires.[24] That's why, all Christians need to ask themselves, "Is it in the holy word, which you declare is the only rule of faith, that you have found the declaration, that the one God is three persons? Have you been taught it by Jesus Christ, or by fallible men?"[25]

---

22 *AT*, brackets mine
23 *TST*
24 Cf. 2 Timothy 3:16, 17; 2 Peter 1:20, 21
25 *An Appeal To Pious Trinitarians*, Henry Grew, 1857, *The Harvest Herald*

Must rely on scriptures alone

It is quite evident as Christians we need to fasten ourselves and validate everything according to the Holy Scriptures alone. Why? Jesus gives us the answer at John 17:17 when he simply states in prayer to his Father: "your word is truth." We are under obligation to cling to truth—whether the world and Christendom accept it or not. Did not Jesus himself say: "I am the way, and the truth, and the life?"[26] 2 Timothy 3:16, 17 reads: "The whole Bible was given to us by inspiration from God and is useful to teach us what is true and to make us realize what is wrong in our lives; it straightens us out and helps us to do what is right. It is God's way of making us well prepared at every point, fully equipped to do good to everyone."[27] God reminds us that his whole Bible is inspired of him. Therefore, this would include the Hebrew Scriptures as well as the Christian Greek Scriptures. The apostle Paul said under inspiration "Everything, remember, in the Scriptures was written beforehand for our instruction."[28] Notice too what is mentioned: "the whole Bible" is "inspired" of God. The literal meaning 'inspired' is God breathed. Simply stated, the Bible is God's own words spoken to mankind. Anything outside the Bible is prone to fallibility. Is this not reason enough to confine us to the pages of God's word?

Another perfectly good reason for continued reliance solely on the Bible is found in the expressions of Gods prophet Isaiah. "The word of our God remains forever."[29] Yes, the Bible is the only book whose contents will endure forever. Why? Because the Bible is the only infallible words ever recorded. Therefore, "No prophecy of Scripture is a matter of one's own interpretation, for no prophecy was ever made by an act of human will, but men moved by the Holy Spirit spoke from God … You do well to pay attention as to a lamp shining in a dark place."[30] Man's so-called wisdom is as "a bit of smoke that appears for a little while, then vanishes."[31] Without question then, it is in our best interest to pay attention to our Grand instructor in order to know "the way [we] should go."[32] In fact, Gods

---

26 John 14:6; *LD*
27 *TB*
28 Romans 15:4; *TCNT*
29 Isaiah 40:8, *NJB*
30 2 Peter 1:19–21; *NASB*
31 James 4:14 *HCSB*, compare 1 Peter 1:24, 25
32 Isaiah 48:17, 18 *HCSB*; compare Proverbs 3:5, 6, brackets mine

word says quite candidly: "O Jehovah, I know that the way of man is not in himself; it is not in man that walketh to direct his steps."[33]

Notice too what is accepted worship by God when Jesus says: "But the hour comes and now is when the true worshippers will worship the Father in Spirit and truth; for the Father seeks such as these to worship Him. God is a Spirit, and it is necessary for the ones who worship Him to worship in Spirit and truth."[34] Yes, God is looking for Theo centric individuals to worship him. Should there be any doubt as to the importance of adhering to the truth established in scripture? For this reason, anyone claiming to be a Christian must speak absolute truth, and adhere only to the Holy Scriptures.[35]

Knowledge or accurate knowledge?

I have come to learn through personal Bible study over the years there is an immense difference between knowledge and having accurate knowledge. This is an imperative point to made here because God through Paul says: "We ... have not ceased praying on behalf of you and requesting that you may be filled with the full knowledge of His will in all wisdom and spiritual understanding."[36] The word knowledge, (Greek Ginosko), by itself means: "to be taking in knowledge, to come to know, recognize, understand."[37] This is a basic understanding of a particular subject. On the other hand, accurate knowledge, (Greek epi-gnosis), refers to an exact, full knowledge, and full discernment of a subject.[38]

To illustrate: we may walk into a jewelry store and select a sparkling diamond. We know—or have come to realize—that diamonds are valuable. In contrast, the Jeweler examines each facet of the diamond and sees its flaws in order to appraise its value and qualities respectively. He has full knowledge, (accurate knowledge), of that diamonds worth. Hence, it is essential that as Christians we study the Bible—our diamond with all its facets—in order to gain an exact or full knowledge of God and his purposes. That is why Paul continues in verse ten of Colossians chapter one: "We also, never cease praying for you ... that you may be fulfilled in your understanding of his will, in full wisdom and spiritual com-

---

33 Jeremiah 10:23; *TBJ*
34 John 4:23, 24; *LCNTV*
35 Cf. Ephesians 4:14, 15, 25
36 Colossians 1:9; *LCTNV*
37 *Vine's Expository Dictionary*, under know
38 *Strong's Hebrew and Greek Dictionary*, G1922

prehension."[39] Thus, having accurate knowledge is much more critical than just knowing that someone is up there in the heavens.

God's very will is found in scripture at 1 Timothy 2:4 that reads: "Who wants all men to be saved and to come into a full knowledge of truth."[40] Some other renderings are: "To reach full knowledge of the truth," or "Who wishes all men to be saved and [increasingly] to perceive and recognize and discern and know precisely and correctly the [divine] truth," and finally "Come into full knowledge of the truth."[41]

For those intent and satisfied on having the talent to recite scriptures, "Although they are continually being taught, these never do acquire a sound knowledge of truth."[42] Knowing and possessing the ability to recite scriptures will not entitle us to everlasting life. Why? Jesus declares with straightforward simplicity: "You keep on searching the Bible, because you think you will find eternal life there; ... but you refuse to come to me so that you can have life."[43] Obviously, much more is required than just a basic knowledge.

An excellent Bible example of the difference between knowledge and accurate knowledge can be observed in the life of the apostle Paul. Before he acquired accurate knowledge, he was known as Saul of Tarsus. He was a scholarly Pharisee[44] who hunted down, persecuted and even took part in the death of Christians.[45] Why? He didn't have accurate knowledge of God's purpose at this time. Perhaps speaking from his own personal experience, Paul says: "For I testify for them, that they have a zeal for God—but not according to correct knowledge ... and how, in my devotion to Judaism, I surpassed many of my contemporaries among my own people in my intense earnestness in upholding the traditions [not accurate knowledge of God] of my ancestors."[46]

As we continue on, I invite you to please pay close attention to what is claimed to be scriptural, opposed to what scriptures actually claim. If we are true sincere worshipers, God will open our spiritual eyes to his light amongst this spiritually be-darkened world of false teachings. God's Word states: "The path of the righ-

---

39 *RL*
40 *VC*
41 *TINT, TAB, MNT*, respectively
42 2 Timothy 3:7; *VC*
43 John 5:39, 40; *JGA*
44 A prominent religious sect of Judaism in the 1st century CE
45 Cf. Acts 22:1–5; 26:10–18
46 Romans 10:2 *TST*; Galatians 1:14 *TST*; brackets mine

teous is like the radiant sun, shining ever more brightly until midday."[47] Notice what God states at Micah 7:9 "He will bring me forth to the light, and I shall behold his righteousness."[48] We do well to pray to God: "Send Your light and Your truth; let them lead me ... Let them bring me to Your dwelling place."[49] "We speak these things, not in the words that mans wisdom teaches. We speak them with the words the Holy Spirit teaches comparing spiritual things with spiritual things."[50]

Because of the infinite amount of lies associated with those claiming to know God's word, unfortunately and with great sadness, I have no choice but to agree with Soren Kierkegaard. He states: "Christendom has done away with Christianity without being quite aware of it."[51] For this reason, more is required than simply knowing that God exist. Remember, God's will is that "all sorts of men should ... come to an accurate knowledge of truth."[52] May you dear reader always make every effort and persist in coming to an accurate knowledge of truth. Always be a student of God's inspired written word.

Questions for meditation

Before we begin our break down of John 17:3, there is a need to gain a proper understanding of how the trinity chain developed. As we do so, I ask you to please keep these questions in mind.

- Is the trinity doctrine in harmony with God's word?
- Who is the Father according to Scripture?
- Who is the only true God according to scripture?
- Did Jesus or his followers teach the trinity?
- Is Jesus Christ Almighty God?
- What is the Holy Spirit according to Scripture?

To be fair we must first acquire a definition of the trinity chain before we are able to proceed. This will initiate our first chapter.

---

47 Proverbs 4:18; *RJC*
48 *NBAV*, also compare Ephesians 1:17, 18; Matthew 5:8; Revelation 3:18; 1 Timothy 6:20, 21; Titus 1:14; Psalm 119:105; Proverbs 1:22, 23; 2:10–13
49 Psalm 43:3; *HCSB*
50 1 Corinthians 2:13, *NSB*
51 *Time Magazine*, December 16th, 1946, p. 64
52 1 Timothy 2:4

Part I

Development of the trinity chain

I was adopted when I was eight years old by a very loving couple, my parents. I could never be more grateful to them for instilling in me the love and heartfelt desire for God and respect for his word the Bible. Mom and Pop, I thank-you. I was raised in the Lutheran faith and my love and belief for God was never a question. I was a regular Sunday church participant and confirmed a Lutheran in my early teens.

I joined the U.S. Air Force with the intentions of making this my life long career. I was stationed in Bitburg Germany with my very own family of three in tow during the month of May 1987. My life was moving along steadily and thought my relationship with God was just as steady and stable. This was all about to change in December of the same year. I began to study the Bible more in depth with a couple whose desire was to worship God in truth as I.[53] During one of our Bible studies I was asked: "Do you believe in the trinity?" I immediately thought 'Of course! Don't all Christians?' Then I answered with a firm "yes!" However, his next question required much more thought and invoked a more personal belief. He asked: 'What does the trinity mean to you?' I have to admit this is the first time anyone has ever asked this of me. After a few moments of silence I replied proudly: 'It is believing in the Father, Son, and Holy Spirit!'

Fellow Bible readers, if this is your understanding, then you are in harmony with God's word. At Matthew 28:19 Jesus says: "… baptizing them in the name of the Father and of the Son and of the Holy Spirit." Regrettably, this is not even close to the definition of the trinity dogma. "Some suppose that Trinitarianism consist in believing in the Father, the Son, and the Holy Spirit. But we all believe in these; we all believe that the Father sent the Son, and gives, to those that ask, the Holy Spirit. We are all Trinitarians, if this is belief in Trinitarianism. But it is not. The Trinitarian believes that the one God is three distinct persons, called Father, Son, and Holy Ghost; and he believes that each is the only true God, and

---

53 We are still extremely close friends till this day. They reside in Scotland with their two daughters

yet that the three are only one God. This is Trinitarianism."[54] What precisely are the churches of Christendom teaching the trinity to be? Let's hear it from Christendom's very own mouth.

Today's definition of the trinity

No matter what faith you may profess to be in Christendom, all have to acknowledge this about the trinity: the word trinity is not found in God's word the Bible. In fact, not one verse in the Bible explains the definition of the trinity. That may be a revelation to some; but it still remains an historical fact.

Now, according to the Catholic Encyclopedia regarding the definition of this trinity doctrine it reads: "the central doctrine of the Christian religion ... In the unity of the Godhead there are three persons, the Father, the Son, and the Holy Spirit, these three persons being truly distinct one from another. Thus, in the words of the Athanasian Creed: 'the Father is God, the Son is God, and the Holy Spirit is God, and yet there are not three Gods but one God' ... The Persons are co-eternal and co-equal: all alike are uncreated and omnipotent."[55] This official definition makes it plentifully obvious that the trinity doctrine is not an uncomplicated or straightforward concept. It basically comes down to this:

- The trinity is said to be three divine persons-the Father, the Son, and the Holy Spirit in the Godhead.
- Each of these separate persons of God is said to be eternal, none coming before or after the other in time.
- Each is said to be Almighty, with none greater or lesser than the other.
- Each is said to be omniscient, knowing all things.
- Each is said to be true God.
- Finally, it is said that there are not three Gods but only one God.

Remember, all of these statements must be present. If any are removed it is no longer a trinity. A chain is only as strong as its weakest link.

Thus, we have in a nutshell what today's definition is pertaining to the trinity doctrine. On the other hand, it is of great significance to note that this explanation has changed from its former conception. At this point I feel it is of necessity to examine the three main and former creeds of Christendom. They are:

---

54 *Review of American Unitarianism*, Boston, 1815, William Ellery Channing, pp. 38, 39
55 *The Catholic Encyclopedia*, Vol. XV, 1912, p. 47

The Apostles Creed, Nicene Creed, and the Athanasian Creed. It's important to briefly review these to show the significant progressive developments from one to the other. Keep in mind that most of Christendom acknowledges and adheres to these creeds. However, before we advance into exploring these three central creeds, there is a need to discuss an exceptional archeological find that predates all of them.

The Didache

This find was actually a book consisting of sixteen chapters and is known as "The Didache."[56] Perhaps it is more widely known as the 'Teaching of The Twelve Apostles.' Although alluded to by the so-called early church fathers, The Didache was recently discovered in 1873 in a monastery in Constantinople. A Greek Orthodox Bishop named Philotheos Bryennios, in 1883 then translated this rare discovery. Several English translations have since been produced.

Our interest in this book should be for two reasons. They are the dating given it by historians as well as its contents. Unlike the creeds we will be conversing about shortly, most historians agree with the date given this book of 100CE or even earlier. In contrast the dates of the three major creeds are still hotly debated. I must interject here that I do not believe the Didache or the creeds to be inspired of God. As I have mentioned earlier only God's word the Bible is inspired of him. Withstanding its not being inspired of God does not take away the value of its contents. This is especially true considering it may have been an active document during or shortly after the last Apostles of Jesus Christ. If there were any notion or concept of the trinity doctrine, one would think it to be mentioned in this book of the Apostles.

I will focus in on chapters seven and ten. Chapter seven considers baptism and interestingly it employs the exact same words Jesus used in Matthew 28:19. It stipulates baptism "in the name of the Father, and of the Son, and of the Holy Spirit." Also captivating is the fact that chapter seven says absolutely nothing concerning the Father, Son, and Holy Spirit being co-equal, or co-eternal. Nor is the word trinity mentioned.

Chapter ten is a bit more fascinating. We notice here a confession of faith in the form of a prayer. It reads: "We thank you, Holy Father, for your holy Name which you have made to dwell in our hearts; and for the knowledge and faith and immortality which you have made known to us through Jesus your servant. Glory

---

56 Pronounced as dee-dah-KHAY, R. Frederick Harrison; see Greek Interlinear Matthew 16:12

to you forever! You, Almighty Master, created everything for your Name's sake … And to us you have graciously given spiritual food and drink, and life eternal through Jesus your servant."[57]

There are eye-opening details that stand out for us. First, this prayer is addressed to the Father, calling him Holy Father and Almighty Master. Twice we notice Jesus is referred to as the Fathers 'servant', a subordinate position. As well, we find no mention of the trinity or persons of God in this book, which is dated around 100CE. Edwin Hatch in *The Influence of Greek Ideas on Christianity* says concerning this prayer: "In the original sphere of Christianity there does not appear to have been any great advance upon these simple conceptions. The doctrine upon which stress was laid was, that God is, that He is one, that He is almighty and everlasting, that He made the world, that his mercy is over all his works. There was no taste for metaphysical discussion."[58]

My observation of this book could not have been said any clearer than that. The fact remains that there is not even a hint of the modern trinity doctrine as of the year 100CE. Perhaps the traditional creeds will shed some light.

Apostle's Creed

Our first article of faith to examine is the Apostle's Creed. It is a very simple, logical, and importantly, for the most part, is based on the Bible. "The present form of what we know as the Apostles' Creed probably did not exist before the sixth century … a briefer form, known as the Roman Symbol, was in use in the Church of Rome at least as far back as the fourth century. With the exception of two or three phrases it was known to Irenaeus and Tertullian, and so was employed in the later part of the second century … Although the development was in part due to the conflict with the Marcionites and although several generations were still to elapse before all the phrases were added which make it as it stands today, it must not be forgotten that the Apostles' Creed had as its nucleus words going back to the first century and first explicitly stated in the post-resurrection command of Jesus to the apostles."[59]

This creed declares: "I believe in God the Father Almighty, Maker of heaven and earth, and in Jesus Christ his only Son our Lord, who was conceived by the Holy Ghost; born of the virgin Mary; suffered under Pontius Pilate, was crucified, dead, and buried; he descended into hell; the third day he rose from the dead; he

---

57 *The Apostolic Fathers*, Vol. 3, Robert A. Kraft, 1965, p. 163
58 1952, p. 252
59 *A History of Christianity* by Kenneth Scott Latourette, 1953, pp. 135, 136

ascended into heaven, and sitteth on the right hand of God the Father Almighty; from thence he shall come to judge the quick and the dead. I believe in the Holy Ghost; the holy Catholic Church, the communion of saints; the forgiveness of sins; the resurrection of body; and life everlasting. Amen."

This is very simple, straight forward, and easy to understand. On the other hand, after reading this are you able to locate the proclamation that says God, Jesus Christ, and holy spirit are "one God?" How about "three persons of God?" Of course, there is no mention of a trinity either. "The Apostolic Fathers wrote between A.D. 90 and 140. Their discussion of the person of Jesus Christ simply repeated the teaching of the New Testament. None of the Apostolic Fathers presented a definite doctrine on this point. In this respect the New Testament, the Apostolic Fathers, and the Apostles' Creed stand in one line."[60]

Nicene Creed

Let us move even further along in history from the time of Christ and see what is revealed. We come to the Nicene Creed. By this time the so-called early church fathers, were heavily debating over the exact relationship Jesus had to God. "Up until the end of the second century at least, the universal Church remained united in one basic sense; they all accepted the supremacy of the Father. They all regarded God the Father Almighty as alone supreme, immutable, ineffable and without beginning ... With the passing of those second century writers and leaders, the Church found itself ... slipping slowly but inexorably toward that point ... where at the Council of Nicaea the culmination of all this piecemeal eroding of the original faith was reached. There, a small volatile minority, foisted its heresy upon an acquiescent majority, and with the political authorities behind it, coerced, cajoled and intimidated those who strove to maintain the pristine purity of their faith untarnished."[61] The *Encyclopedia Britannica* even admits: "Constantine himself presided, actively guiding the discussions, and personally proposed ... the crucial formula expressing the relation of Christ to God in the creed issued by the council, 'of one substance [homoousios] with the Father.' ... Overawed by the emperor, the bishops, with two exceptions only, signed the creed, many of them much against their inclination."[62]

Therefore, it was Roman Emperor Constantine who called a church council, not the church officials, in 325CE. This was to be held in Nice—modern day

---

60   *A Short History of the Early Church* by Harry R. Boer, 1976, pp. 108–110
61   *Second Century Orthodoxy* by J. A. Buckley, 1978, pp. 114–115
62   Volume 6, 1971, p. 386

France—to decide this issue. "Not only was the council of Nicea assembled by Constantine the Great, but all the great councils, the two at Constantinople (381 and 553), Ephesus (431) and Chalcedon (451), were called together by the imperial power. And it is very manifest that in much of the history of Christianity at this time the spirit of Constantine the Great is as evident as, or more evident than, the spirit of Jesus. [Constantine] was, we have said, a pure autocrat ... the history of the Church under his influence now becomes, therefore, a history of the violent struggles that were bound to follow upon his sudden and rough summons to unanimity. From him the Church acquired the disposition to be authoritative and unquestioned, to develop a centralized organization and run parallel to the empire."[63]

Imagine that! A world ruler, who worshiped the Sun-God Sol Invictus, was allowed to decide what relationship Jesus had with God! I can't help but think of Jesus' own words at this time. Referring to his loyal and true disciples he said: "They are no part of the world crowd and it's low aims and ambitions anymore than I am."[64] James, the half-brother of Jesus declares: "Ye adulteresses, know ye not that that the friendship of the world is enmity with God? Whosoever therefore would be a friend of the world maketh himself an enemy of God."[65] That scripture is dreadfully sobering to be sure. Let us not forget the serious words of Jesus when questioned by Pontius Pilate if he was a king: "My Kingdom is not of this world."[66]

It is a historical fact that it was Constantine's ambition to unite his kingdom and perhaps to keep his power, not the furthering of church dogma. Richard E. Rubenstein states in his book: "Having just assumed the throne, Constantine was by no means finished either with power or with committing the sins necessary to retain it. But presiding over the grandest council in Christian history might make up in the community's eyes (and, who knows, perhaps even in God's) for a certain number of moral lapses."[67]

Jonathan Kirsch relates: "His command of Greek-the language of high culture in the Hellenistic world-was notorious and even laughably poor," and Mr. Kirsch continues on by stating: "Constantine never fully grasped the finer points of the argument that he was called upon to decide one way or the other-but he was quick to understand the dangers of dissent against authority, and he knew well how to

---

63 *The Outline of History, The Whole Story of Man*, 1961, p. 439
64 John 17:16, *TLDNT*
65 James 4:4
66 John 18:36
67 *When Jesus Became God*, p. 70

go about suppressing it ... the bitter struggle within early Christianity over the name and nature of the Only True God turned out to be a battle for the heart and mind of one man-the emperor Constantine ... "The selfsame imperial government which use to make a bonfire of Christian sacred books had them [Bishops] adorned sumptuously with gold and precious stones," writes Jerome in frank amazement, "and, instead of razing church buildings to the ground, pays for the construction of magnificent basilicas with guilded ceilings and marble-encrusted walls." So the apocalyptic visions of the book of Revelation were now replaced by realpolitik. When the high clergy of the Christian church beheld Constantine wearing the diadem that had once crowned their persecutors, they no longer saw an agent of Satan but rather "the Lord's angel," and they regarded the sight of the Augustus on the imperial throne as "a picture of Christ's Kingship."[68]

Does this give the impression as if these church leaders were following Jesus' own words, that his Kingdom was no part of this world? History confirms just the opposite. Referring to Constantine, Henry Chadwick says: "his conversion should not be interpreted as an inward experience of grace ... It was a military matter ... In other words, Constantine was not aware of any mutual exclusiveness between Christianity and his faith in the Un-conquered Sun."[69] Norbert Brox adds: "Constantine did not experience any conversion; there are no signs of a change of faith in him. He never said of himself that he had turned to another god ... Constantine did not forsake this god Sol. The spectacular shift consisted in the fact that he changed the cult (the form of worship) of this god and that he chose Christianity for this cult. For him, the God of the Christians was identical with the god he himself worshipped."[70]

Finally, "It should be remembered that even our creed was to some extent decided by him. For it was this Sun-God worshipper-who, though he advised others to enter what he wished should become a catholic and all-embracing religion, refused to do so himself till he was dying-who called together our bishops, and, presiding over them in council at Nicaea, demanded that they should determine the controversy in the ranks of the Christians as to whether the Christ was or was not God, by subscribing to a declaration of his Deity. It is even recorded that he forced the unwilling ones to sign under penalty of deprivation and banishment. From these and other incidents in his career it would appear that, either from policy or conviction, Constantine acted as if he thought the Sun-God and

---

68 *God Against The Gods*, 2004, pp. 126, 167, 169, 179, brackets mine
69 *The Early Church*, pp. 122, 125–127
70 *A History of the Early Church*, translated by John Bowden, 1994, pp. 48–49

the Christ were one and the same deity."[71] "Constantine never wavered from his view that Christianity was the means of worshipping *Summus Deus*, and that Christian clergy were his ministers ... It is less clear that he regarded Christianity as the *sole* means of worshipping God. His retention of the inscription *Soli Invicto Comiti* on the coinage in general circulation in the West, and his choice of the *Dies Solis* (Sunday) as a rest day throughout his dominions point to the opposite direction ... Constantine's first religious conversion had been to the worship of the sun-god Apollo, and though the latter was given a cross on an imperial column at Constantinople he was not entirely superseded."[72]

Let's take a close look at the somewhat final outcome of this creed. It reads: "I believe in one God the Father Almighty, Maker of Heaven and earth, and of all things visible and invisible: And in one Lord Jesus Christ, the only-begotten Son of God, begotten of his Father before all worlds; God of God, Light of Light, very God of very God, begotten, not made, being of one substance with the Father; by whom all things were made; Who for us men and our salvation came down from heaven, and was incarnate by the Holy Ghost of the Virgin Mary, and was made man, and was crucified also for us under Pontius Pilate, he suffered and was buried; and the third day he rose again, according to the Scriptures; and ascended into heaven, and sitteth on the right hand of the Father. And he shall come again with glory to judge both the quick and the dead whose kingdom shall have no end. And I believe in the Holy Ghost the Lord and giver of life, who proceedeth from the father and the Son, who with the father and the Son together is worshiped and glorified, who spake by the prophets. And I believe one catholic and apostolic Church. I acknowledge one baptism for the remission of sins; and I look for the resurrection of the dead, and the life of the world to come. Amen."

The trinity of today is still not to a certain extent established in this creed either. The Father and Son are alleged to be of the same substance or essence and the holy ghost is said to be "Lord and giver of life," yet, all three are still not understood to be "one God" or "three persons of God," albeit we finally start to see a pattern developing. We also notice that the word trinity is not even vaguely mentioned.

In fact, I mentioned before this creed was 'somewhat final.' This is simply because history tells us that after Constantine affirmed the Nicene Creed, he "discovered that the bulk of the population in the heavily Christianized area of Asia Minor had Arian leanings. He was mainly interested in concord and was willing to have the question reopened. Ten years later, in 335, a synod met in Tyre, and

---

71 *The Non-Christian Cross* by John Denham Parsons, 1896, p. 66
72 *The Early Church* by W. H. Frend, 1965, pp. 150, 151, italics his

this time the Arians won: Arius was restored … and Athanasius was exiled. But still the struggle was far from over."[73] Yes, this struggle was certainly far from over. This debate went back and forth through the fifth and possibly even the sixth century before the trinity and all it necessitates was finalized. Thus, the *New Catholic Encyclopedia* is forced to recognize and admit: "Whether the Council intended to affirm the numerical identity of the substance of the Father and Son is doubtful."[74]

Athanasian Creed

Next we have the Athanasian Creed formulated perhaps between 381 and 428CE. However, there is truthfully no certain authoritative date that can be applied here. According to one source: "Athanasias had been dead for five hundred years when it (the creed) appeared."[75] Also, the *New Encyclopedia Britannica* agrees and says: "The creed was unknown to the Eastern Church until the 12th century. Since the 17th century, scholars have generally agreed that the Athanasian Creed was not written by Athanasius (died 373) but was probably composed in southern France during the fifth century … The creed's influence seems to have been primarily in southern France and Spain in the 6th and 7th centuries. It was used in the liturgy of the church in Germany in the 9th century and somewhat later in Rome."[76] Therefore, the hot debate continues.

At any rate, the Athanasian Creed declares this: "We worship one God in Trinity in Unity; neither confounding the persons, nor dividing the substance. For there is one person of the Father, another of the Son, and another of the Holy Ghost. But the Godhead of the Father, of the Son, and of the Holy Ghost is all one: the glory equal, the majesty coeternal. Such as the Father is, such is the Son, and such is the Holy Ghost. The Father uncreated, the Son uncreated, and the Holy Ghost uncreated. The Father incomprehensible, the Son incomprehensible, and the Holy Ghost incomprehensible. The Father eternal, the Son eternal, and the Holy Ghost eternal. And yet they are not three eternals, but one eternal. As also there are not three incomprehensibles, nor three uncreated, but one uncreated, and one incomprehensible.

"So likewise the Father is almighty, the Son is almighty, and the Holy Ghost almighty. And yet there are not three Almighty's, but one almighty. So the Father

---

73 *The Horizon History of Christianity*, 1964, pp. 102–103
74 Volume VII, 1967, p. 115
75 *We Believe*, p. 118
76 15th edition, Volume I, 1985, p. 665

is God, the Son is God, and the Holy Ghost is God. And yet there are not three Gods, but one God. So likewise the Father is Lord, the Son Lord, and the Holy Ghost Lord. And yet not three Lords, but one Lord. For like as we are compelled by the Christian verity to acknowledge every person by himself to be God and Lord, so are we forbidden by the catholic religion to say there be three Gods and three Lords.

"The Father is made of none, neither created nor begotten. The Son is of the Father alone; not made or created, but begotten. The Holy Ghost is of the Father and of the Son; neither made, nor created, nor begotten, but proceeding. So there is one Father, not three Fathers; one Son, not three Sons; one Holy Ghost, not three Holy Ghosts. And in this Trinity none is afore or after other; none is greater or less than another. But the whole three persons are coeternal together, and coequal. So that in all things, as is aforesaid, the Unity in Trinity and the Trinity in Unity is to be worshipped. He therefore that will be saved must thus think of the Trinity."

I had to come up for air a few times in there. Wow! Nonetheless, we have arrived at today's understanding, or lack of, the trinity chain. There are a number of comments that have to be pointed out. First, the length of this creed has doubled in size from the last one and tripled in size from the first. Why the need to continue adding Greek philosophy to Gods written word? It starts sounding suspicious when definitions start to expand. It's like the man that caught a 12-inch fish. By the time the story hits the local newspapers, it's a world record fish!

Next, we see the word trinity mentioned numerously for the first time. Why not in the other two creeds? Then we finally observe written the words that are used so often by Trinitarians today: "There are not three Gods, but one God," as well as "three persons."

It is now that we have the final formulated doctrine of the trinity. It is here I believe that the men who claim to represent God had, in the words of theologian N. Leroy Norquist, "experimented with words, sharpened phrases, until they had refined the relation of the three 'persons' of the Trinity in such a way that they could finally say, 'Unless you believe this you're not a true believer.'" Mr. Norquist points out an extremely important fact that is too often been concealed by Christendom. It is here in this creed that we are introduced for the first time to the term 'three persons' of God. When Trinitarians say they believe in God, what they really mean is they believe in the 'three persons' of God. I want you to be aware of that nowhere in the Bible is God ever spoken of as being three persons! Irrefutably there is never any mention of 'persons' of God either. If the word trinity, and the words 'persons of God' are not in his very own inspired Holy book, then where is this thought coming from? The only response is a twisted man made doctrine.

Jesus says at Matthew 15:9 "These people honoureth me with their lips; But their heart is far from me. But in vain do they worship me, Teaching as their doctrines the precepts of men."[77] God warned the first century Christians through the apostle Paul when he stated: "And men will rise up out of you yourselves speaking perversions in order to draw away the disciples after them."[78] Notice Jesus says they teach as doctrines the 'commands', or 'rules' of men, not God. Harold Bloom gives us something to think about too. He states: "Athanasius, however, insisted that Jesus Christ was not creaturely, nor was the Holy Spirit: The Trinity was an identity of substance, and not merely an analogy. But if God is one being, how can he also be three entities, each capable of separate description? ... the Athanasian Creed won the contest, and Jesus Christ became more God than man, in practice if not quite in theory ... The Trinity is a great poem, but a difficult one, and always a challenge to interpretation. Its sublime ambition is to convert polytheism back into monotheism, which is possible only by rendering the Holy Spirit into a vacuum, and by evading the flamboyant personality of Yahweh. If the Trinity truly is monotheistic, then its sole God is Jesus Christ ... his hyperbolic expansion into the usurper of his beloved *abba*."[79]

Please, ask yourselves this question. 'Is there a verse or verses that you can turn to in your Bible right now that declares a trinity and every part it necessitates?' Speaking about the Nicene, Athanasius' and Apostles' Creeds, Isaac Newton said of the Church: "She doth not require us to receive them by authority of General Councils, and much less by authority of Convocations, but only because they are taken out of the Scriptures. And therefore are we authorized by the Church to compare them with the Scriptures, and see how and in what sense they can be deduced from thence? And when we cannot see the Deduction we are not to rely upon the Authority of the Councils and Synods." He concludes with these words: "Even General Councils have erred and may err in matters of faith, and what they decree as necessary to salvation is of no strength or authority unless they can be shown to be taken from the holy Scripture."[80] Therefore, even Isaac Newton found no support in Scripture for the doctrine of the trinity from the creeds and councils. Still, the important question is: do we?

---

77   *JBP*, cf. 2 Peter 3:14–17
78   Acts 20:30, *LCNTV*, cf. 2 Timothy 4:3, 4; 2 Peter 1:20, 21
79   *Jesus and Yahweh The Names Divine*, 2005, pp. 98–99, 101
80   *Theological Manuscripts*, selected and edited by H. McLachlan, Liverpool 1950, pp. 37–38

Professor of Historical Theology, Yale University, George A. Lindbeck confirms: "In order to argue successfully for the unconditionality and permanence of the ancient Trinitarian Creeds, it is necessary to make a distinction between doctrines, on the one hand, and on the terminology and conceptuality in which they were formulated on the other ... Some of the crucial concepts employed by these creeds, such as "substance," "person," and "in two natures" are post biblical novelties. If these particular notions are essential, the doctrines of these creeds are clearly conditional, dependent on the late Hellenistic milieu."[81]

God says the following at Galatians 1:8–9 "But even if we or an angel from heaven should preach [to you] a gospel other than the one we preached to you, let that one be accursed! As we have said before, and now I say again, if anyone preaches to you a gospel other than the one that you received, let that one be accursed!"[82] Then God adds another word of caution for Christians at Revelation 22:18 "I testify unto every man that heareth the words of the prophecy of this book, If any man shall add unto them, God shall add unto him the plagues which are written in this book."

So what are we to assume and discern from these scriptures in lieu of the claim of the trinity doctrine? God resolutely states "let that one be accursed!" Why? As mentioned in our introduction, God's "word is truth," not manmade creeds, according to Jesus' own words at John 17:17. We are warned at Colossians 2:8 "See to it that no one enslaves you through philosophy and empty deceit according to human tradition ... and not according to Christ."[83] For that reason, as Christians we are to live, eat, drink, and die in complete truth. Jesus certainly did. He says: "I was born for that destiny. And I came to bring truth to the world. Everyone that is on the side of truth listens to my voice."[84] Are we going to listen to Jesus or obey fallible men who infer their own orthodox doctrine into God's word?

"It is all too easy to read the traditional interpretations we have received from others into the text of Scripture. Then we may unwittingly transfer the authority of the Scripture to our traditional interpretations and invest them with a false, even an idolatrous, degree of certainty. Because traditions are reshaped as they are passed on, after a while we may drift far from God's Word while still insisting all our theological opinions are 'biblical' and therefore true ... Many local Bible

---

81　*The Nature of Doctrine: Religion and Theology in a Post Liberal Age*, 1984, p. 92
82　*NAB*, cf. Proverbs 30:6
83　*ISV*
84　John 18:37 *LD*; cf. Psalm 25:5; 119:60; Proverbs 12:19; Zechariah 8:19; Ephesians 4:15–16, 25

teachers and preachers have never been forced to confront alternative interpretations at full strength; and because they would lose a certain psychological security if they permitted their own questions, aroused by their own reading of Scripture, to come into full play, they are unlikely to throw over received traditions."[85]

"God Himself ... cannot lie," says Titus 1:2[86] and Hebrews 6:18[87] declares: "By means of two unchangeable things, the promise and the oath, in neither of which it is conceivable that God could lie." Of Jesus Christ 1 Peter 2:22 reads: "Jesus is a man who "never did anything sinful, and he never said anything that was false or dishonest."[88] Therefore, "Let God be true, and every man a liar," says Romans 3:4.[89]

The point is this: Christians speak truth no matter what. Anything beyond truth—God's word the Bible—is from the Father of the lie, Satan. Jesus made this point crystal clear.[90]

Does your church accept these creeds and trinity doctrine?

You may be thinking or believe that your church does not teach such a doctrine or even approve of these creeds. I invite you to read the following.

- *The Catholic Encyclopedia* under "Trinity" says: "This the Church teaches", after stating a part of the Athanasian Creed.
- "The Athanasian Creed (written between 434 and 440) sums up the fundamental theological beliefs of the Catholic Church."[91]
- The book *Our Orthodox Christian Faith* says: "God is triune ... The Father is totally God. The Son is totally God. The Holy Spirit is Totally God."
- *Eastern Orthodox Church* "teach ... the text of the Nicene Creed, a statement of Christian faith adopted at the council of Nicaea in 325. Orthodox Christians use the original text, which states that the Holy Spirit proceeds from the Father."[92]

---

85 D. A. Carson, *Exegetical Fallacies*, pp. 17, 19
86 *JWCW*
87 *JWCW*
88 *JGA*
89 *NIV*
90 Cf. Matthew 5:37; John 8:44
91 *Christianity: World Religions*, 1991, p. 49
92 *Christianity: World Religions*, 1991, pp. 57, 58

- *Lutheran Church in America*, Article II, section 4, says: "This Church accepts the Apostles', the Nicene, and the Athanasian creeds as true declarations of the faith of the Church."
- *The Lutheran Confessions*, circa 1953, p. 5, Mueller, John Theodore, Says this of Martin Luther: "Luther called the Athansen Creed the grandest production of the Christian Church since the times of the apostles."
- *United Church of Christ* constitution states: "It claims as it's own the faith of the historic Church expressed in the ancient creeds ..."
- *The Protestant Episcopal Church* says it "is far from intending to depart ... in any essential point of doctrine."
- *"Anglicans* ... believe in the ancient faith of Christianity as expressed in the Apostles' Creed and the Nicene Creed."[93]
- *The Church of England* also endorses the Apostles', Nicene and Athanasian creeds.
- *Presbyterian Pastor,* Philip W. Butin, says the doctrine of the Trinity is "the heart and center of Christian faith."[94]
- Majority of *Methodist* bodies endorse the Nicene Creed.
- The Associate General Secretary of the *American Baptist* Convention proclaims regarding the Athanasian Creed: "I am confident that most American Baptist would be in substantial agreement with its contents."
- *Private Thoughts, Bishop Beverage*, part 2, 48, 49, states candidly: "This is a mystery which we are all bound to believe, but yet must exercise great care in how we speak of it, it both being easy and dangerous to err in expressing so great a truth as this is."[95]
- *Protestant Theologian* Dr. James R. White states: "Within the one Being that is God, there exists eternally three coequal and coeternal persons, namely the father, the Son and the Holy Spirit ... We hang a person's very salvation upon the acceptance of the doctrine ... We must know, understand, and love the Trinity to be fully and completely Christian."[96]
- *Protestant scholar* Wayne Grudem says: "We may define the doctrine of the Trinity as follows: God eternally exists as three persons, Father, Son, and Holy Spirit, and each person is fully God, and [yet] there is one God."[97]

---

93 *Christianity: World Religions*, 1991, p. 75
94 *The Trinity, Foundations of the Christian Faith*, 2001, p. 13
95 As cited in *The True Believers Defense Against Charges Preferred by Trinitarians for Not Believing in the Deity of Christ*, Charles Morgridge, Boston: B. Greene, 1837, p.16
96 *The Forgotten Trinity, Recovering the Heart of Christian Belief*, 1998, pp. 15, 26
97 *Systematic Theology*, p. 26

Even if some churches are not enclosed in this list we can be reasonably confident of the support that Christendom has for these creeds and the trinity doctrine.

The first weak link identified

The first weak link of the trinity chain has arrived. Take special care and notice the candid observations from the very ones who adhere to the trinity teaching noted previously, as well as other scholarly references in the following information. I find this to be a genuine eye opener.

- *The Encyclopedia of Religion*, Mircea Eliade, editor in chief, 1987, Volume 15, p. 54 states: "Exegetes and theologians today are in agreement that the Hebrew Bible does not contain a doctrine of the Trinity ... Although the Hebrew Bible depicts God as the Father of Israel and employs personifications of God such as Word (davar), Spirit (ruah), Wisdom (hokhmah), and Presence (shekhinah), it would go beyond the intention and spirit of the Old Testament to correlate these notions with later Trinitarian doctrine. Further, exegetes and theologians agree that the New Testament also does not contain an explicit doctrine of the Trinity. God and the Father is source of all that is (Pantokrator) and also the father of Jesus Christ; 'Father' is not a title for the first person of the Trinity but a synonym for God ... In the New Testament there is no reflective consciousness of the metaphysical nature of God ('immanent trinity'), nor does the New Testament contain the technical language of later doctrine (hupostasis, ousia, sunstantia, subsistenia, prosopon, persona) ... It is incontestable that the doctrine cannot be established on scriptural evidence alone."
- *The New Encyclopedia Britannica*, 15th edition, 1985, Volume 11, Micropaedia, p. 928 says: "Neither the word Trinity nor the explicit doctrine appears in the New Testament ... The doctrine developed gradually over several centuries and through many controversies ... It was not until the 4th century that the distinctness of the three and their unity were brought together in a single orthodox doctrine of one essence and three persons."
- *The New Encyclopedia Britannica*, 1976, Micropaedia, Vol. X, p. 126 reads: "Neither the word Trinity, nor the explicit doctrine as such, appears in the New Testament, nor did Jesus and his followers intend to contradict the Shema in the Old Testament: "Hear, O Israel: The Lord our God is one Lord' (Deut. 6:4) ... By the end of the 4th century ... the doctrine of the Trinity took substantially the form it has maintained ever since."

- *The New Catholic Encyclopedia*, 1967, Volume XIV, p. 295 says: "There is the recognition on the part of exegetes and Biblical theologians, including a constantly growing number of Roman Catholics, that one should not speak of Trinitarianism in the New Testament without serious qualification. There is also the closely parallel recognition on the part of historians of dogma and systematic theologians that when one does speak of an unqualified Trinitarianism, one has moved from the period of Christian origins to, say, the last quadrant of the 4th century. It was only then that what might be called the definitive Trinitarian dogma 'one God in three persons' became thoroughly assimilated into Christian life and thought … The formula itself does not reflect the immediate consciousness of the period of origins; It was the product of 3 centuries of doctrinal development." On p. 299 it sums everything in this way: "The formulation 'one God in three Persons' was not solidly established, certainly not fully assimilated into Christian life and its profession of faith, prior to the end of the 4th century. But it is precisely this formulation that has first claim to the title the Trinitarian dogma. Among the Apostolic Fathers, there had been nothing even remotely approaching such a mentality or perspective."
- *Cardinal John O'Connor* states: "We know that it is a very profound mystery, which we don't begin to understand."
- *Monsignor Eugene Clark* says: "God is one, and God is three. Since there is nothing like this in creation, we cannot understand it, but only accept it."
- *Catholic scholar, Gerard S. Sloyan*, in his book, *The Three Persons in One God*, p. 7 states: "It is a matter beyond all question that there was no knowledge of the Trinity in the Old Testament period …"
- *Catholic theologian Hans Kung* states: "Even well informed Muslims simply cannot follow, as the Jews thus far have likewise failed to grasp, the idea of the Trinity … The distinctions made by the doctrine of the Trinity between one God and three hypostases do not satisfy Muslims, who are confused, rather than enlightened, by theological terms derived from Syriac, Greek, and Latin. Muslims find it all a word game … why should anyone want to add anything to the notion of God's oneness and Uniqueness that can only dilute or nullify that oneness and uniqueness?"[98]
- *Dictionary of the Bible*, John L. McKenzie, Jesuit Scholar, New York, 1965, pp. 899, 900 says: "The trinity of persons within the unity of nature is defined in terms of 'person' and 'nature' which are G [ree] k philosophical terms; actually the terms do not appear in the Bible. The Trinitarian

---

[98] *Christianity and World Religions*

definitions arose as the result of long controversies in which these terms and others such as 'essence' and 'substance' were erroneously applied to God by some theologians ... OT does not contain suggestions or foreshadowings of the trinity of persons such as Father, Son, Word, Spirit, etc."

- *A Handbook of Christian theology, Definition Essays on Concepts and Movements of Thought in Contemporary Protestantism*, 1958, p. 336 states: "The doctrine of the Trinity (or triunity of God) refers to the one being of God as Father, Son and Holy Spirit ... The concept as such is nowhere explicitly expressed in the scriptures, though such passages as Matthew 28:19 and II Corinthians 13:14 are suggestive. The doctrine itself was thus formulated in the Church, as the community sought to explicate the meaning of the revelation in Jesus Christ."
- *Dictionary of Religious Knowledge* says: "Precisely what that doctrine is, or rather precisely how it is to be explained, Trinitarians are not agreed among themselves."
- *Jesuit Joseph Bracken* says: "Priest who with considerable effort learned ... the Trinity during their seminary years naturally hesitated to present it to their people from the pulpit, even on Trinity Sunday ... Why should one bore people with something that in the end they wouldn't properly understand anyway? ... The Trinity is a matter of formal belief, but it has little or no [effect] in day-to-day Christian life and worship."[99]
- *The Nouveau Dictionnaire Universel*, Paris, 1865–1870, edited by M. Lachatre, Vol. 2, p. 1467 states: "The Platonic trinity, itself merely a rearrangement of older trinities dating back to earlier peoples, appears to be the rational philosophic trinity of attributes that gave birth to the three hypostases or divine persons taught by the Christian churches ... This Greek philosopher's [Plato, 4th century B.C.E.] conception of the divine trinity ... can be found in all the ancient [pagan] religions."
- *The Encyclopedia Americana*, 1956, Vol. XXVII, p. 294L says: "Christianity derived from Judaism and Judaism was strictly Unitarian [believing that God is one person]. The road which led from Jerusalem to Nicea was scarcely a straight one. Fourth century Trinitarianism did not reflect accurately early Christian teaching regarding the nature of God; it was, on the contrary, a deviation from this teaching."
- *The Triune God*, Jesuit Edmund Fortman admits: "The Old Testament ... tells us nothing explicitly or by necessary implication of a Triune God who is Father, Son, and Holy Spirit ... There is no evidence that any sacred writer

---

99   *What Are They Saying About The Trinity?*

even suspected the existence of a [Trinity] within the Godhead ... Even to see in [the "Old Testament"] suggestions or foreshadowing's or 'veiled signs' of a trinity of persons, is to go beyond the words and intent of the sacred writers." Then he adds "The New Testament writers ... give us no formal or formulated doctrine of the Trinity, no explicit teaching that in one God there are three co-equal divine persons ... Nowhere do we find any Trinitarian doctrine of three distinct subjects of divine life and activity in the same Godhead."

- *Karl Rahner, The Trinity*, J. Donceel, trans, p. 10 reads: "Despite their orthodox confession of the Trinity, Christians are, in their practical life, almost mere monotheist. We must be willing to admit that, should the doctrine of the Trinity have to be dropped as false, the major part of religious literature could well remain virtually unchanged."
- *Evangelical theologian, Donald Macleod*, in his book, *Shared Life*, p. 9, 11 admits: "no group possessing only the Old Testament has ever come to a knowledge of the doctrine of the Trinity ... if the Old Testament is emphatic about the unity of God, it appears to have little to say about the second aspect of the doctrine of the Trinity, namely, the idea of more-than-oneness in God ... in the oneness of God there were the Father, the Son, and the Holy Spirit. There is scarcely a hint of this in the Old Testament."
- *Jesus and Yahweh The Names Divine* says: "Historicism, be it older or newer, seems incapable of confronting the total incompatibility of Yahweh and Jesus Christ ... The authentic difference came about with the development of the theological God, Jesus Christ, where the chain of tradition indeed is broken ... Marks God remains Yahweh."[100]
- *A Short History of Christian Doctrine* says: "As far as the New Testament is concerned, one does not find in it an actual doctrine of the Trinity."
- *Christian Theology*, Vol. 1, 1983, pp. 321, 322 by Erickson says: "[The Trinity] presents what seems on the surface to be a self-contradictory doctrine. Furthermore, this doctrine is not overtly or explicitly stated in Scripture ... Since the Trinity is not explicitly taught in Scripture, we will have to put together complementary themes, draw inferences from biblical teachings, and decide on a particular type of conceptual vehicle to express our understanding ... It will be important to note the type of witness in the Scripture which led the Church to formulate and propound this strange doctrine."

---

100 Harold Bloom, 2005, p. 7

- *A Religious Encyclopaedia: Based on the real-Encyklopadie of Herzog, Plitt, and Hauck states:* "it is a remarkable fact, that no single passage or verse of the Old or New Testament is received as an assured proof-text of the trinity by the unanimous consent of all Trinitarian writers: some ground their faith on one passage, some on another."
- *Hastings Dictionary of The Bible*—Revised edition by F.C. Grant & H.H. Rowley says: "The doctrine of God as existing in three persons and one substance is not demonstrable by logic or by scriptural proofs."
- *For Christ Sake* by Tom Harpur an Anglican Priest says: "You simply cannot find the doctrine of the Trinity set out anywhere in the Bible. St. Paul has the highest view of Jesus' role and person, but nowhere does he call him God. Nor does Jesus himself explicitly claim to be the second person of the Trinity, wholly equal to his heavenly Father." He continues: "As early as the 8th century, the Theologian St. John Damascus frankly admitted what every modern critical scholar of the NT now realizes: that neither the doctrine of the Trinity nor that of the 2 natures of Jesus Christ is explicitly set out in scripture. In fact, if you take the record as it is and avoid reading back into it the dogmatic definitions of a later age, you cannot find what is traditionally regarded as orthodox Christianity in the Bible at all."
- *Kittels Theological Dictionary of the N.T.* says: "The New Testament does not actually speak of tri-unity. We seek this in vain in the triadic formulae of the N.T."
- *The River of God*, by Gregory J. Riley, p. 62 states: "There was no theoretical framework in scripture that explained the relationship of the Father, Son, and Holy Spirit. No Old Testament author addressed the issue of a separate being, the Holy Spirit, and its ('her', in Hebrew) relationship to the Father; the Spirit of God was God's 'spirit' or breath that carried his power … there are no triadic formulations in the New Testament, such as the command to baptize "in the name of the Father and the Son and the Holy Spirit" (Matt 28:19), and the prayer of the blessing that "the grace of the Lord Jesus Christ and the love of God and the fellowship of the Holy Spirit be with you all" (2 Cor. 13:14). But all of these have to do with how God relates to the church. None explains how the Father, Son, and Holy Spirit relate to each other in essence. That task fell to a particularly influential group of 'heretics'-Gnostic Christians of the second century."
- *The New International Dictionary of New Testament Theology*, Protestant theologian Karl Barth, states: "The N [ew] T [estament] does not contain the developed doctrine of the Trinity. The Bible lacks the express declaration that the Father, the Son, and the Holy Spirit are of equal essence."

- Martin Luther "declared such a term as homoousios[101] to be unallowable in the strict sense, because it represents a bad state of things when such words are invented in the Christian system of faith ... if my soul hates the word homoousios and I prefer not to use it, I shall not be a heretic; for who will compel me to use it, provided that I hold the thing which was defined in the Council by means of the Scriptures?" Adolf Harnack noted about Luther: He "In like manner objected to and rather avoided the terms 'trinitas' (threefoldness, threeness, oneness, trinity)."[102]
- *Grundlinien des Glaubens* (Baselines of the Faith), under 1.2, p. 244fn., Karl Barth (Protestant theologian) states: "The Trinity doctrine cannot be found in the Bible, it is the work of the church."
- *Origin and Evolution of Religion*, Yale University Professor E. Washburn Hopkins says: "To Jesus and Paul the doctrine of the trinity was apparently unknown; ... they say nothing about it."
- *The Paganism in our Christianity*, Historian Arthur Weigall notes: "Jesus Christ never mentioned such a phenomenon, and nowhere in the New Testament does the word "Trinity" appear. The idea was only adopted by the Church three hundred years after the death of our Lord."
- *The Church of the First Three Centuries*, Alvan Lamson states: "The modern popular doctrine of the Trinity ... derives no support from the language of Justin [Martyr]: and this observation may be extended to all the ante-Nicene Fathers; that is, to all Christian writers for three centuries after the birth of Christ. It is true, they speak of the Father, Son, and ... holy spirit, but not as co-equal, not as one numerical essence, not as Three in One, in any sense now admitted by Trinitarians. The very reverse is the fact."
- *The History of Christianity*, Peter Eckler explains: "If Paganism was conquered by Christianity, it is equally true that Christianity was corrupted by Paganism. The pure Deism of the first Christians (who differed from their fellow Jews only in the belief that Jesus was the promised Messiah,) was changed, by the Church of Rome, into the incomprehensible dogma of the trinity. Many of the pagan tenets, invented by the Egyptians and idealized by Plato, were retained as being worthy of belief."
- *Robert I. Gannon*, Catholic clergyman, admits: "The doctrine of the Holy Trinity is extremely difficult to explain, and nobody understands it,"
- *Robert A Heinlein* says: "Anyone who can worship a trinity and insist that his religion is a monotheism can believe anything."

---

101 Greek term meaning of identical substance/being/consubstantial
102 *History of Dogma* by Adolf Harnack, Volume 7, p. 225

- *Jesus and the Meaning of "God"*[103] states: "When the New Testament writers say 'God' they normally mean God the Father, Yahweh the God of Israel and they do not have any idea of a distinction of coequal Persons within God." He adds: "the New Testament nowhere says that the Son of God is God of God. In pre-Nicene days the phrase 'Son of God' could be used to emphasize the *difference* of status between Jesus and God."
- G.H. Boobyer, *Jesus as Theos in the N.T.*,[104] says: "The fact has to be faced that New Testament research over, say, the last thirty or forty years has been leading an increasing number of reputable New Testament scholars to the conclusion that Jesus himself may not have claimed any of the Christological titles which the Gospels ascribe to him ... and certainly never believe himself to be God ... can you hold together, as many New Testament scholars seem to do, the two positions that on the one hand critical study of the Gospels discloses a Jesus with no consciousness of being God and making no claim to be God and on the other hand the belief that Nicene Christology, declaring him 'True God of true God' is a right credalization of the New Testament evidence?"
- *The Harper Collins Encyclopedia of Catholicism* correctly admits: "The doctrine of the Trinity is not revealed in either the Old Testament or the New Testament; however, the essential elements of what eventually became the doctrine are contained in Scripture."[105]
- Trinitarian scholar A. W. Argyle himself admits: "The fully developed Christian Doctrine that God is three Persons in one Godhead is nowhere explicitly stated in the New Testament."[106]
- Trinitarian scholars Roger E. Olson and Christopher Hall also admit: "What do we find in the writings of the Christian leaders during roughly the first sixty years of the second century CE? As we might expect, we do not find the developed Trinitarian language or theology that will blossom from the fourth century on ... we will be disappointed if we expect to find developed Trinitarian reflection in the early post-apostolic writers. It is simply not there."[107]

---

103 P. 38, Cupitt; *Incarnation and Myth: The Debate Continued*, 1979; Stanton, *Incarnational Language in the N.T.*, p. 166, emphasis by Cupitt
104 Vol. 50, 1967–1968, pp. 251, 252
105 P. 1270
106 *God in The New Testament*, 1966, p. 173
107 *The Trinity*, 2002, pp. 16, 20

- Trinitarian Bible scholar Emil Brunner in his book, *The Christian Doctrine of God, Dogmatics* acknowledged: "It was never the intention of the original witnesses to Christ in the New Testament to set before us an intellectual problem—that of Three Divine Persons—then to tell us silently to worship this mystery of the 'Three-in-One.' There is no trace of such an idea in the New Testament. This 'mysterium logicum,' the fact that God is Three and yet One, lies wholly outside the message of the Bible. [This mystery has] no connection with the message of Jesus and His Apostles. No Apostle would have dreamt of thinking that there are Three Divine Persons, whose mutual relations and paradoxical unity are beyond our understanding. No 'mysterium logicum,' no intellectual paradox, no antinomy of Trinity in Unity, has any place in their testimony."[108]
- Protestant Dr. Shirley C. Guthrie states in his book *Christian Doctrine*: "The Bible does not teach the doctrine of the Trinity. Neither the word 'trinity' itself nor such language as 'one-in-three,' 'three-in-one,' one 'essence' (or 'substance'), and three 'persons' is biblical language … language of the doctrine is the language of the ancient church, taken not from the Bible but from classical Greek philosophy."[109]
- Baptist professor of theology at Southwestern Baptist Theological Seminary, Millard J. Erickson, states: "The doctrine of the Trinity as we know it today did not simply spring full blown onto the scene of Christian thought at the beginning of the Church's life. It went through a long process in which the Church weighed varying interpretations of the biblical data and selected those it judged to be more adequate. At the same time, the Church was progressively dealing with different and more refined issues, and in so doing was sharpening the focus of it's thinking … we will see the doctrine of the Trinity being developed, layer by layer."[110]
- A. T. Hanson, Professor of Theology at the University of Hull candidly admits: "No responsible New Testament scholar would claim that the doctrine of the Trinity was taught by Jesus, or preached by the earliest Christians, or consciously held by any writer of the New Testament. It was in fact slowly worked out in the course of the first few centuries in an attempt to give an intelligible doctrine of God."[111]

---

108 Volume I, 1949, p. 226
109 1968, pp. 92, 93
110 *God in Three Persons, A Contemporary Interpretation of the Trinity*, 1995, p. 33
111 *The Image of the Invisible God*, 1982, p. 87

There most certainly could be countless other references quoted, but I believe you understand my position here. What position is that? Those teaching the doctrine of the trinity are simply speaking opposing ideas out of both ends of their mouths—and at the same time. On one hand these learned men—most are Trinitarians—insist the trinity chain is based on God's word the Bible. Yet, as noted above, they readily admit there is no scripture that professes—with definitiveness—this doctrine of the trinity in the Hebrew or Greek Scriptures. However, this is exactly what the religious leaders in Christendom are telling, demanding, and expecting their flocks to believe by faith in order to be saved.

Does this not represent an extraordinarily weak link in this doctrine? The author certainly feels so and I am proud to reveal this to you from scripture. You simply cannot have it both ways. A doctrine is either found in Gods word or it isn't. One book makes this candid observation regarding the explicit description of the trinity in scripture: "Can it really be so intrinsically connected with the gospel of salvation that denying it (not merely failing fully to understand it) results in loss of salvation or at least loss of status as a Christian? It is understandable that the importance placed on this doctrine is perplexing to many Christians and students. Nowhere is it clearly and unequivocally stated in Scripture ... How can it be so important if it is not explicitly stated in Scripture?"[112]

God's word says: "The Spirit makes it clear that as time goes on, some are going to give up on the faith and chase after demonic illusions put forth by professional liars. These liars have lied so well and for so long that they've lost their capacity for truth."[113] Since the trinity doctrine was introduced after Christ and his disciples, who then can we allege the inspiration of this so-called doctrine of faith according to 1 Timothy 4:1? As Jesus said: "Let the reader use discernment."

If the trinity doctrine were taught by Jesus and his followers then by all means as Christians we have an obligation to believe in it. However, we find just the opposite convincing information to expose it as being counterfeit, not only by its progression that took centuries to develop after Christ, but also by Trinitarians own admittance that there is no trinity in scripture. "The adoption of the Trinity doctrine came as a result of a process of theological exploration which lasted at least three hundred years ... it would be foolish to represent the doctrine of the Holy Trinity as having been achieved by any other way ... This was a long, confused, process whereby different schools of thought in the Church worked out for themselves, and then tried to impose on others, their answer to the question,

---

112 *The Trinity, Guides to Theology*, Roger E. Olson and Christopher Hall, 2002, p. 1
113 1 Timothy 4:1, *TM*

"How divine is Jesus Christ?" ... If ever there was a controversy decided by the method of trial and error, it was this one."[114] Thus, Professor Rolf Furuli, a lecturer in Semitic languages at the University of Oslo, Norway writes: "While all the Fathers used the Bible, the evidence suggests that the trinity doctrine was gradually formed under the influence of Greek philosophy ... there is little doubt that the trinity doctrine is a theological teaching that came into being *after* the Bible was completed."[115] And so, our first weak link of the trinity chain is exposed. A chain is only as strong as it's weakest link.

Is the trinity unique to Christendom?

The doctrine of the trinity is certainly not unique to Christendom, as some might believe. Triune gods or god in 'three persons' was a most common belief in ancient religions. In the book *A statement of Reasons* by Andrews Norton says regarding the trinity: "We can trace the history of this doctrine, and discover its source, not in the Christian revelation, but in the Platonic philosophy ... The Trinity is not a doctrine of Christ and his Apostles, but a fiction of the school of the later Platonists." Thus, "Fourth century Trinitarianism was a deviation from early Christian teaching."[116]

In Babylon the planet Venus was revered as special and was worshipped as a trinity consisting of Venus, the moon, and the sun. This was established in the 14th century before Jesus Christ. The Babylonians used a triangle to represent this 'three in one' god. Zeus, Athena, and Apollo represented the Greek triad god. The Romans trinity consisted of Jupiter, Mercury, and Venus. Egypt of course had its triune gods. The most famous was that of Horus, Isis and Seb, (HIS), which interestingly, consisted of father, mother and son.

It is a known fact that as pagans were converted to Christianity, they brought with them their ideas and beliefs and incorporated them into Christian doctrines. "In Indian religion there is the Trinitarian group of Brahma, Vishna, and Shiva; in Egyptian religion there is the group of Kneph, Phthas, and Osiris. In Phoenicia the trinity of gods were Ulomus, Ulosuros, and Eliun. In Greece they were Zeus, Poseidon, and Aidoneus. In Rome they were Jupitor, Neptune, and Pluto. In Babylon and Assyria they were Anos, Illinos, and Aos. Among Celtic nations

---

114 *Reasonable Belief, A Survey of the Christian Faith*, Anthony Tyrell Hanson and Richard Patrick Crosland Hanson, 1980, pp. 174–175
115 *The Role of Theology and Bias in Bible Translation With a special look at the New World Translation of Jehovah's Witnesses*, 1999, p. 147, emphasis his
116 *The Encyclopedia Americana*

they were called Kriosan, Biosena, and Siva, and in Germanic nations they were called Thor, Wodan, and Fricco."[117] Another source reveals: "The trinity was a major preoccupation of Egyptian theologians ... Three gods are combined and treated as a single being, addressed in the singular. In this way the spiritual force of Egyptian religion shows a direct link with Christian theology."[118]

With certainty we are able to deduce that "Such a Hellenization did, to a large extent, take place. The definition of the Christian faith as contained in the creeds of the ecumenical synods of the early church indicate that unbiblical categories of Neoplatonic philosophy were used in the formulation of the doctrine of the Trinity."[119] One dictionary readily admits: "The Platonic trinity, itself merely a rearrangement of older trinities dating back to earlier peoples, appears to be the rational philosophic trinity of attributes that gave birth to three hypostases or divine persons taught by the Christian churches ... This Greek philosopher's [Plato, forth century B.C.E] conception of the divine trinity ... can be found in all the ancient religions."[120]

Sadly, After Christ's apostles died, philosophies and all kinds of pagan, apostate weeds influenced and infiltrated the true wheat class as Jesus and his disciples had foretold.[121]

Bible scholars in Jesus' day vs. scholars of today

The religious leaders and Bible scholars of Jesus day were no different than in ours. Notice what Jesus said to them: "Ye hypocrite, well did Isaiah prophesy of you, saying, This people honoreth me with their lips; But their heart is far from me. But in vain do they worship me, teaching as their doctrines the precepts of men."[122] Just the same, the Apostle Paul warned Christians: "The time is sure to come when, far from being content with sound teaching, people will be avid for the latest novelty and collect themselves a whole series of teachers according to their own tastes; and then, instead of listening to the truth, they will turn to myths."[123] Paul continues and also says not to be "hanging on to Jewish fables

---

117 *God*, Paul Johnson, 1938, published by P.S.L. Johnson, Philadelphia, PA
118 *Egyptian Religion*, Siegfried Morenz
119 *The Encyclopaedia Britannica*, 1976
120 *Nouveau Dictionnaire Universel*, 1865–1870, edited by M. Lachatre, Vol. 2, p. 1467, brackets mine
121 Cf. Matthew 13:24–30; 36–43; Acts 20:29, 30
122 Matthew 15:7–9
123 2 Timothy 4:3, 4, *JB*

and human dogmas which turn them away from the truth."[124] Warning after warning was given to avoid the deceptive reasoning's and false teachings of imperfect men.[125]

It is of great interest as well that these educated Jewish religious so-called leaders were not recognized as a whole to be Jesus' followers. Instead, we find Jesus Christ, after a full night of prayer to his Father, had selected humble farmers, tax collectors, and fishermen. These 'common, unlettered, and ordinary' people were so convinced of what Jesus taught about God that they were willing to die for their belief. The very same honest, humble, teachable and spiritually hungry ones are being drawn to God today through his beloved Son.[126]

Is it a mystery or just plain confusion?

There is another helpful truth that cannot go unnoticed as well as unanswered. When Trinitarians are not able to explain their doctrine from the Bible, (because it's not in the Bible), they will always fall back on this 'safety blanket': "It's a mystery!" This may sound reasonable to some, but there is a question that Trinitarians, (really, all those professing to be Christians), must answer. If the trinity doctrine is the 'central doctrine of the Christian faith', why are we not able to find Jesus explaining this very confusing mystery? Why didn't his followers teach this or at least try to enlighten us about it? Why would Jesus, and all the Bible writers, speak of God as only one person if he were in fact three? This would do nothing except to mislead, confuse and push others away from God, not draw them closer.[127] The Bible proclaims openly of God: "for God is not a God of confusion," or "for God is not [the author] of confusion, but of peace," and "for God is not [a God] of confusion, but of peace."[128]

Besides this, Jesus was known as the Great Rabbi,[129] and yet we ascertain not even an insinuation of this teaching of the trinity from him. Jesus gave not even an illustration without speaking to the crowds, which the scripture declares: "Jesus used parables to tell all these things to the crowds, and he didn't speak to them except in parables. He did this that it might be fulfilled what the prophet said, "I will open my mouth in parables. I will say things which have been secret

---

124 Titus 1:14, *VC*
125 Cf. 2 Corinthians 11:12–15; 2 Peter 2:1, 2
126 Cf. John 6:44; 7:45–49; Matthew 15:1–9; 21:23–32, 43; 23:13–36; Acts 4:13
127 James 4:8
128 1 Corinthians 14:33, *NASB, MKJV, ASV*, respectively
129 Meaning Teacher; compare John 1:38; 13:13

since the creation of the world.""[130] Jesus used so many illustrations his disciples were literally forced to ask: "Why speakest thou unto them in parables?" In reply Jesus said: "To you it is granted to understand the sacred secrets of the kingdom of the heavens, but to those people it is not granted ... because looking, they look in vain, and hearing, they hear in vain, neither do they get the sense of it ... for the heart of this people has grown unreceptive, and with their ears they have heard without response, and they have shut their eyes ... and get the sense of it with their hearts ..."[131]

Notice Jesus connects the understanding of illustrations with our figurative heart? If religious leaders find it necessary to explain the trinity with illustrations to their flocks, why didn't Jesus do so for his disciples to understand? I find it very interesting when I am in the ministry work, and many who profess the trinity try to use all sorts of witty illustrations to explain this doctrine, such as a three-leaf clover, and the water, ice, and steam theory—of course to no avail. I ask of them to please show one illustration concerning the trinity to me from the Bible translation of their choice. I am always met with silence. If there is a need on behalf of imperfect man to try and explain the trinity with illustrations, then again I ask, why didn't the perfect, great teacher Jesus Christ, not illustrate this trinity doctrine? This would seem rather odd, especially for those whose hearts were longing for truth as his disciples. No teaching would have required more explanation than the trinity chain. This would apply especially to fellow Jews, who to this day, still believe in one God ontologically, not 'three persons' of God.

Some have even said: 'It is not for us to understand and know God.' Yet, is this opinion in harmony with God's own word? God says: "If you search for him, he will let himself be found by you," and "Come close to God, and he will come close to you," "The intimacy with Jehovah belongs to those who are fearful of him," "God's purpose in all His dealings with mankind is to cause them to look for Him—hoping they will reach out for Him and find Him, though He isn't far from any of us" and finally "My name is Jav'e, there is no other rival to me; it was not in secret, not in some dark recess of the earth, that my word was spoken. Not in vain I bade the sons of Jacob search for me."[132] Does this sound like a God who doesn't want us to understand or know him?

Unfortunately, the trinity has caused many to view God as unknowable. Andrews Norton, a professor at Harvard Divinity School in the 19th century

---

130 Matthew 13:34, 35, *NMB*, compare Psalm 78:2
131 Matthew 13:10–15, *ASV, NWT* respectively
132 1 Chronicles 28:9, *NWT*; James 4:8, *NEB*; Psalm 25:14; Acts 17:27, *LDB*; Isaiah 45:19, *RAK* respectively

declares: "It appears, then, that while other questions of far less difficulty (for instance, the circumcision of the Gentile converts) were subjects of such doubt and controversy that even the authority of the Apostles were barely sufficient to establish the truth, this doctrine [the trinity], so extraordinary, so obnoxious, and so hard to be understood, was introduced in silence, and received without hesitation, dislike, opposition, or misapprehensions."[133] This is contrary to what the Bible as a whole teaches and emphasizes. For it is the want and desire of God for mankind to know him intimately.

Jesus answers with logic and reason

Why do we not find anywhere, Jesus enemies arguing and disproving the trinity doctrine? This concept of 'three in one' Godhead would have been disgusting to the Jews. "The Epistles are full of statements, explanations, and controversy, having their origin in Jewish prejudices and passions. With regard however to this doctrine [the Trinity], which if it had ever been taught, the believing Jews must have received with the utmost difficulty, and to which the unbelieving Jews would have manifested the most determined opposition, with regard to this doctrine, there is not a trace of any controversy … it must have required, far more than any other doctrine, to be explained, illustrated, and enforced … the doctrine then is never defended in the New Testament, though unquestionably it would have been the main object of attack, and the main difficulty in the Christian system. It is never explained, though no doctrine could have been so much in need of explanation … and still more, this doctrine is never insisted upon as a necessary article of faith; though it is now represented by its defenders as lying at the foundation of Christianity."[134]

Another Bible scholar of the nineteenth century had this to say: "Look at the devotional character of the New Testament. If the Apostles worshipped God in three persons, it will so appear in their conduct and writings; this circumstance will characterize their devout expressions everywhere. And this the more especially, because they were Jews, a people who worshipped God with a strict and most jealous regard to his unity. They could not have changed their practice in this particular without the change being most strikingly most observable. Yet we have no intimation of such a change. They appear to have gone on with the worship of the One God of their fathers, without any alteration. Look at this fact.

---

133 *A Statement of Reasons For Not Believing The Doctrines of Trinitarians, Concerning The Nature of God and The Persons of Christ*, 1883
134 Andrews Norton, pp. 38–39

When Paul was converted, he must have passed—supposing the Trinity to be a Christian doctrine—from believing Jesus a blasphemous imposter, to believing him the Lord Jehovah. Is there the least hint of such an amazing change? He speaks with admiration and rapture of the new views and feelings which he enjoyed with his new faith. But all the rest together was not so astonishing and wonderful as this particular change. Yet he nowhere alludes to it. Is it then possible that it could have been so? That so great a revolution of feeling should have taken place, and no intimation of it be found in any act or expression? He speaks frequently of his prayers. And how? 'Blessed be the God and Father of our Lord Jesus Christ.' 'Making mention of you in my prayers, that the God of our Lord Jesus Christ, the Father of glory, may give unto you the spirit of wisdom.' It is plain therefore to whom Paul directed his worship ... And not once, either in his epistles, or in any other writing of the Bible, is doxology to be found, which ascribes praise to the Father, Son and Spirit [together as one God], or to the Trinity in any form. This fact is worth remarking. The New Testament contains, I think, twenty-eight ascriptions in various forms; and from not one of them could you learn that the doctrine of the Trinity had been dreamt of in that day."[135]

The answer to our opening question is very simple and explained in scripture by Jesus himself. Quoting from Deuteronomy 6:4 he says: "Hear, O Israel! The Lord our God is the one and only Lord."[136] Unfortunately, many sincere Trinitarians have been taught the word 'one' in this verse implies and infers there is more than one person in the one God. The truth is the grammar of this verse concerning the Hebrew word 'one' (Echad), has no plural modifiers to suggest not even a little, that it means anything but one specific individual. "Echad is a numerical adjective and naturally enough is sometimes found modifying a collective noun ... one family, one herd, one bunch. But we should observe carefully the sense of plurality resides in the compound noun and not in the word echad (one) ... It is subterfuge to transfer to "one" the plurality which belongs only to the following noun. It would be similar to saying "one" really means "one hundred" when it appears in the combination "one centipede."[137] Just as well, *Strong's Exhaustive Concordance* gives the definition of echad H259 as: "a numeral from H258; properly united, that is, one; or, (as an ordinal) first ..." Likewise, *Brown-Driver-Briggs Hebrew and English Lexicon* affirms: "echad-1a. One (number), 1e. only, once, once for all, 1f. one ... another, the one ... the other."

---

135 *Testimony of Scripture Against the Trinity*, 1827, Boston
136 Mark 12:29, *NLT*
137 *The Doctrine of the Trinity-Christianity's Self-Inflicted Wound*, Buzzard and Hunting, 1999, pp. 25, 26

Some perfect Bible examples of the application of this word echad (one), are Isaiah 51:2 and Genesis 21:15. Isaiah says: "Look to Abraham your father and to Sarah, who gradually brought you forth with childbirth pains. For he was one [echad] when I called him." If Trinitarians want us to believe that the word 'one' implies multiplicity in Deuteronomy 6:4, then we would have to accept it here as well. We are not allowed to pick and choose scriptures to fit our theology. Hence, according to Trinitarian theology, Abraham would have to be converted into a multi-person since he is called 'one' by God. Of course, this makes no logical sense at all. The same could be spoken of regarding Genesis 21:15 and the other occurrences of the word 'one' (echad).

Anthony Buzzard continues by saying: "It is untrue to say that the Hebrew word *echad* (one) in Deuteronomy 6:4 points to 'compound unity.' The argument is fallacious ... The claim that 'one' really means 'compound oneness' is an example of argument by assertion without logical proof ... *Echad* appears some 960 times in the Hebrew Bible and in no case does the word itself carry a hint of plurality. It strictly means 'one and not two or more.' One bunch of grapes is just that—one and not two bunches ... When the spies returned with evidence of the fruitfulness of the Promise Land they carried 'a single (*echad*) cluster of grapes' (Num. 13:23, NRSV) ... Israel's supreme Lord is 'one single Lord,' 'one Lord alone.' It has been necessary to belabor our point because the recent defense of the Trinity makes the astonishing assertion that *echad* always implies a 'compound unity.' The author then builds his case for a multi-personal God on what he thinks is a firm foundation in the Hebrew Bible. The linguistic fact is that *echad* never means 'compound one,' but strictly a 'single one.' ... It has sometimes been argued that God would have been described as *yachid*, i.e. 'solitary, isolated, the only one,' if there were only one person in the Godhead. The use of *echad* ('one single'), however, is quite sufficient to indicate that the One Person comprises the Deity. Yachid is rare in biblical Hebrew ... The One God of Israel is a single person, unrivaled and in a class of His own. He is One, with all the mathematical simplicity implied by that word."[138]

Let us take a few moments and a closer look at a small number of scriptures containing this word echad (one), and verify that 'one' does not mean trinity—multi-personal—as some wish it to be. Remember, scripture interprets scripture.[139]

Our first verse is found at Genesis 1:5. "And God called the light Day, and the darkness he called Night. And there was evening and there was morning, one

---

138 *The Doctrine of the Trinity*, Buzzard and Hunting, pp. 25–29
139 Cf. Genesis 40:8; 2 Peter 1:21

day." Ask yourselves: Does night and day make up two days or one (echad) day? The answer is obvious. There is literally one day.

Let us view Genesis 2:24. "Therefore shall a man leave his father and his mother, and shall cleave unto his wife: and they shall be one flesh." Using reason, when man and wife are joined in marriage, do they become literally one fleshly being? Hardly! However, they are one (echad) in unity, same purposes, goals, and worship.

Our next example is found at Genesis 41:5. "He [Pharaoh] fell asleep and dreamed a second time: Seven heads of grain, full of good, came up on one stalk."[140] Were these seven heads of grain located on one stalk or many?

Another scripture is Genesis 42:16. "So send one of your number to get your brother, while the rest of you stay here under arrest."[141] How many persons did Joseph want to send, a unity of persons, or one person in the absolute numerical and logical sense? The answer is obvious and found in verse 19: "Let one of your brothers."

Our final scripture I will use is Ezekiel 33:24. "Abraham was just one man."[142] Would you consider Abraham to be more than one person? Is he considered as a compound unity or simply numerically one?

When we allow reason and scripture alone to guide us, these questions are easily answered and more importantly made exceptionally clear. With the correct understanding of the word one (echad), let us return to Deuteronomy 6:4.

According to Mark 12:29 "Yeshua [Jesus] was not a Trinitarian, a statement at once obvious yet also shattering in its implications ... Mark's Jesus, who anguished all night before his end, had been steadfast in devotion to Yahweh alone."[143] Referring to Song of Solomon 6:9: "One there is who is my dove, my blameless one ... she is the pure one," Professor John Sawyer states in comparison to Deuteronomy 6:4 "She is his (the poet's) favourite, the one to whom all his love is directed. Surely, this is what the Shma, [Deut. 6:4], means: Yahweh is the one God above all others who demands total allegiance ... its original meaning as a rather positive statement about the unique nature of Yahweh."[144] For this reason, Jesus' love for his Father was pure as well, showing allegiance only to Jehovah.

---

140 *HCSB*
141 *NAB*
142 *CEV*
143 *Jesus and Yahweh The Names Divine*, Bloom, pp. 97, 178; brackets mine
144 *Biblical Alternatives to Monotheism*, J.F.A. Sawyer, Volume 87, 1984, p. 175, brackets mine

Therefore, If Jesus was teaching a new theology, this would have been the perfect opportune time for him to explain and confess the trinity doctrine. A Biblical scholar of the day, a scribe, asked Jesus "which commandment is first of all?" Then Jesus responded accordingly. Notice the reaction of this scribe: "Teacher," the lawyer acknowledged, "you said the truth. He is One. There is no other than He.'"[145] Afterward, in verse 34, Jesus had discerned that this scribe "answered intelligently." This Jewish scribe believed in the Monotheistic God of the Old Testament. Obviously, Jesus did too. Ian Wilson states in his book: "If Jesus had wanted to institute a formula for the religion he taught, there is one moment, described in Marks Gospel, when he had the perfect opportunity to do so. A scribe is reported as having asked him: "Which is the first of all the commandments?" It was an occasion to which Jesus could have imparted one of those characteristic twists, bringing in something new, something involving himself, if he wished us to believe that he was a member of a Trinity, on an equal footing with God the Father. Instead he looked unhesitatingly to his traditional Jewish roots."[146]

In fact, Jesus Christ was born a Jew, raised a Jew and believed as a Jew. Jesus was known as the Great Teacher,[147] a Jewish title bestowed upon only those fluent in the Jewish heritage and tradition. This can be the only commonsensical conclusion since Jesus was educated and raised by faithful Jewish parents on the subject of the Hebrew Scriptures. This is to be said of Jesus' disciples and his targeted audience—they were Jews. Surely, at least some agitation would have been recorded for us if a new teaching as the trinity doctrine were introduced to the monotheistic Jews. Again, Buzzard and Hunting declare: "Such an innovation would have required the most careful and repeated explanation for men and women who has been steeped from birth in the belief that God was one person only."[148] Also, "It is now, I suppose, fully established and generally admitted that the Jews in the time of Christ had no expectation that the coming Messiah would be an incarnation of Jehovah, and no acquaintance with the mystery of the Trinity."[149]

Therefore, "The thoughtful student must ask himself: if it was hard for the Jews in the early church to let go of the Law, wouldn't it have been even harder to get them to change their view of God? Fifteen New Testament chapters are

---

145 Mark 12:32, *LD*
146 *Jesus, The Evidence*, pp. 176–177
147 Rabbi
148 *The Doctrine of the Trinity, Christianity's Self-Inflicted Wound*, p. 7
149 *The Journal of the Society of Biblical Literature and Exegesis*, 1881

dedicated to changing the Jew's mind on the Law. And if it took that much to deal with the Law, shouldn't we find at least 1 or 2 chapters explaining the change in how God would be viewed from now on? But not a single verse suggests the Jew change his view of God ... [In our examination we noted the] lack of a single verse which 'taught' the doctrine. The Bible has many verses that 'teach' justification, 'teach' repentance, 'teach' baptism, 'teach' the resurrection, but not one verse in the entire Bible 'teaches' the doctrine of the Trinity. No verse describes it, explains it, or defines it. And no verse tells us to believe it ... The more I looked at the Trinity, the more I saw a doctrine rich in tradition, and passionately defended by brilliant and sincere people, but severely weak in reason and badly wanting in Biblical support."[150]

The truth and facts reveal for us just the opposite of what the trinity advocates. Another way to articulate this is to declare, "Jesus simply restated with complete clarity the fundamental tenet of the Jewish religious system, confirming beyond all argument that the true God is one Lord ... and thus one person."[151]

The 'missing link'

Some of you may be wondering why I haven't considered the holy spirit. The answer is really quite simple. The 'third person' of the trinity is rarely a topic of discussion with Trinitarians. Why? When Trinitarians present their 'proof texts', God's holy spirit is never mentioned. Please take a close look at John 1:1; John 20:28; John 8:58; Romans 9:5; Titus 2:13; Hebrews 1:8; 1 John 5:20; et cetera. The holy spirit is simply not mentioned. The trinity then really isn't triune at all. Hence, this would be modalism or dualism at best.

At any rate, every discussion I have been engaged in always comes down to the following: Is the holy spirit an 'It' or an 'He?' It's only logical to draw upon Hebrew and Greek dictionaries as a starting point. The Hebrew word for spirit is ruach. The Greek word for spirit is pneuma. *Vine's Expository Dictionary* says of ruah: "breath; air; strength; wind; breeze; spirit ... First this word means "breath," air for breathing, air that is being breathed." *The Brown-Driver-Briggs and English Lexicon* says of ruach: "7307—breath, wind, spirit ... 1. Breath of mouth or nostrils." Regarding spirit of the Greek (pneuma), *Strong's Exhaustive Concordance of the Bible* says: "G4151—a current of air, that is breath (blast) or a breeze." *Vine's Expository Dictionary* says: "Primarily denotes "the wind" (akin to pneo, "to

---

150 *The Great Debate Regarding the Father, Son, & Holy Spirit*, Robert A. Wagoner, 1997–98
151 Buzzard and Hunting, p. 32

breathe, blow"); also "breath"; then, especially "the spirit," which, like the wind, is invisible, immaterial, and powerful."

Theological Workbook of the Old Testament says: "The basic idea of ruah [the Hebrew word for 'spirit'] (Grk pneuma) is 'air in motion.' ... The ruah 'spirit' of God (from God) is in my nostrils.' (Job 27:7) ... ruah can exhibit a range of meaning. The 'breath' of God may be a strong wind. (Is 40:7) ... His 'spirit' may indicate no more than active power ..."[152]

Cyril C. Richardson states in his book: "The primary notion of Spirit in the Bible is that of God's dynamic activity. The Spirit is his breath, hence his vitality or life. Since a body without breath is dead, breath was viewed as the vitalizing element in man. At man's creation God breathed into Adam's nostril's the breath of life, and thus he became a living soul (Gen. 2:7). As applied to God, then, his breath is his vitality and the means by which he does things and expresses his creative potency."[153] Another book states: "The root meaning of the word spirit in the Old Testament is wind or breath—not a breeze, but the powerful, sweeping desert wind; not a quiet, steady breathing, but agitated, violent breathing. Hence in the Old Testament spirit comes to denote the vital energy, the power of God. God created by his Word (Psalm 145:8), but by his Spirit he vitalized what he created (Psalm 104:30)."[154]

Finally, *A Greek-English Lexicon of the New Testament and Other Early Christian Literature* by Walter Bauer, F.W. Gingrich, and Fredrick Danker, second edition p. 674 states concerning pneuma: "1. blowing, breathing, b. the breathing out of air."

These definitions alone should be sufficient evidence to validate the holy spirit being an 'It.' As always, let's confirm this through scripture. Let's begin with Genesis 1:2.[155] "The earth was a shapeless, chaotic mass, with the Spirit, (ruach, breath), of God brooding over the dark vapors." Is God's breath a person or an impersonal force?

Judges 14:6[156] reads: "The Spirit of the LORD entered Samson with great power and he tore the lion apart with his bare hands." Did a literal 'spirit being' enter into Samson? Or, was it God's invisible active power that allowed Samson to have such strength?[157]

---

152 Volume 2, 1980, pp. 836–837
153 *The Doctrine of the Trinity*, p. 45
154 *Hard Questions*, John A. Simpson, 1977, pp. 48, 50
155 TB
156 NCV
157 Cf. Judges 16:19, 20

Notice Exodus 31:18 "And he gave unto Moses, when he had made an end of communing with him upon mount Sinai, the two tables of the testimony, tables of stone, written with the finger of God." Now compare this verse with 2 Corinthians 3:3[158] "Written, not with ink, but with the Spirit of the Living God; not on stone tablets, but on the tablets of human hearts." Did God inscribe the tablets with a literal spirit person? Is a literal spirit person inscribed on our hearts?

Matthew 3:11[159] states concerning Jesus: "He will baptize you with the Holy Spirit and fire." Were these people baptized with a literal spirit person and literal fire? Of course they weren't. Just as Jesus was, they were baptized with God's power of approval.

Can a spirit person be poured out upon people? For Acts 2:17, 18 says: "I will pour forth of my Spirit upon all flesh ... on my servants and on my handmaidens ... I will pour forth of my Spirit."[160] Compare this with Acts 2:2–4 "And suddenly there occurred from heaven a noise just like that of a rushing stiff breeze, [remember Strong's definition: a breeze], and it filled the whole house in which they were sitting. And tongues as if of fire became visible to them and were distributed about, and one sat upon each one of them [120], and they all became filled with the holy spirit."[161] Can one person, let alone one hundred and twenty persons, be filled with another person? This is illogical.

Finally, we have Jesus Christ being anointed with holy spirit in Acts 10:38[162] "How God anointed him with the Holy Spirit, and with power." Did God anoint Jesus with a literal spirit being, or with power of authority? In other words, did God anoint Jesus with another god? This is illogical and unreasonable. Hebrews 1:9[163] illuminates this when it says: "Therefore God, your God, has anointed you in preference to your associates with the oil that brings gladness." Oil is certainly not a literal person. Oil was poured out upon a person's head to signify authority given to him.[164] Remember, it was prophesied that Jesus would be anointed with holy spirit.[165]

---

158 *TPNT*
159 *WFB*
160 *TMB*, cf. Isaiah 44:3
161 *NWT*, Cf. Luke 1:41; Exodus 31:3; brackets mine
162 *WB*
163 *KL*
164 Cf. Exodus 30:22-33; 1 Samuel 10:1; 1 Kings 1:39
165 Cf. Isaiah 11:1, 2; 42:1; 61:1

It is apparently clear from these few scriptures as well as easy to understand, that the Bible's employment of holy spirit is as something, not someone. Bible students must be aware that in Greek and Hebrew, unlike our English, assigns a gender to each noun. The genders assigned are masculine, feminine, or neuter. This is for grammatical reasons only, not for any theological interpretation. The holy spirit, (Hebrew ruach, Greek pneuma), is always in the neuter form. "the "holy Spirit" is referred to by a "neuter" noun in the Greek. Consequently, it is never spoken of with personal pronouns in Greek. It is a "which," not a "who." It is an "it," not a "he." "the phrase "holy spirit," which as always appears in the neuter form."[166] Anglican scholar, C.F.D. Moule, observes: "In the Old Testament, 'spirit' is used chiefly to denote God's powerful action on and within persons, and especially members of his own people; or occasionally, it means simply the breath of life."[167]

I would also like to add here that God's holy spirit is never referred to in the Bible as 'God the Spirit.' Evangelical scholar, Murray J. Harris agrees by saying: "the New Testament never uses *ho theos* ['God'] of the Holy Spirit."[168]

This subject recalls another interesting, rather highly important point. Worship and prayer are never given to the holy spirit in the Bible either. If the holy spirit is the 'third person' of God—according to Trinitarians—we would rightfully expect to find in scripture worship and prayer being given it. This is far from truth. Trinitarian scholars even admit this. For example, one Anglican scholar declares: "In the New Testament there is no example of prayer being offered directly to the Holy Spirit. This practice came later after the dogma of the Trinity had been clarified."[169] Just as well, Trinitarian Millard Erickson says: "in the New Testament we do not have either texts commanding or texts describing worship of or prayer to the Holy Spirit ... It appears, then, that in the New testament the Holy Spirit was not the recipient, but rather, the instrument, the enabler, of prayer. Prayer was done 'in the Spirit,' or 'by the Spirit,' rather then 'to the Spirit.' If, then, we can find in the New Testament neither instruction nor example of worship of the Holy Spirit, we need to ask at what point such practice did enter the church?"[170]

There are, however, a handful of scriptures seeming to imply the holy spirit to be personified. Let's take a close look at one of these. The holy spirit is called 'helper' (comforter) at John 14:16, 26; 16:7. Many have been quick to point

---

166 *Truth In Translation*, Jason BeDuhn, 2003, pp. 140, 142
167 *The Holy Spirit*, 2000, p. 19
168 *Jesus as God*, p. 43
169 *Our Triune God*, Peter Toon, p. 226
170 *God in Three Persons*, p. 234

these out and say: 'only a person can help or comfort someone!' The Greek word for 'helper' (parakletos) is in the masculine gender. Trinitarians try to assert the holy spirit must be a person due to its given action of masculinity in gender. Remember, gender is used for grammatical reasons only, not for theological ones. In other words, this does not change the literal sex gender of whomever, or whatever, is in question; in this case the holy spirit.

It is simply a matter of following grammatical requirements in the Greek language. If the holy spirit took on masculine gender literally in Greek, Trinitarians would have another serious problem to explain. Why? The holy spirit in the Hebrew is with a feminine gender, (Her). Of course, this is not true, since the gender of a noun is grammatical, not theological. The book, *Our Triune God, A Biblical Portrayal of the Trinity* correctly admits: "The Greek word *pneuma* is, in terms of grammar, neuter in gender (in contrast to *ruach* in Hebrew which is feminine gender and *spiritus* in Latin which is masculine gender)."[171] The Catholic *New American Bible* admits regarding John 14:17 "The Greek word for 'Spirit' is neuter, and while we use personal pronouns in English ('he,' 'his,' 'him'), Most Greek MSS employ 'it.'"

I would also like to point out that many scriptures personify impersonal things. For example, would we consider the following to be persons?

- Wisdom has children — "wisdom is justified by all her children." (Luke 7:35)
- Sin, Death are kings — "death was king … sin was king." (Romans 5:14, 21)[172]
- Wind has a will — "The wind blows wherever it wants to." (John 3:8)[173]
- Sin is crouching — "Sin is crouching at the door." (Genesis 4:7)[174]
- Water, Blood witnesses — "For there are three who bear witness." (1 John 5:7, 8)
- The Law speaks — "As the Law expressly states." (1 Corinthians 14:34)[175]

---

171 Pp. 165–167, 188; italics his
172 RL
173 VC
174 TS
175 JWCW

• Scripture speaks	"But what does the Scripture say?" (Galatians 4:30)[176]
• Stone hears	"This stone ... hath heard all the words of Jehovah." (Joshua 24:27)

Is it possible for these things to have children, act as kings, act as witnesses, speak and hear? All of us would agree the answer to be no. Obviously then, just because the holy spirit is spoken of as being able to speak, hear, grieve, comfort, and help does not make it a 'person' in the literal sense.

"In some cases where the Holy Spirit is described in a personal activity, we should understand this as God using his Holy Spirit as the power or agency through which He acts. Consider, for example, that if a man's hand takes hold of a book and lifts it, this does not make the hand a separate person. The hand is merely the agency through which the man is acting."[177] *The Catholic Encyclopedia* writes: "Nowhere in the Old Testament do we find any clear indication of a Third Person."[178] Just as well, *The New Catholic Encyclopedia* states: "The OT clearly does not envisage God's spirit as a person ... God's spirit is simply God's power. If it is sometimes represented as being distinct from God, it is because the breath of Yahweh acts exteriorly ... The majority of NT texts reveal God's spirit as something, not someone; this is especially seen in the parallelism between the spirit and the power of God. When a quasi-personal activity is ascribed to God's spirit, e.g., speaking, hindering, desiring, dwelling (Acts 8:29; 16:7; Rom 8:9), one is not justified in concluding immediately that in these passages God's spirit is regarded as a person; the same expressions are used also in regard to rhetorically personified things or abstract ideas (see Rom 8:6; 7:17) ... St. Paul uses the word pneuma 146 times. Sometimes it means man's natural spirit, but more often it signifies the divine sanctifying power."[179] *A Catholic Dictionary* reads: "On the whole, the New Testament, like the Old, speaks of the spirit as a divine energy or power."[180]

Also, Catholic theologian, Fortman declares: "The Jews never regarded the spirit as a person; nor is there any solid evidence that any Old Testament writer held this view ... The Holy Spirit is usually presented in the Synoptics [Gospels]

---

176 *NCV*
177 *The Good News Magazine*, p. 31
178 1912, Volume 15, pp. 47–49
179 Volume 13, pp. 574–576
180 By Addis and Arnold

and in Acts as a divine force or power ... The spirit of Yahweh was often described in personal terms. The spirit was grieved, guided men, instructed them, caused them to rest."[181] Professor Millard J. Erickson admits: "The Spirit was not necessarily differentiated as a separate person from Jehovah; rather, the focus was on his manifestation, activity, and power."[182]

Thus, even the mouth of Christendom reluctantly and quietly admits the holy spirit to be God's active power, or force; not a 'third person' of the trinity chain.

Final thoughts

Jesus Christ unquestionably taught a new gospel, but not a new theology. Neither should Christians today teach anything, especially doctrine, other than what the whole Bible unequivocally teaches.[183] In an effort to say the trinity is implied—or rather inferred in the scriptures, some point to so-called triadic formulas such as Matthew 28:19 (Father, Son, Holy Spirit), Ephesians 4:4–6 (Spirit, Lord, God), or 1 Peter 1:2 (God, Spirit, Jesus Christ). Ask yourself: does placing three words, names, or titles together prove in anyway or suggest they are co-equal, co-eternal, or three persons of God? Obviously not!

However, some such as Bruce Metzger is thoroughly convinced that they do. Concerning these triadic verses he says they "reveal how deeply the Trinitarian pattern was impressed upon the thinking of primitive Christianity."[184] In addition, M. Evans, a Roman Catholic regarding Matthew 28:19 says that this verse leads directly to a "threesome language about the one God who is Father, Son, and Holy Spirit."[185]

If we are to accept the above scriptures as the trinity, then what is stopping us from accepting the following triadic formulas as the trinity of God? Mark 13:32 (Angels, Son, Father), 1 Timothy 5:21 (God, Christ Jesus, Angels), 2 Thessalonians 1:6–8 (Jesus, Angels, God), Revelation 1:4–5 (God and Father, seven spirits, God), Revelation 3:5 (I (Jesus), my Father, Angels), Revelation 14:10 (God's wrath, Angels, Lamb).

Now, on the other hand, we have others who readily admit: "The connection of these three subjects does not prove their personality or equality."[186] "The NT

---

181 *The Triune God*, pp. 6, 15
182 *God in Three Persons*, p. 34
183 Cf. Proverbs 30:5, 6; Galatians 1:8, 9; 2 Timothy 3:16, 17
184 *The Jehovah's Witnesses and Jesus Christ*, 1953, p. 73
185 *Are Jehovah's Witnesses Right*, 1990, p. 6
186 *M'Clintock and Strong's Cyclopaedia*

does not actually speak of triunity. We seek this in vain in the triadic formulae of the NT."[187] "There are numerous passages in the New Testament where merely a triple formula, containing words for God, Christ, and the Spirit, appears (1 Cor. 12.4 ff., 2 Cor. 13.13, Eph. 1 ff., 2 Thess. 2.13 f., 1 Pet. 1.2, Rev. 1.4 f.); but these are not in themselves necessarily any indication of an awareness of an eternal and necessary threefoldness in the one Godhead ... within the New Testament, threefold phrases are not confined to God, Christ and Spirit. There is, for instance, 'God, Christ, and the holy angels' (1 Tim. 5.21)."[188] "It is not properly speaking Trinitarian, nor, in terms of Matthew's thing, Trinitarian ... I do not find Matthew's understanding of the triadic phrase in 28:19b to be 'trinitarian' in the sense in which I have defined this term."[189]

Roman Catholic scholar Gerard Sloyan, obviously a Trinitarian, candidly admits: "The witness of the New testament is clear on the variety of triadic formulas, none of which is explicitly 'Trinitarian.' In other words, no theology of the trinity of persons in God had been developed by the time the canonical collection of Scriptures was closed."[190] Another commentary book states: "It is not, properly speaking, 'trinitarian'; there is no element of speculation about the divine essence or the relations between Father, Son, and Holy Spirit."[191] R.G. Crawford is a devout Trinitarian, but regarding Matthew 28:19 he admits candidly: "the text does not teach the later doctrine of three persons in one substance."[192]

Finally, scholar Rolf Furuli pointedly says: "In the New testament there are some passages which mention the Father, the Son and the holy spirit, together (For instance, Matthew 28:19; 2 Corinthians 13:14; Galatians 4:4-6), but there is no description of any relationship between the three. The fact, therefore, is that none of the writers of the biblical books saw the need for an ontological[193] identification of the Father, the Son and the holy spirit, or a description of their relationship with each other. They certainly did not formulate a creedal confession expressing faith in an ontological relationship between the three."[194]

Never forget, not one scripture anywhere in the Bible declares, concerning the trinity, that all three, (Father, Son, and Holy Spirit), are the same in substance,

---

187 *Kittel's Theological Dictionary of The New Testament*
188 *The Holy Spirit*, Moule, 2000, p. 25
189 *The Father, the Son, and the Holy Spirit*, J. Schaberg, 1982, pp. 92, 334
190 *The Three Persons in One God*, 1964, p. 29
191 *The Gospel According to Matthew: A Commentary*, Beare, 1981, p. 545
192 *Is The Doctrine of the Trinity Scriptural?*, 1967, p. 288
193 Having to do with the nature or essence of someone or something
194 *The Role of Theology and Bias in Bible Translation*, 1999, p. 111

power, and eternity. Thus, the *Protestant Cyclopaedia by M'Clintock and Strong* truthfully admits: "It appears that none of the passages cited from the Old Test in proof of the Trinity are conclusive ... We do not find in the Old Test clear or decided proof upon this subject." Also: "No New Testament writings supply explicit assurance of a triune God."[195] Finally, *The Eerdmans Bible Dictionary* concludes: "Triadic formulas in the New Testament are often regarded as implying a developed doctrine of the trinity, but this is to read too much into them."[196]

To conclude this section, I thought it would be somewhat proper to shed some light as to the thinking of the 'Hub of Christendom.' From *"Catholicism's Fear of the Bible"* in the *Catholic Magazine*, March 1944, it reads: "Of all advice that we can offer your holiness, we have kept the most necessary to the last. We must open our eyes well and use all possible force in the matter, namely, to permit the reading of the Gospel as little as possible, especially in the vernacular, in all those countries under your jurisdiction. Let the very little part of the Gospel suffice that is usually lead in the Mass and let no one be permitted to read more. So long as the people will be content with that small amount, your interest will prosper, but as soon as the people want to read more, your interest will begin to fail. The Bible is the book, that more than any other, has raised against us the tumults and tempests by which we have almost perished. In fact, if anyone examines closely and compares the teachings of the Bible with what takes place in our churches he will soon find discord and will realize that our teaching is often different from the Bible and oftener still, contrary to it. And, if the people wake up to this they will never stop challenging us till everything is laid bare and then we shall become the object of universal scorn and hatred. Therefore, it is necessary to withdraw the Bible from the sight of the people, but with extreme caution in order not to cause a rebellion."[197]

We need to ask ourselves: 'what are these so-called holy men trying to hide?' Might it be the false teachings such as the trinity which in their own words: "if anyone examines closely and compares the teachings of the Bible with what takes place in our churches he will soon find discord and will realize that our teaching is often different from the Bible, and oftener still, contrary to it." The answer is

---

195 *Swiss Vocabulaire Biblique*
196 1987 revised edition of 1975, p. 1020
197 The Cardinals of the Roman Court delivered this address to Pope Julius III in 1550 immediately after his elevation to papacy. It is continued in a historical document of Reformation times that is preserved today in the National Library of France in folio B, No. 1088, Vol. 2, pp. 641–650, see also *Chronicles of the Unholy Fathers*, R. W. Rowlands, 2001, pp. 252–253,

quite evident if we are to be honest with ourselves. We should never forget how so many lost their very lives, willingly I might add, in order to possess their own copy of God's word. Tyndale, for example, was burned at the stake simply because of his translation of the Bible in another language not authorized by Christendom. Protestants fair no better I'm afraid. John Calvin had Michael Servetus Burned at the stake for, of all things, not believing in the trinity.

God's word was not meant to look impressive on a bookshelf, coffee table, or altar. God's word was to influence our very being, everyday. The Bible was to be read day and night as the scriptures so often attest to. "His delight is in the law of Yahweh, and in his law doth he meditate day and night."[198]

Dear readers, value your copy of the Bible, and thank God that it isn't under control of religious leaders as it was only a few short hundred years earlier. The Bible is Gods personal letter to each one of us. For this reason, be thankful as Christians today, because the chains of false teachings such as the trinity chain have been revealed and removed. We are no longer slaves to man's fallible wisdom. "You will know the truth, and the truth will set you free."[199]

---

198 Psalm 1:2, *TP*, cf. Deuteronomy 17:19; Joshua 1:8; Psalm 119:97; 1 Timothy 4:15
199 John 8:32, *GNB*

Part II

Who is the only true God? —John 17:3

Titles and personal names

Our First weak link concerning the trinity has been revealed and clarified by persuasive facts since it was established not by the Bible, but rather developed progressively over centuries. Uninspired fallible men accomplished this after the death of Jesus and his apostles.

The Bible is detailed in every way in its description of who God really is. Actually, this would depend on whom you ask. For example, who is the first one to come to your mind when we read at Psalm 23:1 "The LORD is my shepherd?" Most individuals will honestly answer Jesus Christ, as I believed in the past. After all, did not Jesus admit: "I am the fine shepherd" at John 10:11? I bring this to the fore simply because there is a connection between the "LORD" mentioned in Psalm 23 and the identity of the "Father" mentioned by Jesus in John 17:3.

Lord, Father, God, and Mighty God are all ambiguous titles. None of these identify the only true God as a specific name would. To illustrate: if I were to tell you that the President is coming to town, you may wonder which president am I talking about, since there are many presidents worldwide. In contrast, if I said President George Bush Jr. is coming to town, you are instantly able to identify the president because of his personal name.

The importance of a name, especially in Bible times, cannot be overstated. The Bible makes abundantly clear: "There must be many gods and lords."[200] Since this is the case, how are we able to distinguish the "only true God" from all others? The true God answers this at Psalm 83:18 "That people may know that you, whose name is Jehovah, You alone are the Most High over all the earth."[201] The sovereign of the universe distinguishes himself by his personal name Jehovah.

You may be wondering, is it really that important and necessary to know and use God's name Jehovah? It is if your desire is to know him intimately, worship God in truth with accurate knowledge, and desire everlasting life. For his word reads at Joel 2:32 "Whosoever shall call on the name of Jehovah shall be deliv-

---

200 1 Corinthians 8:5, *VC*
201 *KJV*

ered."[202] Another very well known scripture that many know as the Lord's prayer or the Our Fathers prayer, reads this way: "Our Father in the heavens, let your name be sanctified."[203] Notice one observation: "To hallow the name of Jahweh was tantamount in itself to acknowledging the uniqueness and exclusiveness of the cult of Israel per se. Wherever Israel in anyway opened its doors to the cult of another deity, the name of Jahweh was profaned. (Lev. 18:21, 20:3) On the positive side, the name was hallowed by obedience to the commandments, by 'walking in the name of Jahweh' (Mic. 4:5)."[204]

Sanctified or hallowed here means to be held sacred, set apart, be treated as holy. Jesus is instructing us to treat his Fathers name with holiness, to set it apart from others by strict obedience to his will. Are we able to honestly say we are truly accomplishing this if we do not know or refuse to use God's name in our worship of him? God asks of us: "If then I am a father, where is mine honor? And if I am a master, where is my fear? Saith Jehovah of host unto you."[205] On the other hand, God's own son, Jesus Christ said: "I have revealed Thy name," and "I have declared unto them thy name, and will declare it."[206] Since we are instructed to follow Jesus' footsteps closely wouldn't it move us as Christians to not only know the Fathers name, but just as well to make it known to others?[207]

A very well known Trinitarian evangelical, Pat Robertson, had this to say regarding God's name: "There is the God of the Bible, who is Jehovah. When you see LORD in caps, that is the name. It's not Allah, it's not Brahma, it's not Shiva, it's not Vishnu, it's not Buddha. It is Jehovah God ... He is the God of all gods."[208]

My question to Mr. Robertson is why aren't you using God's name Jehovah if you know this name belongs only to "the God of all gods?" The answer to this question will be revealed through the written word of God.

Hence, it behooves all sincere Bible students to investigate whether God's name Jehovah should be used. We must gain a little more insight to this unique personal name of God. Some questions you might be unsure about are: Is Jehovah the correct pronunciation and does it matter? Is God's name important to him? How did Jesus Christ view his Fathers name? Is there a difference between Lord

---

202 Cf. Romans 10:13
203 Matthew 6:9
204 *O.T. Theology*, Vol. I, Von Rad, 1962, p. 184
205 Malachi 1:6
206 John 17:6, 26, *WEY, KJV* respectively
207 Cf. 1 Peter 2:21
208 http://www.rightwingwatch.org/2006/11/robertson

and Jehovah? Why Jehovah and not Yahweh? Finally, what about God's name in the Christian Greek Scriptures?[209] These questions and more will be answered in the following information.

Does God have a personal name?

God's name is found in the Hebrew Scriptures close to seven-thousand times. This summation and common sense alone should inform us at the very least, this repetitive prominence means the name was to last eternally. It is found in the form of what we call the Tetragrammaton, meaning 4 letters. Our corresponding English would be either YHWH or JHVH. Notice that there are no vowels. This is because the Hebrew language did not use vowels in God's written word. Unfortunately, due to superstition, and misinterpreting one of the commandments, "You must not take up the name of Jehovah your God in a worthless way, for Jehovah will not leave the one unpunished who takes up his name in a worthless way,"[210] the traditional Jews still believe that God's name is unspeakable or one will be destroyed. Thus, the exact pronunciation of God's personal name was lost. This is the height of pure haughtiness and nothing else!

As one book put it: "Whenever [Jewish] readers came to the word YHWH, they read adonai ['lord'], lest they should 'blaspheme' God by pronouncing his name out loud. Never did God Himself require them to take such measures, but that is how they interpreted Exodus 20:7 … In order to ensure that they would not take his name in vain, they simply refused to speak His name at all. It is hard to imagine that God intended such an extreme position, considering the fact that his name occurs 6,823 [or 6,828] times in the Old Testament. Furthermore, God inspired a Psalmist to say that he would call on 'the name of [Jehovah]' in response to His goodness: Psalm 116:13, 17 (13) I will lift up the cup of salvation and call on the name of [Jehovah] (17) I will sacrifice a thank offering to you and call on the name [Jehovah].'"[211]

When it came to God's name, instead of placing the proper vowel signs around it, in most cases the Israelites would employ other indicative signs to remind the reader that he should say 'Adho-nai'. From this came the spelling Iehouah, and, eventually, Jehovah became the accepted pronunciation of the divine name in

---

209 New Testament
210 Exodus 20:7
211 *One God and One Lord, Reconsidering the Cornerstone of the Christian Faith,* Graiser, Lynn, Schoenheit, p. 326

English. This form retains the crucial essentials of God's name from the Hebrew original.

At the very least then, modern day Bible translations should include God's name in the Hebrew Scriptures. The majority does not. In fact they continue in line with the Hebrews substituting the Tetragrammaton with LORD in all capitals. Is this in harmony with God's word? Notice what Jesus said to his religious leaders of his day for their traditions: "Thus ye have invalidated the commandment of God, through your tradition. Ye hypocrites!"[212]

The importance of a personal name

As was pointed out previously, God most confidently can be addressed in more ways than one. This I whole-heartedly agree with. The idea that there are many names for God is where I disagree. For example: God, Father, Almighty God, Grand Instructor, Lord, Ancient of Days, Creator, God of Gods, Grand God, God of Truth, The Rock, Supreme One, Sovereign Lord, Most High, Most Holy One, Living God, King of Eternity, et cetera. These are all descriptive titles, not a specific name like Jehovah. "It is worth remarking that the Bible knows nothing of different 'names' of God. God has only one 'name'—Yahweh. Apart from this, all the others are titles or descriptions. This fact is often improperly grasped."[213]

Do you have a close personal relationship with anyone whose name you do not know? Think of your best friend for a moment. Do you address him or her by the titles man, woman, father, mother, friend, et cetera? No one does this. Why? Not only will saying and using their personal name draw us closer to them, it also gives respect, and honor to that individual. For people to whom God is nameless he is often merely an impersonal force, not a real person, not someone that we are able to know and love intimately and to whom we can speak from the heart in prayer, as we would speak to a best friend in confidence.

"Giving the name entails a certain kind of relationship; it opens up the possibility of, indeed admits a desire for, a certain intimacy in relationship. A relationship without a name inevitably means some distance; naming the name is necessary for closeness. Naming makes true communication and encounter possible. Naming entails availability. By giving the name, God becomes accessible. God and people can now meet and address each other."[214]

---

212 Matthew 15:6, *NS*
213 *The Revelation of the Divine Name*, J.A. Motyer, p. 7, fn. 18
214 *Yahweh in NIDOTT&E*, Vol. 4, 1997, T. Fretheim, p. 1297

If there is no name involved when we pray, our prayers may become ritualistic, a repetition of memorized expressions. Jesus said of our prayers to God to "not repeat the same words over and over again as is done by the Gentiles, for they suppose that they will be heard in accordance with the length of their prayers. Do not copy them."[215] In other words, if we truly want to know God intimately, it is only reasonable that one would address him by his personal name, Jehovah. Otherwise, we take a probability on knowing God only as an acquaintance, not our best friend, father, and sovereign of the universe.

It is interesting to note that Jehovah named all the stars, and even commissioned Adam to name all the animals. "Lift up your eyes on high and see. Who has created these? He who is bringing out their host by number, He calls them all by name."[216] "And out of the gr[ound] the LORD God formed [every beast of the field, and every bird of the] s[ky; and brought them] to the man to [see what he would call them; and whatever the man called a living creature, that was its name.]"[217]

"With the Semites a name was a description, a definition; it was also something without which a thing was nonexistent. A new for God might indicate the introduction of a new god to fuse with and take the place of the old god, but it could just as well imply a new definition, a new significance, a new understanding of his being and power."[218] In other words "Yahweh is a name, not a concept, and therefore, grammatically considered, a proper noun. As such it denotes an individual Person, with all that personality connotes, life, and character, the power to act and to communicate with other persons."[219]

Finally, Professor David Clines sums up this section very well. He states: "Somewhere between the fifth and the second centuries B.C. a tragic accident befell God: he lost his name. More exactly, Jews gave up using God's personal name Yahweh, and began to refer to Yahweh by various periphrases: God, the Lord, the Name, the Holy One, the Presence, even the Place … does not the capitalization of 'God' turn it into a personal name? Not really. 'God' can be a dictionary entry, but 'Yahweh' must be an encyclopaedia entry.… At least in our translations of the Bible it should be made plain (as the Jerusalem Bible does) when the personal name of God is being used, rather than having it hidden by such an epithet as 'the Lord.' And the introduction of God's personal name into Christian worship and

---

215 Matthew 6:7, 8; *TST*
216 Isaiah 40:26, *TS*
217 Genesis 2:19, *DSS*
218 *Hebrew Origins*, T.J. Meek, 1950, pp. 93–94
219 *The Book of the Law, Studies in the Date of Deuteronomy*, G.T. Manley, 1957, p. 39

theology could have surprising and creative results ... My point is this: in popular Christian theology the personhood of God is less prominent than it ought to be because God is not referred to by his personal name."[220]

Unquestionably, Jehovah places great value and intimacy in names, specifically his own. Be aware too, that true Christians have a commission from Jesus Christ to make disciples of people of all the nations. "God authorized and commanded me to commission you: Go out and train everyone you meet, far and near ... Then instruct them in the practice in all I have commanded you," and "The good news—the Message of the kingdom—will be preached all over the world, a witness staked out in every country. And then the end will come."[221]

When teaching and training these people of the nations, how would it be possible to identify the only true God as different from the thousands of false gods of the world? There is only one-way: by using his personal name, Jehovah, as his very own word, the Bible does.

How does Jehovah feel about his name?

Naturally, we should always look to the Bible to see how God personally feels about his holy name, Jehovah. I have mentioned earlier that his name is found in the Bible almost seven thousand times. The next most mentioned name in the Bible is David, a little over one thousand times. Next is Jesus, under one thousand times. Interesting. Besides these facts, Jehovah is mentioned almost three times more than all the titles given to him combined. Jesuit McKenzie states: "The God of Israel is called by His personal name [Jehovah] more frequently than by all other titles combined; the name not only identified the person, it revealed his character."[222] That should help us to reason properly concerning the importance of this holy name of God. The actual question then that everyone should be asking, is why has the divine name Jehovah, used in the Hebrew text nearly seven-thousand times, more than all other divine titles put together, and more than any other name, completely disappeared? Observe how Jehovah feels about his own name.

- Isaiah 12:4 "And in that day shall ye say, Give thanks unto Jehovah, call upon his name ... make mention that his name is exalted."

---

220 *Yahweh and the God of Christian Theology*, Vol. 83, D. Clines, 1980, pp. 323–324
221 Matthew 28:19, 20; 24:14; *TM*
222 *McKenzie Dictionary of the Bible*, p. 316

- Ezekiel 36:23[223] "And I have sanctified My great name, That is profaned among nations … I am Jehovah."
- Ezekiel 38:23[224] "And I will vindicate my greatness and my sanctity and make myself known before the eyes of many nations; and they shall know that I am Jehovah.'"
- Malachi 3:16[225] "Then have those fearing Jehovah spoken one to another, And Jehovah doth attend and hear, And written is a book of memorial before Him of those fearing Jehovah, And of those esteeming His name."
- Psalm 34:3[226] "O magnify Yahweh with me, And let us exalt his name together!"
- Psalm 83:18[227] "That people may know that you, whose name is Jehovah, You alone are the Most High over all the earth."
- Psalm 96:8[228] "Give to Yahweh the glory of his name."
- Deuteronomy 32:3[229] "I will proclaim Jehovah's name."
- Matthew 6:9[230] "This is how you should pray: Our Father in heaven, May Your name be kept holy."
- Isaiah 42:8 "I am Jehovah, that is my name; and my glory will I not give to another, neither my praise to graven images."
- Psalm 135:1[231] "Hallelujah! Praise the name of Yahweh!
- Psalm 135:13[232] "O Jehovah, your name endures forever; your fame is known to every generation."
- Psalm 145:1, 2[233] "I will praise you, my God and King, and bless your name each day and forever."
- Psalm 148:13 "Let them praise the name of Jehovah; For his name alone is exalted."

---

223 *YLT*
224 *TBLE*
225 *YLT*
226 *TP*
227 *NWT*
228 *TP*
229 *TBLE*
230 *WFB*
231 *TP*
232 *TB*
233 *TB*

- Psalm 8:1[234] "O Yahweh, our sovereign, How magnificent is thy name In the whole of the earth!"
- Psalm 91:14[235] "I will make him great because he trust in my name."
- Micah 4:5[236] "For all the peoples walk everyone in the name of his god; and we will walk in the name of Jehovah our God for ever and ever."
- Malachi 1:11 "For from the sun's rising even to it's setting my name will be great among the nations … a presentation will be made to my name … because my name will be great among the nations, Jehovah of armies has said."
- Psalm 105:1 "Oh give thanks unto Jehovah, call upon his name."
- Isaiah 45:1–6[237] "I am Yahweh, and there is no other God except me … I am Yahweh and there is no other."
- Exodus 3:15[238] "And God said to Moses again "You are to say to the sons of Israel 'Jehovah, your father's God, Abraham's God, Isaac's God, Jacob's God, has sent me to you'; this is my name forever, and this my identification for generation after generation."

This listing of scriptures is by no means exhaustive, but I trust you understand my point. It is very apparent Jehovah desires his name to be made known in all the earth.

Still, translators want to continue to remove and replace Jehovah with surrogates such as Lord. This has only lead to misleading the readers of God's word. Do you recall Psalm 23:1 from before? It read: "The LORD is my shepherd." Now, let's see how this verse should really be translated according to the original translation. "Jehovah [YHWH] is my shepherd." What a difference this makes for the reader of God's word. It identifies Jehovah, not his son Jesus Christ, as we may have thought.

I will share with you a reply to a letter written by Julie Moore on February 3, 1979, from the New International Version translation committee. The late Edwin H. Palmer Th.D. cordially and candidly explains why the committee chose not to use God's name in their translation. He says: "Here is why we did not: You are right that Jehovah is a distinct name for God and Ideally we should have used it. But we put $2.25 million into this translation and a sure way of throwing it down

---

234 *TP*
235 *TLB*
236 *TMB*
237 *NJB*
238 *TBLE*

the drain is to translate, for example, Psalm 23 as Yahweh is my shepherd."[239] This response is very powerful indeed.

How did Jesus view his Father's name?

How about Jesus' view on his Father's name? Let's review an example in Jesus' life. How did Jesus view God's name when confronted by the devil? When Satan tempted Jesus, he answered each and every time with a scripture that highlighted the divine name. At Matthew 4:4 Jesus quotes Deuteronomy 8:3 which says: "And he humbled thee, and suffered thee to hunger, and fed thee with manna, which thou knewest not, neither did thy father's know; that he might make thee know that man doth not live by bread only, but by everything that proceedeth out of the mouth of Jehovah doth man live." At Matthew 4:10 Jesus quotes Deuteronomy 10:20 "Thou shalt fear Jehovah thy God; him shalt thy serve; and to him shalt thou cleave, and by his name shalt thou swear." Jesus Certainly did not follow unscriptural traditions set out by the Jewish leaders—especially knowing that his own name meant Jehovah is salvation.

Already I have proven quite convincingly, God's name certainly belongs in his own written word. If we remove it we deserve punishment from God, and rightfully so, for according to Revelation 22:18–19 "I give fair warning to all who hear the words of the prophecy of this book: If you add to the words of this prophecy, God will add to your life the disasters written in this book; If you subtract from the words of this book of this prophecy, God will subtract your part from the Tree of Life and the Holy City that are written in this book."[240]

Even if you believe this warning applies to the book of Revelation alone, would not the same principle apply to all of God's word? Notice the following at Deuteronomy 4:2 "Ye shall not add unto the word which I command you, neither shall ye diminish from it, that ye may keep the commandments of Jehovah your God which I command you." The Bible continues with the admonition: "Every word of God is true … Add nothing to his words, lest he accuse you and you be seen as a liar."[241] Evidently then, Jehovah insists on not adding or subtracting a single word from his whole utterance, the Bible.

Jesus Christ was adamant on declaring his Father's name to others. Observe his words at John 17:6, 26 "I have made thy Name known to the men whom thou hast given me from the world … So have I declared, so will I declare, thy Name

---

239   *Search for the Sacred Name*, Firpo W. Carr, pp. 49–50
240   *TM*
241   Proverbs 30:5, 6; *RJC*

to them."[242] Let us not forget what many of us refer to as the Lord's prayer or the Our Father's prayer at Matthew 6:9. Here Jesus says: "Father of us, O Spiritual One, Your Name be truly honored."[243] What is the Father's name that should be set apart and honored from all others? It is Jehovah. For Ezekiel 38:23 and 36:23 confirms this when we read: "And I will magnify myself, and I will make myself known in the eyes of many nations; and they shall know that I am Jehovah ... And I will sanctify my great name ... and the nations shall know that I am Jehovah, saith the Lord Jehovah."

Pretty clear, isn't it? No doubt Jesus had in mind the words found at Deuteronomy 32:3 "For I will proclaim the name of Jehovah." We should at the very least meditate on the very prayer that was ingrained in us as children and imitate Jesus Christ by sanctifying Jehovah's name.

No scholarly evidence of removal of divine name?

This brings to the fore an interesting point, which some have erringly, perhaps unknowingly acknowledged. They have said: 'As far as the name "Jehovah" being removed from Old Testament text, there is not a shred of scholarly evidence that I have seen to substantiate this.' I am quite shocked that anyone could suggest this, simply because the evidence is right in front of them and in their copy of the Bible. For example, take a look at *The New Living Bible* introduction p. A23 under *The Rendering of Divine Names*. It says: "We have rendered the Tetragrammaton (YHWH) consistently as "the LORD."" Have these translators not removed God's name with a substitute? They candidly admit it!

How about some other examples? The *King James Bible*, in the Index under the subheading Lord: "In the OT, when large and small capitals are used for LORD, the original Hebrew reads YHWH." This translation kept God's name in only four places out of the seven thousand times in the original Hebrew. Regrettably, the *New King James* has removed God's name altogether.

The *New American Standard Bible* says under the subheading *The Proper Name of God in The OT*: "There is yet another name which is particularly assigned to God as his special or proper name, that is, the four letters YHWH (Exodus 3:14 and Isaiah 42:8). This name has not been pronounced by the Jews because of reverence for the great sacredness of the Divine name. Therefore, it has been consistently translated LORD."

---

242   *GHCM*
243   *CPV*

The *New International Version* Preface says: "In regard to the Divine Name YHWH, commonly referred to as the Tetragrammaton, the translators adopted the device used in most English versions of rendering that name as "LORD.'" The *RSV*, *NRSV*, and the *GNB* read much the same.

J. M. Powis Smith and Goodspeed produced a modern day translation of the Bible—*An American Translation*—in 1935. In their preface they explain: "In this translation we have followed the orthodox Jewish tradition and substituted the Lord for the name Yahweh and the phrase the Lord God for the phrase the Lord Yahweh. In all cases where Lord or God represents an original Yahweh small capitals are employed ... anyone, therefore, who desires to retain the flavor of the original text has but to read Yahweh wherever he sees LORD or GOD." On reading this a question should immediately come to our mind. If reading Yahweh instead of LORD "retains the flavor of the original text," why did the translators not use Yahweh in their translation in the first place?

Please notice what Julian Obermann says: "Such rendering of the word (YHWH) as kyrios, dominus, marya, 'the Lord,' does not represent the intention of the Hebrew writers themselves, but reflects a device of theologians in postbiblical times by which the utterance of the name of God was to be avoided."[244] These and other translators say they were following orthodox Jewish tradition. However, is this wise for a Christian translator of Gods word? Remember, it was the Pharisees—the preservers of orthodox Jewish tradition—who rejected Jesus and put him to death. Jesus says of these men: "You are nullifying the work of God by your tradition."[245]

"The most thorough and complete banishment of Bible words to be found at all is the utter vanishing of the covenant name of the god of Israel—Jehovah. To begin with, this is one of the great boasts of the translators (p. vi of the Bible's Preface). But in the text itself no trace of the word occurs. It is a carefully planned and executed blackout of the covenant Name."[246]

An interesting comment comes from C.H. Titterton. He says: "No doubt the great reason why the Jews have lost the pronunciation of the glorious and fearful name is this, that the fear of the name came upon them owing to the punishment inflicted upon them for their sins, and so they became afraid to utter it."[247] Obviously, this removal and substitution really deteriorates the Word of God. I

---

244 *The Divine Name YHWH in the Light of Recent Discoveries*, Vol. 68, J. Obermann, 1949, p. 304
245 Matthew 15:6; *LD*
246 *The New Bible-Pro and Con.*, William Carey Taylor, p. 70
247 *Who is Jehovah?* Titterton, 1924, p. 30

don't think it is necessary to continue on with this point to establish that God's name has been removed and replaced with clever titles. Most translations will admit this in their preface. Does yours?

A difference between LORD and Jehovah?

You may ask: would it make a difference if God's name were substituted with titles? We have already examined the example of Psalm 23:1. I will use another example to prove that yes, it does make a difference to the reader. The example is found in Psalm 110:1.

It reads in The *NLT*: "The LORD said to my Lord, sit in honor at my right hand until I humble your enemies." Right away you may notice where I am heading with this. It sounds like God talking to another part of himself. This is of course what Trinitarians want: God as a group of persons, two anyways. Yet, if you search in any Hebrew Interlinear, you will find that this is not the case at all. The first 'LORD' is the divine name, Jehovah, when translated properly. The second 'Lord' is the word Adoni.[248] In regards to this second use of "my Lord," Protestant Bible scholar Albert Barnes candidly remarks: "A lord or master is a superior. The word here does not necessarily imply Divinity, but only superiority. David calls him his superior, his Lord, his Master, his Lawgiver; and expresses his willingness to obey him."[249]

Again, Anthony Buzzard highlights an important point: "It is amazing that a number of commentaries wrongly assert that the second lord [of psalm 110:1] is adonai[250] ... In fact the Hebrew for 'my lord' is not adonai but adoni, which is never used of God but often of the king of Israel and other human superiors. This surprising error of fact is symptomatic of widespread confusion of God with the Messiah ... No one reading Ps. 110:1 could imagine that the Messiah was the Lord God. The Messiah is the Lord's anointed ... the same error about the word 'lord' in Psalm 110:1 appears frequently in evangelical literature ... neither the Jews nor Jesus misunderstood their own language on this critical matter of defining God and His Son. They never thought that Psalm 110:1 had introduced distinctions in the Godhead ... Traditional orthodoxy has substituted its own definition of Lord, as it applies to Jesus, and advanced the extraordinary and very un-Hebrew idea that God is more than a single person, in opposition to the

---

248 Pronounced ad-owe-KNEE
249 *Barne's Notes, Notes on the New Testament, Matthew and Mark*, p. 238
250 Pronounced ad-owe-NYE

definitive oracular utterance of Psalm 110:1 ... The whole Trinitarian argument from this Psalm fails because the facts of the language are wrongly reported.""[251]

Therefore, this verse should read: "Jehovah said to my Lord." Thus, "It was impossible for the Apostles to identify Christ with Jehovah. Psalm 110:1 and Malachi 3:1 prevented this."[252] One Journal admits: "When Jesus is called 'Lord' the N.T. does not mean that he is Jehovah, but a Lord distinct from the one Lord God. He is the Lord Christ or, more fully, 'the Lord Jesus Christ.' There are indeed two lords, but the second is not Deity, but the Son of God and Messiah."[253] Senior Lecturer in New Testament Exegesis, Professor I. Howard Marshall, states in the *Tyndale New Testament Commentaries*: "We may note that there is an ambiguity in the English use of the word 'Lord' which is not present in the Hebrew Psalm where the first word translated 'Lord' is YHWH, the name of God, and the second word is 'adon which can be used of lords and masters. In both cases the Greek text has kyrios, and this facilitated the transfer to Jesus of the other Old Testament texts which referred to Yahweh. Here, however, it is simply the attribute of lordship which is given to Jesus; he is not equated with Yahweh."

A final thought here is a quote from the *Today's English Version* translation: "The Lord of Psalm 110.1 is understood absolutely of God, while my Lord is used of the Promised Messiah. If David then refers to the Messiah (who is also his 'son') as my Lord, this automatically reveals that the Messiah is superior to David. Matthew is not so much concerned to prove the Davidic origin of Jesus (this is assumed in the structure of his Gospel), but rather to demonstrate that Jesus, who is both descendant of David and Messiah, is superior to David."[254]

The importance of proper translating of God's name Jehovah has been revealed. In order for a sincere student of God's word to find accurate knowledge, the meaning of possible confusing scriptures—such as Psalm 110:1—must be translated correctly through use of God's personal and Holy name, Jehovah.

Why Jehovah & not Yahweh?

For many the question arises: Why Jehovah and not Yahweh? There is a very simple answer. Jehovah is the English form of God's name and the most recognized and verbally used worldwide. Notice the following.

---

[251] *The Doctrine of the Trinity*, pp. 48–49, 52, 56–57
[252] *International Critical Commentary on 1 Peter*, R.A. Biggs
[253] *Confusing the Lord God and the Lord Messiah*, JRR, Vol. 3, 1994, p. 3
[254] *A Handbook On The Gospel Of Matthew*, Newman, Stine, 1988, p. 699

- Francis Denio says: "Jehovah misrepresent Yahweh no more than Jeremiah misrepresents Yirmeyahu. The settles connotations of Isaiah and Jeremiah forbid questioning their right ... Much the same thing is true of Jehovah. It is not barbarism. It has already many of the connotations needed for the proper name, of the covenant God of Israel. There is no other word which can faintly compare with it ... In the sixteenth century Protestant and Roman Catholic scholars alike began to use this word freely. At the outset they believed that the Hebrew points were correctly used ... The literature of devotion appropriated it more and more as time went on. Few collections are without the one beginning: Guide me, O thou great Jehovah."[255]
- *The Catholic Encyclopedia*, Vol. 8, 1910 edition, p. 329 notes: "Jehovah, the proper name of God in the Old Testament."
- *The Catholic Encyclopedia*, Vol. 8, 1913 edition, p. 329 adds: "Jehovah, the proper name of God in the Old Testament; hence the Jews called it 'the name' by excellence, the great name, the only name."
- Alan S. Duthie says: "In the OT, God's name should appear as a name, either Jehovah or Yahweh (ch.6); One of the forms of the Divine name should appear for the original YHWH through out the OT, and especially in Exodus 6:3, 'by my name Jehovah' and 1Kings 18:39, 'Jehovah, he is God', which hardly makes sense without the actual name. However, in place of the name, many Bible translations use 'the LORD' (in capitals) ... but capitals are inaudible when read aloud and are readily ignored. A few Bibles do not even use capitals for Lord (LB, AB, etc)."[256]
- J.B. Rotherham, in *The Emphasised Bible*, p. 23, used the form Yahweh throughout the Hebrew Scriptures. However, later in his Studies in the Psalms he used the form Jehovah. He explained: "Jehovah—The employment of this English form of the Memorial name ... in the present version of the Psalter does not arise from any misgivings as to the more correct pronunciation, as being Yahweh; but solely from practical evidence personally selected of the desirability of keeping in touch with the public ear and eye in a matter of this kind, in which the principal thing is the easy recognition of the Divine name intended."(London 1911 p. 29) Mr. Rotherham also says regarding the *KJV* use of the Divine name only four times: "If it was wrong to unveil the Tetragrammaton at all, then why do it in these instances? If, on the other hand, it was right to let it be seen in these cases, then why not in all?"

---

255 *Journal of Biblical Literature*, 1927, pp. 146–149
256 *Bible Translations and How to Choose Between Them*, p. 38

- The *Shocken Bible*, by Everett Fox says: "The reader will immediately notice that the personal name of the Biblical God appears in this volume as 'YHWH.' That is pretty standard scholarly practice, but it does not indicate how the name should be pronounced … While the visual effect of 'YHWH' may be jarring at first, it has the merit of approximating the situation of the Hebrew text as we now have it, and of leaving open the unresolved question of the pronunciation and meaning of God's name … Historically, Jewish, and Christian translations of the Bible into English have tended to use 'Lord' with some exceptions (notably, Moffatt's 'The Eternal'). Both old and new attempts to recover the 'correct' pronunciation of the Hebrew name have not succeeded; neither the sometimes-heard 'Jehovah' nor the standard scholarly 'Yahweh' can be conclusively proven."
- *Johann David Michaelis* in his German translation of the Old testament of the 18th century says: "the name Jehovah [Jehova in German] is used in equally long sections [of the Bible] and the supreme being continually called Jehovah God, like with the intent of conveying to the reader that the God of whom Moses is speaking is that one God who made himself known to him by the name Jehovah and who distinguished himself from all other gods by means of this peculiar name … so I consider it a matter of integrity in translation to identify it, even though it might not always be pleasing to the German ear … several of my friends insisted that I not at all insert this foreign word … Jehovah is a Nomen Propium, and, just as properly as I retain other nomina propia [such as] Abraham, Isaac, Jacob, or, taking names of other gods as examples, Baal, Ashtaroth, Dagon-they may be as foreign-sounding as they like—it can well occur in the case of Jehovah … why then should the name of the Only True God sound more offensive? I do not therefore see why I should not use the name Jehovah in the German Bible."
- *The American Standard Bible of 1901* in its preface says the following: "The change first proposed in the Appendix—that which substitutes "Jehovah" for "LORD" and "GOD" …—is one which will be unwelcome to many, because of the frequency and the familiarity of the terms displaced. But the American Revisers, after a careful consideration, were brought to the unanimous conviction that a Jewish superstition, which regarded the Divine name as too sacred to be uttered, ought no longer to dominate in the English or in any other version of the Old Testament, as it fortunately does not in the numerous versions made by modern missionaries. This Memorial Name … and emphasized as such over and over again in the original text of the Old Testament, designates God as the personal God, as the covenant God,

the God of revelation, the Deliverer, the Friend of his people;—not merely the abstract "Eternal One" of many French translations, but the ever living Helper of those who are in trouble. This personal name, with it's wealth of sacred associations, is now restored to the place in the sacred text to which it has an unquestionable claim."[257]

- Gustav Friedrich Oehler concludes: "From this point onward I use the word Jehovah, because, as a matter of fact, this name has now become more naturalized in our vocabulary, and cannot be supplanted."[258]
- Jesuit scholar Paul Jouon states: "In our translations, instead of the (hypothetical) form Yahweh, we have used the form Jehovah … which is the conventional literary form used in French."[259]
- Francis B. Denio, who studied and taught Hebrew for forty years has this to say: "Jehovah misrepresents Yahweh no more than Jeremiah misrepresents Yirmeyahu. The settled connotation of Isaiah and Jeremiah forbid questioning their right. Usage has given them the connotations proper for designating the personalities, which these words represent. Much the same is true of Jehovah. It is not barbarism. It already has many of the connotations needed for the proper name of the covenant God of Israel. There is no other word that can faintly compare with it. For centuries it has been gathering these connotations. No other word approaches this name in fullness of associations required. The use of any other word falls so far short of the proper ideas that it is a serious blemish in a translation."[260]
- *Bible Translator and Baptist Minister Jay P. Green Sr.* says: "In the history of the English language however, the letter J has a written counterpart in the German J, although the latter J in German is pronounced like an English Y. The bulk of Theological studies having come from German sources, there has been an intermixed usage in English of the J and the Y. Our English translations of the Bibles reflect this, so we have chosen to use J, thus Jehovah, rather than Yahweh, because this is established English usage for Biblical Names beginning with this Hebrew letters. No one suggests that we ought to change Jacob, Joseph, Jehoshaphat, Joshua etc. to begin with a Y, and neither should we at this late date change Jehovah to Yahweh."
- *Steve T. Byington* in his *The Bible in Living English* translation regarding the name Jehovah says: "The spelling and pronunciation are not highly

---

257 Preface, p. 4
258 *Theolgie des Alten Testaments*, 2nd ed., Stuttgart, 1882, p. 143
259 *Grammaire de L'hebreu Biblique*, Rome, 1923, fn, p. 49
260 *On the use of the word Jehovah*, JBL 46, 1927, pp. 147–148

important. What is highly important is to keep it clear that this is a personal name. There are several texts that cannot be properly understood if we translate this name by a common noun like "Lord"."

- *Professor E.W. Hengstenberg, Dissertations on the Genuiness of the Pentateuch*, 1847, Vol. p. 247 says: "The name JEHOVAH has been naturalized and taken its place in our religious vocabulary. JAHVEH, although **_literally_** more correct, is *practically* less suitable, since, as matters now stand, in it's departure from ecclesiastical usage, it would flavour the idea of an Israelitish national God ... But write JAHVEH as often as we please, JEHOVAH will retain it's place in popular usage. We should therefore act more wisely to write JEHOVAH, and satisfy ourselves with explaining the precise matter of fact."[261]
- *Translating the Divine Names, BT,* Vol. 3, H. Rosin, 1952, pp. 181, 182 says: "The pronunciation 'Yahweh' is no more than a scholars guess ... When however, it is only the consonants YHWH which are certain, is it still important then which vowels are interpolated? And does not then the traditional currency which the blended form 'Jehovah' has had of old, and the place it has secured for itself in many versions, (and hymns) in numerous variations, weigh heavily in the balance? Is it really so important that we pronounce the name correctly? Is it not more important that we learn to pronounce the *Name* again? Would this not contribute to the Biblical realism of our preaching?"
- *Introduction to the Old Testament,* 1952, p. 94, Professor Robert H. Pfeiffer, of Harvard and Boston Universities declares: "Whatever may be said of the dubious pedigree, 'Jehovah' is and should remain the proper English rendering of Yahweh, the God of Israel who revealed his name to Moses in the burning bush."
- *The Psalms in Modern Speech and Rhythmical Form,* J.E. McFayden, 1916, pp. 98, 99 says: "It is worth remembering that, for popular purposes, the form Jehovah has the high authority of no less great and conscientious a scholar than the late Professor W. Robertson Smith."
- *The Imperial Bible-Dictionary of 1874* observes: "[Jehovah] is everywhere a proper name, denoting the personal God and him only; whereas Elohim partakes more of the character of a common noun, denoting usually, indeed, but not necessarily nor uniformly, the Supreme ... The Hebrew may say the Elohim, the true God, in opposition to all false gods; but he never says the Jehovah, for Jehovah is the name of the true God only. He says again

---

261 Italics his

and again my God ...; but never my Jehovah, for when he says my God, he means Jehovah. He speaks of the God of Israel, but never of the Jehovah of Israel, for there is no other Jehovah. He speaks of the living God, but never of the living Jehovah, for he cannot conceive of Jehovah as other than living."

As you can no doubt perceive already, the form Jehovah is certainly plausible, satisfactory, and really the only reasonable choice. There are countless other references that could be revealed. Remember, the exact pronunciation was lost. "Evidence indicates, nay almost proves, that Jahweh was not the true pronunciation of the Tetragrammaton ... The name itself was probably JAHOH."[262] "The pronunciation Yahve used in some recent translations is based on a few ancient witnesses, but they are not conclusive. If one takes into account personal names that include the divine name, such as the Hebrew name of the prophet Elijah (Eliyahou) the pronunciation might just as well be Yaho or Yahou."[263]

A Hebrew Scholar, Gerard Gertoux relates to us a very interesting thought concerning the pronunciation of the divine name, the Tetragrammaton. "Flavius Josephus [A Jewish Historian between 37-100 c.e.] ... Who knew the priesthood of this time very well, made it clear when the Romans attacked the Temple, the Jews called upon the fear-inspiring name of God [*Flavius Josephe*—La guerre des juifs (V, 438) Tome III, 1982 Ed. Les Belles Lettres p. 172]. He wrote he had no right to reveal this name to his reader [*Flavius Josephe*—Les Antiquites Juives (II, 275) ou (II, 12, 4) 1992 Ed. Cerf p. 130]; however, he did give information of primary importance on the pronunciation he wanted to conceal. One can read the following remark in the work The Jewish War V:235 'The high priest had his head dressed with a tiara of fine linen embroidered with a purple border, and surrounded by another crown in gold which had in relief the sacred letters [Tetragrammanton]; these ones are four vowels.' This description is excellent; moreover, it completes the one found in Exodus 28:36-39. However, as we know, there are no vowels in the Hebrew but only consonants ... Now, it is obvious that the 'sacred letters' indicated the Tetragram written in paleo-Hebrew, not Greek. Furthermore, in Hebrew these consonants Y, W, H, do serve as vowels; they are in fact called 'mothers of reading ...' The H was used as a vowel only at the end of words, never within them. So, to read the name YHWH as four vowels would

---

262 *Periodical for Old Testament Knowledge*, Williams, 1936, Vol. 54, p. 269
263 *French Revised Second Version*, p. 9

be IHUA that is IEUA, because between two vowels the H is heard as a slight E."[264]

Because the exact pronunciation of God's name is not truly identifiable, some claim that the name Jehovah should not be used at all. If this is true then thousands of other names in the English translations should not be used either. The greatest example is that of the name Jesus. This is an English (from Latin) form of his name. The Hebrew is Yeshu'a or perhaps Yehoshu'a. The Greek would be Iesous'. Jesus is our conversational English way of pronouncing his name, and no one finds fault with using Jesus instead of Yeshu'a. Wouldn't you agree? Another example would be the name of Jeremiah. His name would need to be changed to Yirmeyah' or Yirmeya'hu. Of course, this would not be advantageous to the English language, hence we say Jeremiah.

There are countless others that have gone from Hebrew to English, our common language. Some of these would include the following: Isaiah, Jehu, Jehoash, et cetera. Why aren't these names kept in their original language? In order for us to understand the Bible (unless you are able to read Greek, Hebrew, or Aramaic), it needs to be translated into the tongue of the people. I am sure that you would concur that Jesus' name does not need to be changed back to the original—Yehoshua, correct? Neither should his Fathers name, Jehovah.

This brings us to another candid point that I think is quite priceless. What is the meaning of Jesus name? According to Weymouth this name means: JEHOVAH IS SALVATION.[265] So anytime anyone uses this name, Jesus—which is not the original pronunciation in the 1st century—he is using and supporting the use of the divine name Jehovah. I truly hope you remember this every time you utter Jesus' name, especially as you read about him daily in your copy of the Bible. I certainly do.

A final illustration is this: If you had written a book which includes upwards of some eight hundred thousand words and repeated your name in it seven thousand times, then you find out that the publishers have taken your name out of your own book, how would you feel? If you are able to humbly and honestly answer this question, then imagine how the Universal Sovereign, Almighty God Jehovah feels about his own personal name having been removed—or at the very least substituted—from his inspired book!

So Translators or any serious student of God's word who object to his name, doing so on justification of problems regarding pronunciation or because of Jewish

---

264 *The Name of God*, 2002, pp. 111-112
265 *The New Testament in Modern Speech*, ftn. 21 under Matthew 1:21; see also *Vine's Complete Expository Dictionary of Biblical Words*, 1985, p. 333

tradition, might be compared to those whom Jesus said: "Blind guides! You strain out a gnat and swallow a camel!"[266] Jesus also stated: "Now why do you keep looking at the splinter in your brother's eye, and pay no attention to the plank in your own eye? How do you have the nerve to say to your brother, 'Brother, please let me pick the splinter out of your eye,' without even noticing the plank in your eye? You phony, first get the plank from your eye, and then you will see better to pick the splinter from your brother's eye."[267] In other words, they stumble over the smaller problems but end up creating a major problem—by removing the name of the greatest being in the universe from the book that he inspired. How very wrong, arrogant, and exceedingly disappointing.

Does kyrios ever refer to Jehovah?

Now the last issue I want to address is what's said concerning the Greek word Kyrios (Lord). Many have said in essence that it never refers to Jehovah. So an all-important question for us today is: "Does a translator have the right to render Kyrios as Jehovah in the Christian Greek Scriptures?[268] Let us look at the three main reasons we would say yes to this question.

1. "If the New Testament writers did in fact only use Kyrios, their understanding would have been that Kyrios was equivalent to YHWH. For the Jewish writer it was no different then writing YHWH. The modern translator has the right to use this same process and use a word that is equivalent to YHWH in English. Jehovah/Yahweh.
2. When translating New Testament quotes and allusions from the Hebrew Old Testament, which one has higher authority? The quote or the source of the quote? No one can object to using the original source of the quote as higher authority. The only ones who would reject this line of reasoning are the ones who use the lack of manuscript evidence to support their trinity doctrine.
3. The external evidence and history of the Hebrew and Greek Scriptures of the OT point heavily to original NT mss [manuscripts] using the Tetragrammaton."[269]

---

266 Matthew 23:24; *LD*
267 Luke 6:42; *CPV*
268 New Testament
269 All points quoted from *The Lord and the Tetragrammaton*, Mazzaferro, pp. 17–18

Besides, all manuscripts of the Septuagint[270] contained the divine name right up to the middle of the 5th century CE. Here is a list of the Septuagint [LXX] manuscripts that contain the Divine Name.

1.	4QLXX Lev (b)	1st century CE
2.	LXX P. Fouad Inv. 266	1st century BCE
3.	LXX VTS 10b	1st century CE
4.	LXX VTS 10a	1st century CE
5.	LXX IBJ 12	1st century CE
6.	LXX P. Oxy. VII 1007	3rd century CE
7.	Sym P. Vindob.G.39777	3rd/4th century CE
8.	Aq Burkitt	5th century CE
9.	Aq Taylor	5th century CE

Regarding God's name in the Greek scriptures, please pay close attention to the following findings.

- *W.E. Vines expository Dictionary* 1985, p. 379 under Lord, Lordship A. Nouns: (g) kurios is the Septuagint and New Testament representative of Hebrew Jehovah ('LORD' in English Versions), see Matthew 4:7; James 5:11,etc …
- *George Howard* of the University of Georgia says this: "The removal of the Tetragrammanton from the New Testament and it's replacement with the surrogates KYRIOS and THEOS blurred the original distinction between the Lord God and the Lord Christ, and in many passages made it impossible which one was meant…. Once the Tetragrammanton was removed and replaced by the surrogate 'Lord', scribes were unsure whether Lord meant God or Christ. As time went on, these two figures were brought into even closer unity until it was often impossible to distinguish between them. Thus it may be that the removal of the Tetragrammanton contributed significantly to the later Christological and Trinitarian debates which plagued the Church of the early Christian centuries."[271]
- *In The Cairo Geniza*, Oxford, 1959, p. 222, Dr P. Kahle states: "We now know that the Greek Bible text as far as it was written by Jews for Jews did not translate the Divine name by kyrios; but the Tetragrammaton, written with Hebrew or Greek letters, was retained in such MSS. It was the

---

270 Greek translation of the Hebrew Scriptures
271 *The Name of God in the New Testament*, Bar 4.1, March 1978, p. 15

Christians who replaced the Tetragrammaton by kyrios, when the Divine name written in Hebrew letters was not understood anymore."

- *In The Journal of Theological Studies*, Oxford, Vol. XLV, 1944, pp. 158, 159, Professor W. G. Waddell says: "In Origen's Hexapla ... the Greek versions of Aquila, Symmachus, and LXX [Septuagint], all represented JHWH by PIPI, in the second column of the Hexapla the Tetragrammaton was written in Hebrew characters."[272]

- *Professor George Howard*, Associate Professor of Religion and Hebrew at the University of Georgia relates: "In 1944, W.G. Waddell discovered the remains of an Egyptian papyrus scroll, (Papyrus Fuad 266), dating to the first or second century B.C., which included part of the Septuagint. In no instance, however, was YHWH translated kyrios. Instead the Tetragrammaton itself—in square Aramaic letters—was written into the Greek text. This parallels the Qumran Covenanter's use of the paleo-Hebrew script for the Divine Name in a document which was otherwise written in square Aramaic script ... We have three separate pre-Christian copies of the Greek Septuagint Bible and in not a single instance is the Tetragrammaton translated kyrios or, for that matter, translated at all. We can now say with near certainty that it was a Jewish practice, before, during, and after the New Testament period to write the divine name in paleo-Hebrew or square Aramaic script or in transliteration right into the Greek text of Scripture."

- *R.B. Girdlestone*, late principle of Wycliffe Hall, Oxford, states the following: "If that [Septuagint] version had retained the word [Jehovah], or had even used one Greek word for Jehovah and another for Adonai, such usage would doubtless would have been retained in the discourses and arguments of the N.T. Thus our Lord, in quoting the 110th Psalm 110:1, instead of saying, 'The Lord said unto my Lord,' might have said, 'Jehovah said unto Adonai.' ... Suppose a Christian scholar engaged in translating the Greek Testament into Hebrew, he would have to consider, each time the word [kyrios] occurred, whether there was anything in the context to indicate its true Hebrew representative; and this is the difficulty which would arise in translating the N.T. into all languages, if the title Jehovah had been allowed to stand in the [Septuagint translation of the] O.T. The Hebrew Scriptures would be a guide in many passages: thus, wherever the expression 'the angel of the Lord' occurs, we know that the word Lord represents Jehovah; a similar conclusion as to the expression 'the word of the Lord' would be arrived at,

---

272 Brackets mine

Robert L. George   65

if the precedent set by the O.T. were followed; so also in the case of the title 'the Lord of Hosts.'"[273]
- *Papyrus Grecs Bibliques*, by F. Dunand, Cairo, 1966, p. 47, fn. 4, quotes Jerome of 384CE as saying: "The ninth [name of God] is the Tetragrammaton, which they considered … unspeakable, and it is written with these letters, Iod, He, Vau, He. Certain ignorant ones, because of the similarity of the characters, when they would find it in the Greek books, were accustomed to read PIPI."[274]
- *McKenzie's Dictionary of the Bible* under the heading, "Lord," p. 517: "The use of kyrios in the synoptic Gospels … is also a designation of God in quotations from the LXX or as a substitute for the name of God, and in the common profane sense of owner or master."
- *J. Parkhurst* says: "In the NT, likewise, KURIOS, when used as a name of God … most usually corresponds to hwhy Jehovah, and in this sense is applied."[275]
- *J.H. Thayer* says under Kurios: "c. This title is given a. to God, the ruler of the universe (so the Sept. for adonai, eloah, elohim, Jehovah and Jah)."[276]
- *Liddel and Scott*, 1968 ed., p. 1013 A Greek English Lexicon, under Kurios: "B. 4. O KURIOS, = Hebr. Yahweh, LXX Ge. II. 5, al."
- *G.D. Kilpatrick* states in his *Etudes de Papyrologie Tome Neuvieme* that between the periods 70-135CE "there were three major changes in the transmission of the text. The change from scroll to codex, the Tetragrammaton was replaced by Kyrios and nomina sacra (sacred names) were abbreviated."[277]
- *Literary Remains*, 1836–1839, Vol. 4, S.T. Coleridge, pp. 226, 227 states: "Have we not adopted the Hebrew word, Jehovah? Is not the **Kurios**, or Lord, of the LXX a Greek substitute, in countless instances, for the Hebrew Jehovah? Why not then restore the original word, and in the Old Testament religiously render Jehovah by Jehovah, and every text of the New Testament, referring to the Old, by the Hebrew word in the text referred to?"
- *New Testament Abstracts Magazine*, March 1977, p. 306 says: "In pre-Christian [manuscripts] of the OT, the divine name was not rendered by 'kyrios' as has often been thought. Usually the Tetragram was written out in Aramaic or in paleo-Hebrew letters … At a later time, surrogates such as

---

273 *Synonyms of the Old Testament*, 1897, p. 43, brackets mine
274 Brackets mine
275 *A Greek and English Lexicon to the New Testament*, revised ed., 1845, p. 347
276 *A Greek English Lexicon of the New Testament*, 1889, p. 365
277 Pp. 221–222

'theos' [God] and 'kyrios' [Lord] replaced the Tetragram ... There is good reason to believe that a similar pattern evolved in the NT, i.e. the divine name was originally written in the NT quotations of and allusions to the OT, but in the course of time it was replaced by surrogates."

- *Jesuit Magazine Entschluss/Offen*, April 1985, Wolfgang Feneberg states: "He [Jesus] did not withhold his father's name YHWH from us, but he entrusted us with it. It is otherwise inexplicable why the first petition of the Lord's Prayer should read: 'May your name be sanctified!' ... In pre-Christian manuscripts for Greek-speaking Jews, God's name was not paraphrased with kyrios [Lord], but was written in the Tetragram form in Hebrew or archaic Hebrew characters ... we find recollections of the name in the writings of the Church Fathers."

- *The New International Dictionary of New Testament Theology* says: "Recently discovered texts doubt the idea that the translators of the LXX have rendered the Tetragrammaton JHWH with KYRIOS. The most ancient mss (manuscripts) of the LXX today available have the Tetragrammaton written in Hebrew letters in the Greek text. This was custom preserved by the later Hebrew translator of the Old Testament in the first centuries (after Christ)."[278]

- R.B. Girdlestone, *Synonyms of the Old Testament*, 1897, p. 43 declares: "If that version (LXX) would have kept the term (YHWH), or had used the Greek term for JEHOVAH and another for ADONAY, such a use would surely been followed in the discourses and in the reasonings of the NT. Therefore our Lord, in quoting the 110th Psalms, instead of saying: 'The LORD has said to my LORD' could have said: "JEHOVA has said to ADONI." Supposing that a Christian studios was translating in Hebrew the Greek Testament: every time that he met the word KYRIOS, he should have had to consider if in the context there was something that indicated the true Hebrew correspondent; and this is the difficulty that would have arisen in translating the NT in whatever language if the name JEHOVAH would have been left in the Old Testament (LXX). The Hebrew Scriptures would have constituted a standard for many passages: every time that the expression "the LORD'S angel" recurs, we know that the term LORD represents JEHOVA; we could come to a similar conclusion for the expression "the LORD'S word", according to the precedent established in the OT; and so it is in the case of the name "the LORD of armies."

---

278 Volume 2, p. 512

As you are able to certainly recognize, the divine name, Jehovah, falls within the dictionary, lexical and semantic range of Lord/Kyrios, and that is why many other versions or translations, not just English ones, have seen fit to also include the divine name in their Christian Greek Scriptures. "When our New Testament portion of the Bible was being written by men such as Matthew, Mark, Luke, and others, they quoted from the Hebrew Scriptures hundreds of times … Many of these quotations include places where the Tetragrammanton occurred. One would imagine that when these NT … writers quoted from the Old Testament that they would have quoted all the words from the Sacred Scriptures, and would not have changed any of them, including God's personal name."[279]

Today, for example, Thomas Newberry in his *The Englishman's Bible* of 1883 has a shoulder note 'J.' to represent Jehovah at Matthew 1:20, 22, 24, et cetera. Also, it should be noted that most of the Hebrew New Testament translations contain the divine name when referencing a scripture from the Old Testament. *The Jewish N.T.*, by David H. Stern, 1989, is just one example. He has side notes throughout wherever it occurs, "Adonai—the LORD, Jehovah." I have included for your convenience a detailed list of Seventy-Eight different translations of the Christian Greek Scriptures containing God's name. Also provided is a list of Twenty-Seven Hebrew New Testaments containing the divine name of God. These lists are at the end of this section.

As a result, the offense and true center of attention, according to this author, should be on those who have removed the divine name almost seven thousand times; not on those who seek to restore it to its original place in God's own word. Hopefully, you now know, taken the Bible as a whole, Jehovah is more than an acceptable form of Kyrios or Theos where it applies to the Father, as it is the only personal name attached to the Father. Notice the following.

- ISAIAH 64:8[280]   "And now, O [Jehovah], You are our Father. We are the clay, and You our potter. And we are all the work of Your hand."
- ISAIAH 63:16[281]   "For Thou art our Father. Because Abraham knoweth us not, and Israel hath not acknowledge us; do Thou, O Lord [Jehovah], our Father, do Thou deliver us.

---

279   *The Lord and the Tetragrammaton*, Mazzaferro, pp. 7–8
280   *TS*, brackets mine
281   *LXX*; brackets mine

- PSALM 2:7[282]

> From the beginning Thy name is upon us."

> "Let me proclaim Yahweh's decree; he has told me, "You are my son, today I have become your father."

It is also a name to last forever, "'Jehovah the God of your forefathers, the God of Abraham, the God of Isaac and the God of Jacob, has sent me to you.' This is my name to time indefinite, and this is the memorial of me to generation after generation."[283]

Great opposition to the Christian Greek Scriptures

When meditating on the intense persecution of the first century Christians, we often conjure up—and rightly so—torture and death by ruthless Romans. While Christians were enduring unspeakable hardships, there was another subtle persecution developing that is not often talked about. There was an outright hatred regarding the Jewish Christian writings (Gospels) that were already in circulation. These Jewish Christians were known as Minim, (heretics), by the Jewish Rabbis.

Concerning the great opposition to the Christian Scriptures Lawrance H. Schiffman writes in his book *Who Was A Jew?* "While the benediction against the *minim* [heretics] was certainly the most important step taken by the tannaim, [the Pharisaic-Rabbinic teachers between 63bce and 200ce], to combat Jewish Christianity, they also took steps to emphasize that the Christian Scriptures were not holy. First, the Jewish Christians themselves wrote scrolls of the Bible (*sifre minim*). The question here was the sanctity of the entire text. Second, beginning in the second half of the first century, early recensions of the Gospels and Epistles began to circulate. The sanctity of those sections of these Christian texts which quoted the Hebrew Scriptures directly also had to be determined. In view of the role of the Gospels and Epistles as a vehicle for the dissemination of Christianity, it is easy to understand why the Rabbis went out of their way to divest them of sanctity and halakhic, [the Jewish way of life], status."[284]

It is quite significant to notice why these Rabbis were so intent on destroying the Christian Scriptures. It is because these texts quoted the Hebrew Scriptures. Why is this point so significant to our discussion? Mr. Schiffman continues by

---

282 *JB*
283 Exodus 3:15; *NWT*
284 P. 62, par. 1, brackets mine

quoting a very famous Rabbinic passage called T. Shabbat 13(14):5 "We do not save from a fire (on the Sabbath) the Gospels and the books of the minim ("heretics"). Rather, they are burned in their place, they and their Tetragrammata. [YHWH] Rabbi Yose Ha-Gelili says: During the week, one should cut out their Tetragrammata [YHWH] and hide them away and burn the remainder. Said Rabbi Tarfon: May I bury my Sons! If (these books) would come into my hand, I would burn them along with their Tetragrammata. [YHWH] For even if a pursuer were running after me, I would enter a house of idolatry rather than enter their (the Jewish Christians') houses. For the idolaters do not know Him and deny Him, but these (Jewish Christians) know Him and deny Him ... Said Rabbi Ishmael: If in order to bring peace between a husband and his wife, the everpresent has commanded that a book that has been written in holiness be erased by means of water, how much more so should the books of the minim which bring enmity between Israel and their Father who is in Heaven be erased, they and their Tetragrammata [YHWH] ... Just as we do not save them fro a fire, so we do not save them from a cave-in nor from water nor from anything which would destroy them."[285]

Next Mr. Schiffman comments on the above saying: "The passage contains no disagreement regarding what to do if the Gospels or other books of the minim (texts of the Hebrew Scriptures) are caught in a fire on the Sabbath. These books are not to be saved, as they have no sanctity. There is, however, debate regarding what to do with such texts during the week. Rabbi Yose Ha-Gelili suggests removing the Tetragrammata and burning the rest. Apparently, he feels that regardless of who wrote it, the Tetragrammanton retains its sanctity. Rabbi Tarfon permits the burning of the texts with their divine names ..."[286]

Professor George Howard, Associate Professor of Religion and Hebrew at the University of Georgia apparently agrees when he concludes: "The Divine name, YHWH, was and is the most sacred word in the Hebrew language. So it is hardly likely that Jews of any sort would have removed it from their Bibles. Furthermore, we know now from discoveries in Egypt and the Judean desert the Jews wrote the Tetragrammaton in Hebrew even in their Greek texts. In all likelihood Jewish Christians felt the same way about the Divine name and continued to preserve it in Hebrew in their Bibles. A famous rabbinic passage (Talmud Shabbat 13.5) discusses the problem of destroying heretical texts (very probably including books of Jewish-Christians). The problem arises for the rabbinic writer, because the heretical texts contain the divine name, and their wholesale destruction would include the destruction of the divine name. This further suggests that Jewish Christians

---

285 P. 62, par. 2, brackets mine
286 Pp. 62–63, par. 3

did not translate the divine name into Greek ... Thus, toward the end of the first Christian century, the use of surrogates (kyrios and Theos) must have crowded out the Hebrew Tetragrammaton in both Testaments."

The Rabbis were religiously heated from the Jewish Christians use of God's name, the Tetragrammaton (*YHWH*), in their Gospels and other texts. There was no debate on whether these Jewish Christians were using God's name Jehovah, but rather on how to destroy the Gospels that contained God's name. This is exceptional proof that God's enduring name Jehovah was used and written by Christians in their 1st century circulated Gospels.

Hallelujah

All of the previous information should at the very least, give all of us more motivation and incentive to search more thoroughly to locate accurate knowledge. This information really sets up the next step in additional proof as to the name Jehovah being in the Christian Greek Scriptures.

When you hear the word 'Hallelujah,' what comes to your mind? Could it be perhaps the musical masterpiece, Handel's Messiah? Or you may think about the famous American patriotic song 'The Battle Hymn of the Republic,' which is better known as 'Glory, Hallelujah.' This word, Hallelujah, is so often spoken and sung in churches across the world, but regrettably, most have no idea as to what they are saying or singing, and this is truly a great disgrace.

The exact meaning of the word 'ha-lelu-Yah' is 'Praise Jah you People!' "Literally 'praise Yahweh', transliterated 'hallelujah'."[287] Jah is the shortened form of the name of God, Jehovah. It appears in the Bible more than Fifty times, often as part of the expression 'Hallelujah.'

Many names in the Bible contain 'Jah' as part of their names. For example: Elijah (my God is Jah), Abijah (my father is Jah), Jedidiah (beloved of Jah) and of course Jesus (salvation of Jah or, Jah saves). Just as well to note is the fact this abbreviated form, 'Jah', of the Tetragrammaton in Revelation, does appear in the present Greek manuscripts available today. If clergy, scholars, really anyone, has a problem with the name Jehovah being placed in the New Testament, then what are these ones to say regarding Revelation 19:1-6? It is quite clear; this evidence is only irritating to those who despise truth. Lets take a close look at revelation 19:1–6.

---

287 *The Brown-Driver-Briggs Hebrew and English Lexicon*, 1979, p. 39

- Revelation 19:1[288]   "Hallelujah! Salvation, glory, and power belong to our God."
- Revelation 19:3[289]   "A second time they said: Halleluyah!"
- Revelation 19:4[290]   "Then the 24 elders and the four living creatures fell down and worshiped God, who is seated on the throne, saying: Amen! Hallelujah!"
- Revelation 19:6[291]   "Then I heard something like the voice of a vast multitude, like the sound of cascading waters, and like the rumbling of loud thunder, saying: Hallelujah—because our Lord God, the Almighty, has begun to reign!"

G.W. Wade translates Revelation 19:1–6 in this fashion: "After this I heard, as it were, a great sound of voices from a vast multitude in Heaven, exclaiming, 'Praise ye Jehovah; Salvation and Glory and Power are our God's because reliable and just are His judgments; because He has brought to judgment the Great Harlot, who was corrupting the earth by her immorality, and because He has avenged His servants' blood shed by their hands.' And a second time they cried, 'Praise ye Jehovah; and the smoke from her ruins ascends for ever and ever.'"[292]

There is another highlight in the book of Revelation that has been overlooked as well. It involves the use of specifically identifying Jehovah by what Judaism refers to as 'The Name', or Ha-Shem, in replace of Jehovah. The importance of this expression is found in three instances in Revelation. They are Revelation 3:12; 14:1, and 22:4. Notice the expression found in these verses. Revelation 3:12 "I'll make each conqueror a pillar in the sanctuary of my God, a permanent position of honor. Then I'll write names on you, the pillars: the Name of my God."[293] Revelation 14:1 continues: "A Lamb stood on Mount Zion, and with him one hundred forty-four thousand, having his Father's name written in

---

288   *HCSB*; footnote reads: Lit. Praise Yahweh
289   *TA*
290   *HCSB*, see also Revelation 1:4, 5
291   *HCSB*, see also Revelation 1:8
292   *The Documents of the New Testament-Translated and Historically Arranged with Critical Introductions*, 1934, p. 426
293   *TM*

their foreheads."[294] Finally, Revelation 22:4 states: "They will see his face, and his name will be on their foreheads."[295]

Could these scriptures be in reference to the Tetragrammaton, Jehovah? Dr. S.M. McDonough thinks there is a possibility of this. For he affirms: "All of this indicates that John probably had the Tetragrammaton in mind when he spoke of the name 'on' people in Revelation."[296] The author agrees.

Thus, it is rather evident of the importance of God's name, Jehovah, to first century Christians. Notice what the *Zondervan Pictorial Bible Dictionary*, 1964 p. 571 has to say. "In the Scriptures there is the closest possible relationship between a person and his name the two being practically equivalent so that to remove the name is to extinguish the person. To forget God's name is to depart from him." *Today's Dictionary of the Bible* relates: "As is always the case in the ancient Near East, this name is not simply a label for identification, but much more profoundly a revelation of the divine nature. This means that the meaning of the four consonants YHWH as they appear in the Hebrew Ex. 3:15, 6:3 must be seen as a heightening of the awareness of the nature of God as he revealed himself to Moses. There is a contrast drawn in chapter three between the way God revealed himself to the Patriarchs and the way he will now reveal himself to Israel. Before, he was Elohim Shaddai (God Almighty), but now he will be YHWH. It is generally agreed that the divine name here used is a form of the verb hayah, 'to be' [better 'to become'], as the various renderings of the name would indicate … God's very name is a promise to his people."[297]

Just as well, another reference work explains: "Yahweh, 'he will be.' … It is the personal name of God, as distinguished from such generic or essential names as El, Elohim, Shadday, etc. Character knowledge of God as a person; and Jehovah is His name as a person."[298] The revealing of these truths are exceptional points to remember. Please keep in mind that accepting Jehovah as God's name in no way shames our King and Savior Jesus Christ. It actually brings us closer to Jesus, whose very own name means Jehovah is Salvation.

I will end this section with a quote from one Bible translator, John W. Davis, a missionary in China during the 19th century. Please listen attentively to what he says. "If the Holy Ghost says Jehovah in any given place in Hebrew, why does the Translator not say Jehovah in English or Chinese? What right has he to say, I

---

294 *NSB*
295 *TNIV*
296 *Yahweh at Patmos*, 1999, p. 113
297 Pp. 330–331
298 *The International Standard Bible Encyclopedia*, Vol. II, pp. 1254, 1267

will use Jehovah in this place and a substitute for it in that? If anyone should say that there are cases in which the use of Jehovah would be wrong, let him show the reason why; the onus probandi [burden of proof] rest upon him. He will find the task a hard one, for he must answer this simple question,—If in any given case it is wrong to use Jehovah in the translation, then why did the inspired writer use it in the original?"[299]

The Father Jehovah is the only true God

Since the sacred name Jehovah is represented in the Hebrew Scriptures nearly seven thousand times, it would seem logical that God's name might be associated with a variety of titles as well. We have already seen and discussed the title 'Lord.'[300] However, there is a much more significant title Jehovah uses to explain his relationship with us in terms we are able to comprehend as humans.

For example, if you wanted to explain to someone equality within the family arrangement, what would you use? We would use twins or perhaps siblings. What if you needed to explain authority using the family arrangement? We would compare the Father to the son, correct? This title Father is used at John 17:3 and is always used of Jehovah in the absolute sense. It is an endearing title, one that begs God's people to trust in him explicitly as a child would his parents; specifically their Father. "For thou art our Father, though Abraham knoweth us not ... thou, O Jehovah, art our Father"[301] This is irrefutable: Jehovah God is undeniably the Father. This wonderful, appealing title, Father, is given exclusively to Jehovah and no one else. Even Trinitarians do not equate Jesus as being the Father. For a fact their creeds admit: "these three persons being truly distinct one from another."[302]

Why would Jehovah choose to be called Father to Israel? Lets refresh our minds for a moment, and reflect on all the loving deeds Jehovah had done in their behalf. First, is not Jehovah the source of life? "For with you [Jehovah] is the source of life."[303] Was it not Jehovah who adopted the small, seemingly insignificant nation of Israel from all others as his firstborn? "For I [Jehovah] am a father to Israel ... my first-born."[304] Is it not Jehovah that provided food, clothing, and

---

299 *The Chinese Recorder and Missionary Journal*, Vol. VII, Shanghai, 1876
300 Psalm 23:1; 110:1
301 Isaiah 63:16; *TMB*
302 *The Catholic Encyclopedia*, 1912, Vol. XV, p. 47
303 Psalm 36:9; *NWT*, brackets mine, compare Deuteronomy 32:6; Isaiah 64:8
304 Jeremiah 31:9, *ASV*, brackets mine

shelter for his firstborn? "Oh give thanks unto Jehovah; for he is good ... who giveth food to all flesh."[305] Jehovah certainly deserves to be called "Our Father" for he is our provider of all things.

Through prophecy, Jehovah is even recognized to be the Father of Jesus Christ. "He said to Me, "You are My Son; today I have become Your Father," He will be My son, and I will be his father."[306] Jesus himself admits this at Mark 14:36[307] "Abba, Father! All things are possible for You. Take this cup away from Me. Nevertheless, not what I will, but what You will."

This word Abba should not be passed over as just another everyday ambiguous title. Notice how Gary Zeola translates this verse. "And He was saying, "Dad *[Gr. Abba]*, Father! All *[things]* are possible to You; take this cup away from Me; but not what I desire, but what You *[desire]*."[308] Mr. Zeola expresses the term Abba as Dad, a much more personal closeness such as a toddler calls his Father 'Daddy'. I like Eugene H. Peterson's rendering of Mark 14:36 "Papa, Father, you can—can't you?—get me out of this."[309] This closeness is noticeable at 2 John 1–3[310] "In truth and love, God the Father and Jesus Christ, the Son of the Father send you grace, mercy and peace." *Albert Barnes's Notes on the Bible* says: "Abba is used by the Saviour as a word denoting filial affection and tenderness." *Adam Clarke's Commentary on the Bible* notes: "Abba, Father ... intimates filial affection and respect, and parental tenderness, seems to have been used ... to show complete submission to his Father's will." Hence, the affectionate title Father [Abba] is given to Jehovah, and Jehovah only. "We bless Jehovah, the Father."[311]

Jehovah is Father of Jesus Christ

If Jesus Christ affectionately in prayer calls God his Abba (Dad), then we should be able to verify this subordinate yet inseparable filial relationship throughout the Scriptures. Indeed, this is exactly what Bible students become aware of. "It was

---

305   Psalm 136:1, 25
306   Psalm 2:7; 1 Chronicles 22:10; *HCSB*, compare Hebrews 1:5; Mark 1:11; Luke 9:35; 2 Peter 1:17
307   *HCSB*
308   *ALT*
309   *TM*, emphasis added
310   *NSB*
311   James 3:9, *NSB*

God who said to him: You [Jesus] are my [Jehovah's] Son; I today have become your father."[312]

Over and over again we read about this incomparable relationship between Jehovah and his son Jesus. The Bible writers themselves understood God to be the Father of Jesus. Notice the apostle Paul's renderings. "How blessed is God! He's the Father of our Master, Jesus Christ," "I ask—ask the God of our Master, Jesus Christ, the God of glory," "Thank God the Father of our Lord Jesus Christ," "All praise to the God and Father of our Master, Jesus the Messiah!" and finally "The eternal and blessed God and Father of our Master Jesus."[313] Paul makes it clear that "There is one God and Father of all, who is over all."[314]

The Father Jehovah several times verifies his love for Jesus while on earth. His words are so ever appealing. "And lo, a voice out of the heavens, saying, This is my beloved Son, in whom I am well pleased."[315] Jehovah continues another time saying: "This is my Son, my chosen: hear ye him."[316] Where did these voices originate? The heavens. The Father of Jesus Christ was in the heavens. Jesus confirms this on many occasions such as Matthew 16:17 "my Father who is in heaven."[317]

Only one biblical conclusion

God's word makes it so very uncomplicated for us to comprehend who he truthfully is. Isaiah 64:8 assert: "O Jehovah, thou art our Father." If Jesus Christ identifies Jehovah as his Father, who are we to disagree or assert another way? This scriptural truth happily brings us to our second and most important weak link of the trinity chain.

Who is the only true God? Jesus declares at John 17:1, 3 "Father, … you, [are] the one and only true God."[318] The Bible, in Jesus Christ's own words declares the Father Jehovah to be the only true God. When we compare this Biblical teaching with Christendom's ideas that Jesus is Jehovah, much confusion arises. Why? Remember, the trinity teaches that Jesus Christ and the Father are "truly

---

312   Hebrews 5:5; *NSB*; cf. Psalm 2:7, brackets mine
313   Ephesians 1:3; 1:17 *TM*; Colossians 1:3 *NSB*; 2 Corinthians 1:3; 11:31 *TM*
314   Ephesians 4:6; *NSB*
315   Matthew 3:17
316   Luke 9:35
317   Cf. Matthew 5:16; 45; 6:1, 9; 7:11; 10:32, 33; 16:17
318   *TM*, brackets mine

distinct one from another."[319] In other words, the trinity teaches that Jesus is not the Father. This the Bible agrees with.

Nonetheless, as just mentioned, many in Christendom are frantically debating that Jesus is Jehovah of the Hebrew Scriptures. If Trinitarians want to believe this then they must accept the biblical fact that Jehovah is the Father, as I have just proved through scriptures. This is unfeasible for Trinitarians because this theory would make Jesus the Father as well, contrary to their Trinitarian teaching. Oh, what a large man-made unscriptural web they have weaved! A chain is only as strong as it's weakest link.

"What is the testimony of "The faithful Witness" of the Truth? Addressing his "Father," Joh 17:1-3, he plainly and positively declares THE FATHER TO BE "THE ONLY TRUE GOD." You believe that the Father is one person. If then you believe that "the only true God" is three persons, does not your faith stand in the wisdom of men," which denies the testimony of Jesus Christ, that ONE person is "the ONLY true God?" Please to consider the testimony of the inspired apostle, 1Co 8:6. It is not only that "there is but one God," but that this one God is "THE FATHER." He plainly distinguishes the Father as the "one God" "or whom are all things."[320] Thus, our second weak link of this trinity chain is revealed.

John 17:3 could not be more clear-cut and to the point. Jehovah is the only true God. Many Greek scholars acknowledge this as well. "That they may know you, the only one who is really God."[321] Also: "The 'one God' of OT monotheism is 'to us one God the Father.'"[322]

Are there any scriptures that refer to Jesus as true God? Are there any that refer to the holy spirit as true God? Honesty and biblical facts demand the answer is no. Finally, I want to share a quote from Origen regarding John 17:3. He states: "God on the one hand is very God (autoheos, God of himself); and so the Savior says in his prayer to the Father, "That they may know Thee the only true God;" ... The true God, then, is "The God," and those who are formed after him are gods, images, as it were, of Him the Prototype.""[323]

Who are we to believe? Interestingly, God's word says: "God is not a man to lie, or a son of man to change his purpose."[324] The trinity has accomplished nothing except to deceive, confuse, and lie about whom the only true God really

---

319 *The Catholic Encyclopedia*, 1912, Vol. XV, p. 47
320 *An Appeal To Pious Trinitarians*, Henry Grew, 1857, *The Harvest Herald*
321 *Greek-English Lexicon of the New Testament: Based on Semantic Domains*
322 *The Expositor's Greek Testament*, Vol. 2, Nicoll, 2002, p. 841
323 *Ante-Nicene Fathers*, reprint series, Vol. II, p. 323
324 Numbers 23:19; *FF*

is. Where have lies originated? Jesus said: "You are of your father the Devil, and you want to carry out your father's desire's. He was a murderer from the beginning and has not stood in the truth, because there is no truth in him. When he tells a lie, he speaks from his own nature, because he is a liar and the father of liars. Yet because I tell the truth, you do not believe Me ... The one who is from God listens to God's words. This is why you don't listen, because you are not from God."[325] The Bible simply says that the Father Jehovah is the only true God.[326]

Obviously then, any teaching beyond this is from the Father of the lie, Satan. "You must not go beyond what the Scriptures say."[327] When God is permitted to interpret his own word, then, and only then, "You'll understand the truth, and the truth will liberate you."[328]

Here is a list of the Christian Greek Scriptures that contain some form of God's name Jehovah, within their translations.

---

325 John 8:44–47; *HCSB*
326 See John 17:3; Isaiah 63:16; 64:8
327 1 Corinthians 4:6; *ENT*
328 John 8:32 *CPV*; see Genesis 40:8

List of English Bible's containing divine name in NT

Author & Translation	Date	Name	Examples
1- Henry Hammond, *A Paraphrase &Annotations upon the Books of the NT*	1653	Jehovah	Acts 8:10, 15:17
2- John Elliot, *NT, American Indian Lang*	1661	Jehovah	Acts 2:39,47; 3:19
3- Phillip Doddridge	1739–56	Jehovah	Lk 1:68; Mk 12:29
4- E. Harwood, *A Literal Translation of the NT*	1768	Jehovah	Matt 21:9; 22:44
5- Gilbert Wakefield, NT	1795	Jehovah	Rev 19:1,3,4,6
6- Campbell, *Four Gospels*	1796	Jehovah	Footnote Lk 20:43
7- Newcome, NT	1796	Jehovah	Matt 22:44, Mk12:36, etc.
8- Nathaniel Scarlett [Facsimile]	1798	Jehovah & Tet.	Cover page, Footnote in Matthew & John
9- D. Macrae, *A Revised Translationof the Sacred Scriptures*	1798–99	Jehovah	Matt 22:44; Rev 1:8
10- R. Caddick, *The NT in Hebrew & English*	1798–1805	Tet.	Always
11- R. Fellowes, *Memoir of the Life & Doctrine of Christ by the Four Evangelist*	1804	Jehovah	Matt 22:44

12- Johann Babor Tedesco, NT	1805	Jhova	Lk 4:18, 19
13- T. Belsham, *The NT an improved Version upon the basis of Archbishop Newcome*	1808	Jehovah	Matt 22:34; Mk 12:46; etc.
14- B. Boothroyd, *A New Family Bible & Improved Version*	1817	Jehovah	Lk 20:42; Acts 2:34
15- Abner Kneeland, NT	1822	Jehovah	Matt 22:44; Mk 12:36; etc
16- John S. Thompson, *The Gospel History According to the Four Evangelist*	1829	Jehovah	4x's on pp. 192,395,397(2)
17- J.B. McCaul, *The Epistles to the Hebrews*	1836	Jehovah	Hebrews 7:21
18- J.T. Conquest, *The Holy Bible*	1842	Jehovah	Matt 22:44; Mk 12:36; etc
19- John Lingard, *A New Version of the Four Gospels*	1846	Jehova	Matt 22:44
20- T.W. Peile, *A New Translation Epistles to the Romans*	1854	Jehovah	Romans 11:34
21- William Kelly, *Two Nineteenth Century Versions of the NT by John Darby & Kelly*	1860	Jehovah	18x's
22- Herman Heinfetter, *A Literal Translation of the NT from the Text Of the Vatican Manuscript*, London	1863	Jehovah	Mark 12:29, 30

23- Herman Heinfetter, *An English Version of the NT*	1864	Jehovah	Always
24- George Taplin, *Scripture Selections*	1864	Jehovah	John 3:16
25- John M. Darby New Translation	1879	Jehovah	Footnotes in Matt/Rev
26- Herbert, *NT Letters*	1880	Jehovah	Consistently
27- Benjamin Wilson, *Emphatic Diaglott*	1886	Jehovah	18x's, Matt 21:9; 21:42; etc
28- B.W. Johnson, *The Peoples NT*	1891	Jehovah	Footnote Matt/Rev
29- G.B.Stevens, *The Message of the Apostles*	1900	Jehovah	Acts 2:1; 3:7; 7:6
30- Ballentine American Bible, 5 Vol. NT	1901	Jehovah	Ro-7x's; 1Co-5x's; 2Co-1x
31- T.C. Hall, *The Messages of Jesus According to the Synoptist*	1901	Jehovah	Sometimes
32- W.W. Smith, *The NT in Braid Scots*	1901	Jehovah	Matt 22:44; Lk 20:37
33- Charles K. Kent, *The Message of the Apostles*	1902	Jehovah	Many Times
34- Perkiomen Press NT [Ballentine]	1909	Jehovah	Acts 2:25, 34
35- Ellen G. White	1911	Jehovah	Many Times

36- W.G. Rutherford	1914	Jehovah	6x's in Romans
37- Helen B. Montgomery [2nd Edition]	1924	Jehovah	Luke 1:38
38- Ray Allen, *Book of Mark*	1927	Jehovah	Few Times
39- George N. LeFevre, NT	1928–29	Jehovah	Many Times
40- B.W. Bacon, *Studies in Matthew*	1931	Jehovah	Matt 21:9, 42, 44, 23:39, 27:10
41- B.W. Bacon, *The Gospel of Hellenist*	1933	Jehovah	Gv 10:12,38
42- W.H Isaacs, *New Testament Epistles in English Prose*	1933	Jehovah	Some
43- G.W. Wade, *The Documents of the New Testament*	1934	Jehovah	Rev 19:1,3,4,6
44- J.W.C. Wand, *NT Letters*	1946	Jehovah	8x's Ro 9:29, 11:14; Heb etc
45- Traina *Sacred Name NT*	1950	Yahweh	Many Times
46- P.G.Parker, *The Clarified NT*	1955	Jehovah	Matthew 22:44
47- William Beardslee, *Book of Mark*	1962	Jehovah	Few Times
48- *Vincent Roth NT*	1963	Jehovah	Many Times
49- *Restoration of Original Sacred Name New Testament*	1970	Yahweh	Many Times
50- *The Restoration of Original Sacred Name Bible Missionary Dispensary Bible Research*	1970	Yahvah	Always

51- W.A. Carleton, *The Growth of the Early Church*	1970	Jehovah	Acts 2:35
52- Dr. Dymond, NT, manuscript only	1972	Jehovah/Yahweh	
53- G.B. Stevens, The Epistles of Paul in Modern English	1980/1898	Jehovah	Always
54- G.W. Cornish, *From the Trenches Corinthians & Ephesians*	1981	Jehovah	1 Corinthians 10:9
55- J.O. Meyers, *The Sacred Scriptures*	1981	Yahweh	Always
56- *New World Translation of the Holy Scriptures,* Reference edition	1984	Jehovah	277x's
57- Marley Cole, *Living Destiny*	1984	Jehovah	43x's
58- A.B. Traina, *The Holy Name Bible Revised*	1989	Yahweh	Always
59- H. Jahn, Excesses Ready Research Bible	1993	Yahveh	Always
60- W. Kelly, *Two Nineteenth Century Versions of the NT Revised*	1995	Jehovah	Some
61- *The Christian Bible*	1995	Yehweh	Few Times/Mostly fn.
62- *New American Bible*	1995	Yahweh	Matt 1:21; Lk 1:13
63- Yisrayl Hawkins, *The Book of Yahweh, The Holy Scriptures*	1996	Yahweh	Always

64- T.R. Weiland, *God's Covenant People*	1997	YHWH	Always
65- *The Scriptures, A Paraphrase & Version of the NT*	1998	Tet.	Many Times
66- Thomas Newberry, *The Holy Bible*	1998	Jehovah	Many Times
67- Frank Daniels, *The Non-Ecclesiastical NT*	1999	Yahweh	Many Times
68- Vivian Capel, *21st Century NT*	2000	Jehovah	Many Times
69- *21st Century Version of the Christian Scriptures-The Gospel Of Matthew*	2000	YHWH	Many Times
70- *Sacred Scriptures*-Family of Yah Ed	2001	Yahweh	Always
71- Dallas James, *The Holy Bible-Urum-Thumin Version* Vol. V	2001	YHWH	Matt 1:1; John 1:19
72- *2001 Translation, An American English Translation*	2001	Jehovah	Many Times
73- *Sacred Name KJV*, Scripture Research Association	2001	YHVH	Always
74- Rhichard Lattier, *Restored Name KJV*	2002	YHVH	Always
75- *The Scriptures*, Institute for Scripture Research	2002	Tet.	Many Times
76- Jim Madsen, *New Simplified*	2004	Jehovah	Consistently
77- *Holman Christian Standard Bible*	2004	Yahweh	Revelation 19:1 fn.

78- *The Sacred Scriptures* Assemblies of Yahweh	2004	Yahweh	Always
79- Gary Zeolla, *Analytical-Literal Translation*, 2nd Edition	2005	Yahweh	Matt 1:21; Lk 1:31

List of Hebrew Bible's containing divine name in NT

(Courtesy of *The Lord and the Tetragrammaton* by Howard Mazzaferro)

Author & Translation	Date
1- Gospel of Matthew, di Shem-Tob ben Isaac Ibn Shaprut	1385
2- Psalms and Matthew, di A. Margaritha, Lipsia	1533
3- Gospels, di F. Petri, Wittemberg	1537
4- Matthew and Hebrews, di S. Munster, Basilea	1537
5- Gospel of Matthew, di J. Quinquarboreus, Parigi	1551
6- Gospel of Matthew, a cura di J. du Tillet, Parigi	1555
7- Gospels, di J. Claius, Lipsia	1576
8- New Testament, di E. Hutter, Norimberga	1599
9- New Testament, di W. Robertson, Londra	1661
10- Gospels, di G.B. Jona, Roma	1668
11- New Testament, di Dominik von Brentano, Veienna e Praga	1796
12- New Testament, di R. Caddick, Londra	1798–1805
13- New Testament, di T. Fry, Londra	1817
14- New Testament, di W. Greenfield, Londra	1831
15- New Testament, di A. McCaul e altri, Londra	1838
16- New Testament, di J.C. Reichardt, Londra	1846
17- Luke, Acts, Romans, Hebrews, di J.H.R. Biesenthal, Berlino	1855

18- New Testament, di H. Heinfetter, Londra	1863
19- New Testament, di J.C. Reichardt e J.H.R. Biesenthal, Londra	1866
20- New Testament, di I. Salkinson e C.D. Ginsburg, Londra	1891
21- Romans, di W.G. Rutherford, Londra	1900
22- Gospel of John, di M.I. Ben Maeir, Denver	1957
23- A Concordance to the Greek New Testament, di Moulton e Geden	1963
24- New Testament, di J. Bauchet e D. Kinnereth, Roma	1975
25- New Testament, United Bibles Societies, Gerusalemme	1979
26- New Testament, di F. Delitzsch, Londra	1981
27- New Testament, Bible Society, Gerusalemme	1986

PART III

Does Almighty God have a God?

Jesus Christ has a God?

Who is Almighty God? In every instance of posing this question to Trinitarians in my ministry, they will always reply: 'Jesus Christ.' Again, there is never any mention of Jehovah and the holy spirit. Although the Trinitarian chain teaches that all 'three persons' are Almighty God,[329] their main focus is on Jesus Christ. Simply stated Jesus Christ is the Trinitarians God.

Almighty God is translated in his own word the Bible from the Hebrew word El (God) Shaddai (Almighty). The basic meaning is all-powerful. The *Jewish Encyclopedia*,[330] states referring to Almighty: "It is possible, however, that the original significance was that of 'overmastering' or 'overpowering strength,' and that this meaning persist in the divine [title]." In other words, Almighty God needs to depend on no one for strength and energy. In fact he is the source of power, self-sufficient. "The opening affirmation, "I believe in God the Father almighty" (in the original Greek the word translated "almighty" means "all governing" or "all controlling," as one who governs all the universe)."[331] Therefore, other mighty ones get their power, energy, and authority from Almighty God.

To illustrate: a large corporation may have many managers to oversee a smooth operation. However, there is one all-powerful, all-controlling manager, the CEO, who gives these others their authority. Hence, it is the same with Almighty God. With this definition it would be impossible for an Almighty God to have a God above him. Otherwise, the title and term Almighty is pointless. The real question that needs to be answered then is: if Jesus Christ is Almighty God, does he have a God above him?

I have projected the above question to many and the answer is the same no matter what faith you profess to be while believing in the trinity. The response is a definite 'no'. If Jesus Christ truly occupies the position of Almighty God, then I most certainly have to agree with the answer 'no', based on the Biblical definition. Unfortunately, when serious students read their Bibles and search for accurate knowledge, they come across some seemingly very difficult questions to answer.

---

329 See part I of this book
330 Vol. IX, 1976, p. 162
331 *A History of Christianity*, Latourette, 1953, p. 135

For example, at John 20:17, Jesus proclaims: "Don't hold on to me! I have not yet gone to the Father. But tell my disciples that I am going to the one who is my Father and my God, as well as your Father and your God."[332] The obvious question is how is it possible for Jesus to have a Father and God, if he is the Almighty God? This question deserves our attention and must be answered.

Another scripture to inquire about is located at Matthew 27:46. Jesus is experiencing the most shameful and torture like death at the hands of his enemies and has been hanging upon a stake[333] for several agonizing hours. Very close to his last breath of life he cries out: "My God, My God, why have you abandoned me?"[334] Please consider this: if Jesus is Almighty God who is self sufficient, as well as all-powerful, why is he crying out to another God? To whom could the Almighty pray? To himself? That would be meaningless. Why? God is the hearer of prayers. Psalm 65:2 plainly sates: "O thou that hearest prayer."[335] It is well attested to in the scriptures that Jesus Christ prayed often to his Father in the heavens. Thus, can an Almighty God really feel abandoned and left alone?

A Biblical thought that has to be explained, is the death of Jesus Christ. Is it possible for Almighty God to die? A correct response is 'of course not!' This is in harmony with God's word at Habakkuk 1:12. It reads: "Surely you, Yahweh, are from ancient times, my holy God, who never dies!"[336] Regarding this verse in Habakkuk scholar C.D. Ginsburg says the following: "All the ancient records emphatically states that this exhibits the corrected text by the Sopherim and that the original reading was: "Art thou not from everlasting? O Lord my God, mine Holy One, thou diest not.""[337] This is also in harmony with the rest of God's word. For we read at Psalm 90:2, "Even from everlasting to everlasting, You are God."[338] It is plain to see from scripture Jehovah has no beginning and no end. For he declares of himself at Revelation 1:8 "I am the Alpha [beginning] and the Omega [ending], says Jehovah God, the One who is and who was and who is coming, the Almighty."[339]

Yet, as Christians, we know the Messiah, Jesus, died in the fullest sense. "The Messiah died for our sins, exactly as Scripture tells it," "Jesus Christ—Loyal

---

332 *CEV*
333 See cross
334 *GWN*
335 *JD*
336 *NJB*; cf. *EB; NRSV; AT*
337 *Introduction to the Massoretico-Critical Edition of the Hebrew Bible*, 1897, p. 358
338 *NASB*
339 *NWT*; brackets mine

Witness, Firstborn from the dead."[340] If Christ "is still dead, then all our preaching is useless and your trust in God is empty, worthless, hopeless; in that case all Christians who have died are lost! And if being a Christian is of value to us only now in this life, we are the most miserable of creatures."[341] Therefore, Jesus cannot be the Almighty Jehovah who cannot die!

In the book *Jehovah's Witnesses a Challenge* writes: "Another stumbling block in the complete spectrum of the clergy's theologies, which are obviously personal, proves to be "God's mortality; with Jesus Christ God had actually died. On Good Friday God died completely for three days", Pastor Dr. M. Schlicht, Bardowick, explains, without clarifying who resurrected the completely dead God again. This is simply unbelievable."[342]

These are very thought provoking questions being theological and Bible based thoughts you may not have considered. However, seeking accurate knowledge as well as worshipping God in truth demands that we carefully mull over them.

The normal response from Trinitarians after reading these scriptures is 'Jesus Christ is the God-man. These two instances are when he was a man on the earth.' First of all, I may have missed it, but where in all scripture is this prefaced? Nowhere! Presbyterian Pastor and New Testament Professor, Mark D. Roberts honestly admits: "We would be wrong, however, to envision the earliest Christians as somehow thinking in the complex terms of later theology. They did not talk of God as Trinity or refer to Jesus as fully God and fully human."[343] Another scholar likewise remarks: "The doctrine of the double nature of Christ, like that of the Trinity, is a doctrine of inference. Neither doctrine is declared in any verse, nor can they be expressed in the language of Scripture. Scattered verses are assembled in quasi-syllogistic form, inferences are drawn from newly-created contexts, and it is assumed that the Messiah is both a mortal man and the almighty God … I know of no allusion in the Bible to the doctrine of the Two Natures, either with or without modification."[344]

Second, are there other examples of this anywhere in scripture? Nowhere! For the moment, lets indulge this 'theological theory.' After Jesus was resurrected all Trinitarians that I have met agree amongst themselves, that he ascended into the heavens as fully God. If this were the case, then now for a certainty it would be impossible for the Almighty God to have a God. Trinitarians all agree to this. I

---

340 1 Corinthians 15:3; Revelation 1:5; *TM* respectively
341 1 Corinthians 15:14, 18–19; *TLB*
342 Helmut-Dieter Hartmann, 2001, p. 77
343 *Jesus Revealed*, 2002, p. 133
344 *The Doctrine of the Double Nature of Christ*, Snedeker, 1998, pp. 6–7

will concur with Trinitarians when they say God's word does not contradict itself. Therefore, what does the Bible really teach?

Jesus Christ is not Almighty God

We will begin our research in the book of Revelation. This inspired book of God was written on the island of Patmos in 96CE by the beloved disciple of Jesus Christ, the apostle John. Since Jesus was resurrected to the heavens in 33CE, according to Trinitarian theology, Jesus has been Almighty God for Sixty-Three years since his resurrection. Remember, the definition of Almighty God means all-powerful, dependant on no one. Hence it would be impossible for the Almighty God to have a God. Is this what we find in the book of Revelation?

Please, notice Revelation 1:6. It reads: "He [Jesus] made us to be a kingdom, to be priest unto his God and Father."[345] This poses a serious problem for Trinitarians. If Jesus Christ has a God and Father while in the heavens, it is impossible for him to be the Almighty God. This is the third and final weak link to the trinity chain. I have not met one Trinitarian who can explain this scripture based on the Trinitarian doctrine and most importantly, on the Bible. They move quite quickly to another subject. Why? As I believe this book has revealed and made quite convincingly understandable, the trinity doctrine is not based on the inspired word of God.

Now, remember Jesus' words "My God! My God?"[346] Revelation chapter three sets matters straight regarding the Trinitarian assumption that Jesus was a God-man. In the Bible book of Revelation chapter three, Jesus says: "before my God," "temple of my God, name of my God, city of my God, from my God."[347]

Five times while in the heavens Jesus calls Jehovah his God! How many more times would it take before Trinitarians start believing what Jesus Christ says and stop believing the man made uninspired fallible traditional doctrine of the trinity? "Make sure you don't allow anyone to rob and plunder you of your pure faith and hope thru the ideas and conclusions of their hollow and deceptive reasonings. Their arguments may sound ever so reasonable, but they are based on man's feeble and worldly-wise conclusions, not on the teachings of truth that Christ brought us from God."[348]

---

345 *RVNT*
346 Matthew 27:46
347 Verse 2, 12
348 Colossians 2:8; *LDB*

What is the truth concerning Jesus Christ which has been revealed to us through Scripture? Out of his own mouth proceeds this fact; he has a God and Father. He cannot be the Almighty God, Jehovah.[349] Jehovah is called Almighty throughout his word. The book of Job alone mentions Jehovah as the Almighty Thirty-One times. Lets take a close look at the scriptures that call Jesus Almighty. Wait a minute, that's right, there are none. The same can be said of the holy spirit. Almighty God is the Father, Jehovah; the living God of everyone, including Jesus Christ. This is our third weak link to this trinity chain. A chain is only as strong as its weakest link.

More scriptural proof Jesus has a God

Another scripture that is often ignored by Trinitarians is found at Hebrews 1:9. It reads concerning Jesus Christ: "Therefore God, even your God, has anointed you."[350] The apostle Paul in Rome between 60-61CE wrote Colossians. You will be quick to notice this is over Twenty-Seven years after Jesus' resurrection in the heavens. There is no doubt to Jesus' God and Father being Jehovah.

A side point to this scripture also reveals that God anointed Jesus. Who is greater in authority; the one who anoints or the one being anointed? The one who is sent or the one sending forth?[351] Murry writes regarding this issue: "One sent is as he who sent him ... The messenger [the Shaliach] is thereby granted authority and dignity by virtue of his bearing the status of the one who sent him. This is the more remarkable when it is born in mind that in earlier times the messenger was commonly a slave."[352]

Professor Marriane Thompson agrees and states: "Rather than predicating the virtual equality of the one who is sent with the one who sends, John tends to stress that the one who sends is greater than the one who is sent."[353] Of course, Jesus makes this point plentifully obvious saying: "I can do nothing on my own authority; as I hear, I judge; and my judgment is just, because I seek not my own will but the will of him who sent me."[354]

In addition, can Almighty God be given anything he doesn't already possess? For example, pay close attention to what Matthew 28:18 says, "All authority hath

---

349 Cf. Genesis 17:1; 35:11
350 *NSB*
351 Cf. John 13:16
352 *Gospel of Life: Theology in the Fourth Gospel*, p. 18
353 *The God of the Gospel of John*, 2001, p. 94
354 John 5:30; *RSV*

been given unto me in heaven and on earth." Who gave Jesus his authority? John 5:26, 27 states: "For just as the Father has life in himself, so he gave also to the Son to have life in himself. And he [the Father, Jehovah] gave him [Jesus] authority to do judging, because Son of man he is."[355] Who gave authority to do judging and to have life within himself to Jesus Christ? Jehovah says he himself gave authority to Jesus. Do we believe him?

Also, what are we to say when scriptures reveal that Jehovah will reward resurrected anointed Christians with this gift of self-existence? For 1 John 3:2 says: "we are now children of God ... But we know that when it [or, He] shall be revealed, we will be like Him, because we will see Him just as He is!"[356] Will this make them equal to God, since they will forever possess a state of deathlessness? 1 Corinthians 15:51, 52 affirms: "We indeed will not all sleep [fig., die] ... and the dead will be raised incorruptible [or, imperishable]."[357] Simply because one has been given life within himself does not make this one the only true God.

Philippians 2:9 is a very telling scripture about Jesus. It reads: "This is why God has highly exalted Him [Jesus], and given Him [Jesus] the name that is above every other name."[358] If Jesus Christ is almighty God, can he be exalted to a superior position than what he already owns? Can God be given a name that he doesn't already possess? This is of course to go beyond all logical and scriptural sense. However, Jesus as God's Son can be exalted by his God Jehovah, as well as be given a name above every other name by his God Jehovah.

Again, Revelation 1:1 shows that Jesus needs to be given insight from a higher source, his God and Father. It reads: "The unveiling [Apocalypse] of Jesus Christ which God gave him."[359] This occurs after Jesus has been raised from the dead and has been seated at the right hand of God for Sixty-Three years. Both in heaven and on earth, the true God Jehovah, his Father, gives Jesus his authority, exalted position, and life. John 13:3 reads: "Jesus knew that the Father had given everything into His hands, that He had come from God, and that He was going back to God."[360]

There are many other scriptures proving the subordinate role of Jesus, but I will share one more that completes this. John 12:49 reads: "For I spake not of myself; but the Father having sent me, he gave me a command, what I should say,

---

355 *KJ*; brackets mine
356 *ALT*
357 *ALT*
358 *TNTBW*; brackets mine
359 *MNT*
360 *HCSB*

and what I should speak."[361] Here, the Father sends Jesus and gives him a command as what to say and speak. Could anyone dare give a command to the living Almighty God as what to say and speak? No, but Jesus can be told what to say and speak simply because he is God's Son, a subordinate position, not Almighty God himself.

Edgar Foster agrees and states: "The Bible makes it clear that Jesus is not God, but subordinate to God and inferior to Him. In the book of Revelation, Jesus repeatedly calls the Father "my God" (Rev. 3:12). How could God possibly have a God? Surely, John 14:28 unambiguously substantiates Jesus' lesser position in relation to the Father (Cf. John 20:17)."[362]

Clearly, Jesus is not the living true God, but has a God, Jehovah, who gives him everything and is the source and origin of all life, including his Son. Howard Mazzaferro inquires: "Where does it say Jehovah would never give another or let another have authority to demonstrate these abilities, especially his only Son? The Bible says that Jehovah is the only savior, but he let Israelite men be saviors.[363] The Bible says that Jehovah is the only God, but he let Moses be a God to Aaron.[364] Jehovah is King of eternity, but he let David [and Solomon] be a King on his throne.[365] Therefore, Jesus is not God, King, Savior, or Lord because of his nature; it is because Jehovah, for the purpose of his eternal plan has given all this to his only Son."[366]

There is an all-important Bible verse, which really illuminates the subordinate role of Jesus towards his God and Father, Jehovah. It reads regarding Jesus Christ: "Then will come the end—when he surrenders the Kingdom to his God and Father … for he must reign until God 'has put all his enemies under his feet.' … (But, when it is said that all things have been placed under Christ, it is plain that God is excepted who placed everything under him.) … the Son will place himself under God who placed everything under him, that God may be al in all."[367] We notice Jesus surrenders the Kingdom to "His God and Father." The apostle Paul, under inspiration from God, makes it so simple for us to understand. Jesus has a God and Father, Jehovah. This is the God whom Jesus surrenders, or rather hands over the Kingdom to. But this isn't all. In verse Twenty-Eight Jesus 'places himself

---

361 *HBJS*
362 *Christology and the Trinity An Exploration*, 1997, p. 24
363 Cf. Judges 3:9, 15
364 Cf. Exodus 4:16; 7:1
365 Cf. 1 Chronicles 29:23
366 *The Lord and the Tetragrammaton*, p. 43; brackets mine
367 1 Corinthians 15:24–28; *TCNT*

under God.' If God represents 'three persons' of God—according to Trinitarian theology—how is it that Jesus, the 'second person' of God, subjects himself to God? Does he subject himself to himself? Not only is this theological theory unfathomable, more importantly, this is not what the Bible says in these verses.

William Barclay, a British Bible scholar comments on these verses saying: "Paul clearly and deliberately subordinates the Son to the Father. What he is thinking of is this. We can use only human terms and analogies. God gave to Jesus a task to do, to defeat sin and death and to liberate man. The day will come when the task will be fully and finally accomplished, and then, to put it in pictorial terms, the Son will return to the Father like a victor coming home and the triumph of God will be complete ... It is a case of one who, having accomplished the work that was given him to do, returns with the glory of complete obedience as his crown. As God sent forth his Son to redeem the world, so in the end he will receive back a world redeemed."[368]

Another well-known Bible scholar, Arthur W. Wainwright agrees and observes: "When all the enemies of God have been overthrown, the Lord Christ will hand over his kingdom to the Father. Here Paul seems to be teaching a subordinationism which is not limited to the earthly life of Christ but which is ultimate and absolute. The final status of the Son is one of subjection to God. And in this passage God is not Father, Son, and Holy Spirit, but Father only."[369]

Simply stated then is, Jesus Christ is subordinate to his Almighty God and Father Jehovah, whether here on the earth, or in his role as king in the heavens.

We shouldn't forget the prophecies that are relating to Jesus. "For whatsoever things were written aforetime were written for our learning."[370] Jesus himself says: "all the things written in the law of Moses and Prophets and in the Psalms about me must be fulfilled."[371] Jesus acknowledges the following as referring to himself, the Messiah.

Lets begin with Isaiah 11:1–2 and be instructed by Jehovah. It states: "And there shall come forth a shoot out of the stock of Jesse ... and the spirit of Jehovah shall rest upon him [Jesus] ... and of the fear of Jehovah."[372] We are able to gather an important point from this prophecy of Jesus Christ.[373] Is it possible for

---

368 *The Letters to the Corinthians, Revised Ed., The Daily Bible Series*, 1975, pp. 151–152
369 *The Trinity in the New Testament*, 1962, p. 187
370 Romans 15:4
371 Luke 24:44; *LD*
372 Brackets mine
373 Cf. Romans 15:12; Revelation 5:5; 22:16

the Almighty God to have fear of himself? This would be illogical and ridiculous. Yet, Jesus is said to have the 'fear of Jehovah.' Only someone in an inferior position is able to comprise fear of another. This is what we find in Jesus' own words at John 14:28 "The Father is greater than I."

Another significant scripture is to be found at Micah 5:4. This prophecy with reference to Jesus Christ says he (Jesus) "shall stand, and shall feed his flock in the strength of Jehovah, in the majesty of the name of Jehovah his God." Ask yourself: Whose strength or power is Jesus shepherding with? 'The Strength of Jehovah!' If Jesus were Almighty God he would rely on the strength and power of no one. Yet, Jesus is said to require Jehovah's Strength. Why? Jehovah is Almighty God and the source of all power, not his Son, Jesus Christ.[374] "The Omnipotent Jehovah cannot be thus dependant on another. "I live by the Father," Joh 6:57. "My Father is greater than I", Joh 14:28. The connection proves that this refers to his highest nature. His prayer, Joh 17:5, for the glory of his divine nature which he had with the Father "before the world was" proves the dependence of his nature."[375]

Then we have Jesus being responsible for shepherding in "the name of Jehovah his God." Is it possible to make the relationship between Jesus and Jehovah any more obvious? There can be no doubt; Jehovah is Jesus' God and Father. "Then shall the Son also himself be subject unto him that put all things under him, that God (not the Trinity, but "THE FATHER," as verse 24 proves) may be ALL in ALL." Is not this divine testimony fatal to trinitarianism? Our blessed Lord as God, has a GOD. Heb 1:8,9. The Father has no god above him."[376]

Conclusively therefore, we find in scripture that Jesus has a Father and a God who is his spiritual head. "But I am anxious that you should understand that … God is the Head of Christ."[377]

How is it then Jesus is a God?

Some of you may be wondering by now: why does the Bible call Jesus Christ God or a god in some scriptures? Scholar Marianne Thompson precisely observes: "confusion regarding 'meaning of god' and 'concepts about God' can be illustrated by the question of identity most frequently asked about Jesus: Does the NT call Jesus God? Once an affirmative answer is received, the inquirer then

---

374 Cf. Isaiah 40:26; Psalm 36:9; Jeremiah 32:17
375 *An Appeal to Pious Trinitarians*, Grew, 1857, *The Harvest Herald*
376 Henry Grew
377 1 Corinthians 11:3; *TCNT*

assumes that we understand who Jesus is: Jesus is God. However, the crucial question here is, What does the NT mean when it calls Jesus God?"[378]

We have just clarified from the Bible that only Jehovah, the Father, is the only true Almighty God. Therefore, some have said to me, 'Jesus must be a false god.' Why? Isaiah 43:10 asserts: "I [Jehovah] alone am God. There is no other God; there never was and never will be."[379] Although this verse will be discussed in detail later, Brian Holt makes an important point: "Jehovah was talking about how there were no man-made gods that could rival Him or equal His power. The Israelites often looked to other gods for help and Jehovah was letting them know there were not other gods that could help them. They were figments of their imagination, manifested in man-made idols."[380]

This argument by Trinitarians—that Jesus would be a false god since there is no god except Jehovah—may seem reasonable at first hearing of it. But as always, further study and reliance on God's word proves otherwise. This type of man-made reasoning is considered equivocation; language used with the intent to deceive. In other words, Trinitarians argue that since we know there is only one true Almighty God, and God says there was no god formed before or after him—Isaiah 43:10—then according to John 1:1—"The word was God"—Jesus has to be the Almighty God. Otherwise he is a false god. This is equivocating because again, man is trying to define who can be called god through his own wisdom.

Trinitarians, and many others have an austere belief that any other god in addition to the Almighty has to be a false god. God himself declares he, "made foolish the wisdom of the world."[381] Trinitarians ignore God's wisdom and point of view relating to agency of god, one acting as a representative given that position by Almighty Jehovah himself. Even John Calvin admits: "I said you are gods. Scripture gives the name of gods to those on whom God has conferred an honourable office. He whom God has separated, to be distinguished above all others [His Son] is far more worthy of this honourable title ... Christ applies this [Psalm 82:6; John 10:34] to the case at hand, that they receive the name of gods, because they are God's ministers for governing the world ... In short, let us know that magistrates are called gods, because God has given them authority."[382]

Ask yourself: if Jehovah designated an individual(s) as god, would that one be considered a false god? Of course not. To suggest otherwise would be to label

---

378 *The God of the Gospel of John*, p. 19
379 *TLB*, brackets mine
380 *Jesus—God or Son of God?* P. 53
381 1 Corinthians 1:20; *WFB*
382 *Commenting on the Gospel According to John*, pp. 419–420

Jehovah a liar. Jehovah in his wisdom has provided Bible examples of those that were made gods to represent him as his agents. "The main point of the Jewish law of agency is expressed in the dictum, a persons agent is regarded as the person himself. Therefore any act committed by a duly appointed agent is regarded as having been committed by the principle."[383]

Even Murray J. Harris, an Evangelical states regarding other gods in the Bible besides the Almighty: "Human rulers or judges, regarded as divine representatives or as bearers of divine authority and majesty (Exod. 21:6; 22:8 [cf. 1 Sam. 2:25]; Judges 5:8; Psalm 82:1, 6) b. Spiritual or heavenly beings, including God (Gen. 1:27) and angels (Psalm 8:6 [Engl. V.5]) c. Angels (Ps. 97:7; 138:1) d. Heathen gods with their images (Exod. 20:23; Jer. 16:20) ... both el, [meaning 'god'] and Elohim [meaning 'gods'], have extended or 'irregular' applications to angels or to persons who represent on earth divine power, judgment, or majesty."[384]

Jesus Christ is without question the greatest example. Not only is Jesus called the "Chief Agent,"[385] but he himself says in a prayer concerning his disciples: "They have ... certainly come to know that I came out as your representative, and they have believed that you [the Father Jehovah], have sent me."[386] A Catholic Jesuit remarks: "The Servant of Yahweh is a light to the nations, an agent of salvation (Is 42:6; 49:6)."[387] "What then can we make of all this? That the Jews used the term 'god' to refer to anyone with real or imagined power. The word elohim literally means 'mighty ones'. While there is only one true Almighty God, there are many mighty ones having power. Certainly the Logos, the second most powerful one in the Universe could be so described."[388]

I believe Henry Grew explains this Biblical point well. "The Father the PRINCIPLE, the Son the AGENT. Now behold the harmony of divine truth. "God created all things BY Jesus Christ." Eph 3:9. "By whom he also made the worlds." Heb 1:2. All his works of love and power, were what "God did BY him." Ac 2:22. "God our Saviour" SAVES US BY, or "through, Jesus Christ our Saviour." Tit 3:4-6. He "shall raise us up also (from the grave) BY Jesus." 2Co 4:14. "God will judge the world in righteousness BY" him. Ac 17:31. All this the Saviour confirms in his own declaration, "I came down from heaven not to do my own will, but the will of him that sent me." Joh 6:38. The humanity did

---

383 *The Encyclopedia of the Jewish Religion*, Werblowski, Wigoder
384 *Jesus as God, the New Testament Use of Theos in Reference to Jesus*, pp. 24, 26
385 Acts 5:31; *NWT*
386 John 17:8 *NWT*; cf. John 7:29; 16:27; Acts 3:15; Hebrews 2:10; brackets mine
387 *The Dictionary of the Bible*, McKenzie
388 *Gems from the New Testament*, Capel, 1998, p. 55

not come down from heaven. The divine and "only begotten Son of God" came down, and took the body "prepared" for him. Heb 10:5. Does not this prove the inferiority of his highest nature to the supreme God? Does not the supreme God seek to do the will of another rather than his own?"[389]

Psalm 8:5 says: "For thou hast made him [man] but a little lower than God."[390] The Hebrew word here for angels—godlike ones—is Elohim, literally meaning 'gods'. Perhaps this verse sounds familiar to you? Please compare Psalm 8:5 with Hebrews 2:6 and 7. The Apostle Paul quotes from this Psalm and declares: "Son of man ... Thou madest him a little lower than the angels." Yes, the apostle Paul equates angels to godlike ones and the Son of man (Jesus Christ) was made lower than these. Is it possible for the Almighty God to be made lower than his own creation, the angels? This would be illogical.

"The angels are occasionally called "gods," but this is not their usual designation. This designation is not used in a religious sense, as is the case with the pantheons of gods found in the Babylonian, Greco-Roman and other ancient (and modern) religious systems. The angels are "gods" in a purely generic sense—they are simply sons of YHWH, and the designation "gods" had no higher religious value to worshippers of YHWH than the designation "angels" (though the two descriptions highlight different attributes and functions). Also, the "belief" of Paul and others in many gods did not amount to "belief" in a religious sense; rather, it was a "belief" in the sense of "acknowledgement." Only when more than one god is worshipped in a religious sense can we speak of polytheism, and only when one supreme god is worshiped and the worshiper believes in the existence of other gods in a religious sense can we speak of henotheism."[391]

The examples of angels being called godlike or gods (mighty ones), is probably easy for us to swallow. We already recognize angels to be more powerful than humankind. How about man being given authority as god? Is this possible?

Remember, Jesus Christ said at John 10:34, 35 "In your own law it says men are gods. So if the scriptures, which cannot be untrue." What scripture was Jesus referring to? Psalm 82:6 which reads: "I myself have said, 'You are gods.'" These 'gods' were men appointed as human judges by Jehovah. "Jesus' argument is that this Psalm proves that the word 'god' can be legitimately used to refer to others than God Himself. His reasoning is that if there are others whom God can address as 'god' or 'sons of the Most High,' why then should the Jews object to

---

389 *An Appeal to Pious Trinitarians*, Grew
390 Fn. reads: the angels Heb. Elohim
391 *The Role of Theology and Bias in Bible Translation*, Furuli, p. 207

Jesus' statement that He is 'the Son of God' (v.36)?"[392] Yes, these particular judges were acting contrary to God's laws, being wicked and showing injustices.[393] Nonetheless, they were still appointed by Jehovah to act as his representatives, agents or gods on earth.

There is another extraordinary example in the Bible of a human appointed as god to others. Exodus 7:1 reads: "THEN the Lord spoke to Moses saying, Behold I have made thee a god to Pharoah, and Aaron thy brother shall be thy prophet."[394] Also, Exodus 4:16 declares: "He will speak to the people for you. He will be your spokesman, and you [Moses] will serve as God to him."[395] One source admits: "The closest analogy to the use of the word (or title) 'god' for Jesus, however, is the use of such a term for Moses. Already Ex. 7.1 says that God makes Moses god to Pharoah; and even before that Ex. 4:16 makes nearly the same claim (*le lohim*, 'as god') of Moses in his relation to Aaron … One may suspect, on the basis of this evidence, that there was some connection between the equation of Jesus with God in the Fourth Gospel and the comparison of Jesus to Moses."[396]

Since Moses has been appointed 'as God' by Jehovah, would this make him a false God? No! To suggest otherwise would be to label Jehovah a liar. If mere imperfect men can and are appointed to represent Jehovah as gods, how much more so is it appropriate to identify Jesus Christ, the Son of God, as a god being the perfect, exact representative?[397] For this is what we discover prophesied about him: "For unto us a child is born, unto us a son is given; and the government shall be upon his shoulder: and his name shall be called … Mighty God."[398]

The bottom line is this. In the pages of Gods word, even though Jehovah designates and appoints others as gods—including his Son Jesus—it makes ever so very clear and simple who the only true Almighty God is. For the Bible declares of Jehovah: "For Yahweh is a great God, a king greater than all the gods,"[399] "Give ye thanks to Yahweh … Give ye thanks to the God of gods,"[400] "Worship him

---

392 *MacArthur Study Bible*, p. 1605
393 Cf. verse two
394 *LXX*
395 *HCSB*; brackets mine
396 *Schismatics, Sectarians, Dissidents, Deviants: The First On Hundred years of Jewish-Christian Relations, Sanders*, 1993, pp. 93–94
397 Cf. John 7:29; Hebrews 1:3
398 Isaiah 9:6
399 Psalm 95:3; *NJB*
400 Psalm 136:1, 2; *EB*

all ye gods ... For thou, Jehovah, art the Most High above all the earth; thou art exalted above all gods."[401] Finally, may we shout as God's children: "Jehovah is the [true] God! Jehovah is the [true] God!"[402]

---

[401] Psalm 97:9; *JD*
[402] 1 Kings 18:39; *NWT*

Part IV

The conclusion of the matter

Which anchor is your 'chain' attached to?

In the middle of the ocean, a thunderous storm is raging. The high seas are surrounding and wanting to envelope a desperate ship. The Captain gives the order to lower its anchor to help keep his ship balanced and pointed in the right direction. Bursts of wind, rain, and mountainous like waves lash out at the helpless ship. The captain, his crew, and all the passengers' lives depend on the chain, on every link connected to that anchor. All night, through the storm, the chain holds it fast. The next morning, each link was found to be as strong as the next, making the chain unbreakable—for a chain is only as strong as its weakest link.

My question to you dear reader is: What anchor is your 'spiritual chain' with its many links attached to? Is it God's word the Bible, or the "teaching of human wisdom?"[403] Does your 'spiritual chain' contain links of truth, or weak links, which, contain "endless arguments that never amount to anything," and "ideas through the empty traditions of human beings and the empty superstitions of spirit beings?"[404] These are questions no imperfect human—no matter how seemingly intelligent—can answer for us. Only God's perfect inspired Word is able to reveal the answer. Please keep in mind, our lives, everlasting life, depend on the answer we choose.

The Apostle Peter warned Christians at 2 Peter 2:1–3, "But there were men who preached lies among the people, just as there will also be among you those who teach lies. They will secretly bring in their own destructive teachings … And many will follow their immoral ways and *cause* people to *slander* the way of truth."[405]

The Apostle Paul as well warned Christians: "In later times certain ones shall fall[406] away from the faith, paying attention to deceitful spirits and doctrines of demons … but profane and old wives' myths refuse … not paying attention to Jewish myths and commandments of men who turn away from the truth. They profess to know God but by their works they deny (Him), being contemptible

---

403 1 Corinthians 2:13 *RL*; cf. 2 Timothy 3:16
404 Colossians 2:8 *TM*; cf. John 17:17
405 *WFB*; emphasis his
406 Lit. "apostatize"; *LCNTV*

and disobedient."[407] These false prophets would throw "over the truth of God for lies."[408]

In contrast, God's word also declares in the last days: "Many shall run to and fro, and [true] knowledge shall be increased ... for the earth shall be full of the knowledge of Jehovah, as the waters cover the sea ... for the earth shall be filled with the knowledge of the glory of Jehovah, as the waters cover the sea."[409]

It is our responsibility to discern which category the trinity chain belongs. Is it part of the true links of knowledge that would be abundant on the earth in the last days? Or, is it links of inspired expressions from demons? One source relates: "To those outside the Christian faith, the doctrine of the Trinity seems a very strange teaching indeed. It seems to violate logic, for it claims that God is three and yet he is one. How can this be? And why would the church propound such a doctrine? It does not appear to be taught in Scripture, which is the Christian's supreme authority in matters of faith and practice. And it presents an obstacle to faith for those who otherwise might be inclined to accept the Christian faith. Is it a teaching that perhaps was a mistake in the first place, and certainly is a hindrance and an embarrassment to Christianity? ... This teaching does not seem to be stated in the Bible. Is it taught there? If not, perhaps the church was mistaken in formulating such a strange teaching. We must look closely at the biblical testimony to determine whether this doctrine is indeed found there ... There is no virtue in continuing to hold such a difficult doctrine of the Trinity if it is not actually taught in the Bible."[410] Let's review.

Review of weak link one

In Part I we learned the word trinity and 'persons of God' are not found in God's word the Bible. Rather, this trinity chain was developed slowly, link by link, progressively for centuries after Jesus Christ and his apostles. Christendom readily admits this: "There is the recognition on the part of exegetes and Biblical theologians, including a constant growing number of Roman Catholics, that one should not speak of Trinitarianism in the New Testament without serious qualification ... when one does speak of an unqualified Trinitarianism, one has moved from the period of Christian origins to, say, the last quadrant of the 4th century. It was only then that what might be called the definitive Trinitarian dogma 'one God

---

407 1 Timothy 4:1, 7; Titus 1:14, 16; *LCNTV*
408 Romans 1:25; *TUNT*
409 Daniel 12:4; Isaiah 11:9; Habakkuk 2:14
410 *Making Sense of the Trinity*, Erickson, 2000, pp. 13, 18

in three persons' became thoroughly assimilated into Christian life and thought ... it was the product of 3 centuries of doctrinal development ... The formulation 'one God in three persons' was not solidly established, certainly not fully assimilated into Christian life and it's profession of faith, prior to the end of the 4th century. But it is precisely this formulation that has first claim to the title the Trinitarian dogma. Among the Apostolic Fathers, there had been nothing even remotely approaching such a mentality or perspective."[411]

Roman Catholic writer Thomas Hart says the following: "The Chalcedonian formula [the council's decision declaring Jesus both God and man] makes genuine humanity impossible. The councilor definition says that Jesus is true man. But if there are two natures in him, it is clear which will dominate. And Jesus becomes immediately very different from us. He is omniscient, omnipotent, omnipresent. He knows the past, present and future ... He knows exactly what everyone is thinking and going to do. This is far from ordinary human experience. Jesus is tempted but cannot sin because he is God. What kind of temptation is this? It has little in common with the kinds of struggles we are familiar with."[412]

One Eastern Theologian, John of Damascus[413] had this to say regarding the trinity chain: "you will not find in scripture the Trinity, of homousian or the two natures of Christ either. But we know those doctrines are true. And so, having acknowledged that icons, the Trinity and the incarnation are innovations."[414]

One more source boldly remarks: "We maintain that the doctrine of the Trinity was of gradual and comparatively late formation; that it had its origin in a source entirely foreign from that of the Jewish and Christian Scriptures; that it grew up, and was ingrafted on Christianity, through the hands of the Platonizing Fathers; that in the time of Justin, and long after, the distinct nature and inferiority of the Son were universally taught; and that only the first shadowy outline of the Trinity had then become visible ... The modern popular doctrine of the Trinity ... derives no support from the language of Justin [Martyr]: and this observation may be extended to all the ante-Nicene Fathers; that is, to all Christian writers for three centuries after the birth of Christ. It is true, they speak of the Father, Son, and prophetic or holy Spirit, but not as co-equal, not as one numerical essence, not as Three in One, in any sense now admitted by Trinitarians. The very reverse is the fact. The doctrine of the Trinity, as explained by these Fathers, was essentially different from the modern doctrine. This we state as a fact as suscep-

---

411 *The New Catholic Encyclopedia*, 1967, Vol. XIV, pp. 295, 299
412 *To Know and Follow Jesus*, 1984, p. 46
413 C. 675–749
414 *The Christ of Christendom*, Cupitt, from *The Myth of God Incarnate*, p. 133

tible of proof as any fact in the history of human opinions ... We challenge anyone to produce a single writer of any note, during the first three ages, who held this [Trinity] doctrine in the modern sense."[415] These findings were then verified through the ever-changing traditional creeds.

We shall not forget also, the one who presided over the Trinitarian hearings. Constantine, a worshipper of the Sun-God Sol Invictus, "Recognized in Jesus Christ a continuation of pagan tradition."[416] As Christians are we to put aside, hide, and forget the atrocities committed by Constantine after he extended favor upon Christendom and was considered a Christian? For "He had a father-in-law, whom he impelled to hang himself; he had a brother-in-law, whom he ordered to be strangled; he had a nephew twelve or thirteen years old, whose throat he ordered to be cut; he had an eldest son, whom he beheaded; he had a wife, whom he ordered to be suffocated in a bath."[417]

"These atrocious crimes were perpetrated after Constantine became a Christian, or at least after he extended his patronage to the Church. Before he embraced or patronized Christianity, his character was less sullied, and he appeared incapable of such enormities."[418] "He [Constantine] gradually advanced in the knowledge of truth, he proportionally declined in the practice of virtue; and the same year of his reign in which he convened the Council of Nice was polluted by the execution, or rather murder, of his eldest son."[419]

Notice these words by Catholic Cardinal John Henry Newman: "Let us allow that the whole circle of doctrines, of which our Lord is the subject, was consistently and uniformly confessed by the Primitive Church ... But it surely is otherwise with the Catholic doctrine of the Trinity. I do not see in what sense it can be said that there is a consensus of primitive [Church authorities] in its favour ... the doctrine of our Lord's divinity itself partly implies and partly recommends the doctrine of the Trinity ... the Creeds of that early day make no mention in their letter of the Catholic doctrine [of the Trinity] at all. They [the early Christian writings] make mention indeed of Three; but that there is any mystery in the doctrine, that the Three are One, that They are coequal, coeternal, all increate [uncreated], all omnipotent, all incomprehensible, is not stated, and never could

---

415 *The Church of the First Three Centuries*, Lamson, 1869, pp. 52, 75–76, 341
416 *Jesus and Yahweh The Names Divine*, Bloom, p. 98
417 *Philosophical Dictionary*, Voltaire, Under Constantine
418 *Crimes of Christianity: Christ to Constantine*, Foote, Wheeler, 1887, Vol. I
419 Gibbon, chapter XX, brackets mine

be gathered from them. Of course we believe that they imply it, or rather intend it."[420]

Even after this admittance by Cardinal Newman, the Catholic Church still places Constantine on high; and so did fourth century Christendom. When "Constantine died … his body was laid in state for several days, and finally interred with gorgeous rites. According to Jortin, he had the honor of being the first Christian who was buried in a church. The true believers paid almost divine honor to his name, his tomb, and his statue, and called him a saint equal to the apostles. And as the clergy had bestowed upon him, during his life, the most fulsome praise even when he was committing the most flagitious crimes, so now, after his death, they had the effrontery to declare that God had endued his urn and statue with miraculous powers, and that whosoever touched them were healed of all diseases and infirmities."[421] A 'saint equal to the apostles?' I think not!

Could we as Christians, ever imagine Jesus Christ choosing a pagan world ruler not only to represent him, but worse yet, to decide who Jesus was and his relationship to God? Remember Jesus' words? "My Kingdom is not of this world … they [Jesus' followers] are not of the world even as I am not of the world."[422] Why did our King, Jesus, say these things? Simply because "the rest of the world around us is under Satan's power and control," and "Don't you realize that making friends with God's enemies, makes you an enemy of God?"[423]

For true worshipers of God, the Bible says in the last days we would be able to distinguish the righteous ones from the wicked. Malachi 3:18 declares: "You will come back to seeing the difference between a right-doer and a wrong-doer, between a worshiper and a non-worshiper of Jehovah."[424] Jesus Christ's words ring so very clear referring to false religious teachers at Matthew 7:16–20 "You can detect them by the way they act, just as you can identify a tree by its fruit. You need never to confuse grapevines with thorn bushes or figs with thistle's. Different kinds of fruit trees can quickly be identified by examining their fruit. A variety that produces delicious fruit never produces an inedible kind. And a tree producing an inedible kind can't produce what is good. So the trees having the inedible fruit are chopped down and thrown into the fire. Yes, the way to identify a tree or a person is by the kind of fruit produced."[425]

---

420 *An Essay on the Development of Christian Doctrine*, 2nd Ed., 1845, pp. 14–18, 40–42
421 *Crimes of Christianity: Christ to Constantine*, 1887, Vol. I
422 John 18:36; 17:16; *LCNTV*; brackets mine
423 1 John 5:19; James 4:4; *TLB*
424 *TBLE*
425 *TLB*

What sort of fruits was Constantine producing? What category would our Savior Jesus Christ have placed Constantine? Jesus continues at Matthew 7:21–23 "Not all who sound religious are really godly people. They may refer to me as 'Lord,' but still won't get to heaven. For the decisive question is whether they obey my Father in heaven. At the judgment many will tell me, 'Lord, Lord, we told others about you and used your name to cast out demons and to do many other great miracles.' But I will reply, 'You have never been mine. Go away, for your deeds are evil.'"[426] Who are we to believe as Christians, Jesus or false religious leaders?

This trinity chain is not unique to Christendom, as they would like to believe. It is a part of this world that belongs to Satan. There were many triune gods from Egypt onward. Siegfried Morenz declares: "The trinity was a major preoccupation of Egyptian theologians ... Three gods are combined and treated as a single being, addressed in the singular. In this way, the spiritual force of Egyptian religion shows a direct link with Christian theology."[427]

Concerning God himself his Word tells us: "For God is not a God of confusion."[428] Yet, we find Trinitarians speaking of God as a 'mystery' when unable to explain God from the Bible. As Christians, we know and believe Jesus Christ, to be the greatest teacher to have ever walked this earth. Scripture plainly states: "Jesus spoke with illustrations to the crowds. He did not speak anything without using illustrations."[429] If anyone was able to explain God as a trinity, certainly Jesus Christ could have done so through use of illustrations. However, we find no such recorded message in the Bible. Instead, Jesus reconfirms his Jewish heritage at Mark 12:29 quoting from Deuteronomy 6:4 saying: "Jehovah our God is one[430] God [Jehovah]."[431]

Hence, Ian Wilson states: "It was an occasion to which Jesus could have imparted one of those characteristic twist, bringing in something new, something involving himself, if he wished us to believe that he was a member of a Trinity, on an equal footing with God the Father. Instead he looked unhesitantly to his traditional Jewish roots."[432]

---

426 *TLB*
427 *Egyptian Religion*
428 1 Corinthians 14:33; *NASB*
429 Matthew 13:34; *NSB*
430 Echad; one only
431 *NSB*, brackets his
432 *Jesus, The Evidence*, pp. 176, 177

Did Jesus' Jewish friends and followers discern him to be a trinity or a 'second person of the trinity?' "Considering how strongly conscious the Jews were of their monotheism, it is interesting to note that as far as the NT evidence goes the Jewish opposition did not charge the Christian movement with tritheism or polytheism, a common Jewish criticism later."[433] "If anything can be inferred with certainty as to the belief of the Jews concerning the mode of the Divine existence, it is that they knew nothing of the Orthodox dogma of the Trinity ... It will not do to say that the Apostles left other essential Christian doctrines without any direct, explicit statement of them. It is not true. They had a commission from their Master, and they discharged it ... Peter, who preached to the Jews the first Christian discourse after the Church had risen from the grave of its Founder, told them that "Jesus of Nazareth," "whom they had put to death," was "a man approved of God by works which God did by him," and that God had raised him up. Words could not be more explicit ... from no other words spoken by the Apostles to the Jews, as recorded, could they have gathered a plain statement of the Trinity."[434]

As a final position of clarity: "Jewish faith in God rules out any arrangement of this kind [co-equality between Jesus and God]. It was held that God, the God of Israel, is absolutely sole in his power, cannot be divided or co-equally shared. The New Testament writers never questioned this principle nor think of themselves as possibly infringing upon it. They never distinguished co-equal persons within one God; the idea was unthinkable. It was also unthinkable to say Jesus was identical with one God. So it was very difficult to see how they could have entertained the ideas of the divinity of Christ and the Trinity."[435]

We also discussed a 'missing link' in this trinity chain, the holy spirit. The holy spirit is never called God, Almighty God, 'God the Spirit' or third 'person of God' in the Bible. The holy spirit is never mentioned in Trinitarian 'proof texts' such as John 1:1, John 8:58, John 20:28, et cetera. Rather, we gained accurate knowledge of the holy spirit to be something not someone. Notice the direct words of Hans Kung: "Perceptible and yet not perceptible, invisible and yet powerful, real like energy charged air, the wind, the storm, as important for life as the air we breath: this is how people in ancient times frequently imagined the "Spirit" and God's invisible working ... "Spirit" as understood in the Bible means the force or power proceeding from God, which is opposed to "flesh," to created, perishable reality: that invisible force of God and power of God which is effective creatively or

---
433 *Dictionary of the Bible*, Hastings, 1963, pp. 337, 338
434 *A Half-Century of the Unitarian Controversy*, Ellis, 1857, pp. 464, 465
435 *The Debate About Christ*, Cupitt, 1979, p. 108

destructively … It comes upon man powerfully or gently, stirring up individuals or even groups to ecstasy."[436]

Bruce Vawter explains: "The wind of divine proportions might also be "the spirit [i.e., the life—giving breath] of God" moving upon the waters preparatory to the beginning of creation. "For the Spirit of God has made me, the breath of the Almighty keeps me alive" (Job 33:4): in Hebrew the words for spirit, breath, wind, all symbols of power, are one in the same."[437] Notice these renderings of Genesis 1:2.

- GNB   "and the power of God was moving over the water."
- RAK   "over its waters, stirred the breath of God."
- NJB   "with a divine wind sweeping over the waters."
- NRSV   "while a wind from God swept over the face."
- AT   "a tempestuous wind raging over the surface."
- NWT   "and God's active force was moving to and fro."

The New Catholic Encyclopedia states: "The OT clearly does not envisage God's spirit as a person … God's spirit is simply God's power. If it is sometimes represented as being distinct from God, it is because the breath of Yahweh acts exteriorly … the majority of NT texts reveal God's spirit as something not someone; this is especially seen in the parallelism between the spirit and the power of God."[438] Jesuit John McKenzie declares: "There is apparent a development in the direction of hypostatization of the Spirit, not in the sense that it is conceived as a person but as a substantial source of force and activity. It is the creative force of Yahweh (Gn. 1:2; Jb 33:5)."[439]

Even the 'hub' of Christendom readily, yet ever so silently, admits the holy spirit to be God's active power, force, not the third person of the trinity. Hence, the 'missing link.'

Finally, we have come to recognize the first weak link of this trinity chain. Christendom insists the trinity is based upon God's word the Bible and is the central doctrine of all Christians. However, out of the very same mouths of Christendom they confess there is no scripture that professes the Trinity Chain.

---

436 *On Being a Christian*, 1997, pp. 468, 469
437 *On Genesis*, 1977, p. 41
438 *Spirit of God*, Vol. XIII, pp. 574–576
439 *Dictionary of the Bible*, 1965, p. 841

For example, Catholic Jesuit and theologian Edmund Fortman relates to us: "The Jews never regarded the spirit as a person; nor is there any solid evidence that any Old Testament writer held this view ... The Holy Spirit is usually presented in the Synoptics [Gospels] and in Acts as a divine force or power."[440] Another Catholic Jesuit Priest, John McKenzie admits: "The New Testament writers could not have said that Jesus Christ is God: God meant the Father. They could and did say that Jesus is God's Son."[441]

Anglican Priest Tom Harper in his book *For Christ Sake* states: "You simply cannot find the doctrine of the Trinity set out anywhere in the Bible. St Paul has the highest view of Jesus' role and person, but nowhere does he call him God. Nor does Jesus himself explicitly claim to be the second person of the Trinity, wholly equal to his heavenly Father ... neither the doctrine of the Trinity nor that of the 2 natures of Jesus Christ is explicitly set out in scripture ... you cannot find what is traditionally regarded as orthodox Christianity in the Bible at all."

Also, Protestant theologian Karl Barth says: "The NT does not contain the developed doctrine of the Trinity. The Bible lacks the express declaration that the Father, the Son, and the Holy Spirit are of equal essence."[442] "We maintain that the doctrine of the Trinity was of gradual and comparatively late formation; that it had its origin in a source entirely foreign from that of the Jewish and Christian Scriptures; that it grew up, and was ingrafted on Christianity, through the hands of the Platonizing Fathers ... The modern popular doctrine of the Trinity ... derives no support from ... Christian writers for three centuries after the birth of Christ."[443]

Finally, we have the admittance of the Director of the Commission of faith and Order, National Council of Churches of Christ in the United States saying: "No doctrine of the Trinity in the Nicene sense is present in the New Testament ... There is no doctrine of the Trinity in the strict sense in the [writings of the] Apostolic Fathers, but the trinitarian formulas are apparent. The witness of this collection of writings to a Christian doctrine of God is slight and provides no advance in synthesis or theological construction beyond the biblical materials."[444]

Remember, if Christendom admits the trinity chain cannot be found in scripture, and yet they continue to teach this man-made embarrassment, then there

---

440 *The Triune God*, pp. 6, 15
441 *Light on the Gospels*, 1976, p. 188
442 *The New International Dictionary of New Testament Theology*
443 *The Church of the First Three Centuries*, Lamson, 1860, pp. 52, 70, 71, 75, 76
444 *The Trinitarian Controversy, Source of Early Christian Thought*, Rusch, 1980, pp. 2, 3

can absolutely be only one conclusion: their chain is only as strong as it's weakest link. In other words, since the trinity chain is the result of many man-made weak links, it is not strong but rather pathetically fragile. The historical facts are thus in order. "Jesus did not become God until the fourth century."[445]

Once again, if this trinity chain is not founded upon the Christian anchor, the Bible, there is only one conclusion of it's origin: "The Spirit makes it clear that as time goes on, some are going to give up on the faith and chase after demonic illusions put forth by professional liars. These liars have lied so well and for so long that they have lost their capacity for truth ... Stay clear of silly stories that get dressed up as religion. Exercise daily in God—no spiritual flabbiness please!"[446] "Continually, the Johannine Gospel appears to militate against the Trinity doctrine since John says that the Son is subordinate to the Father and freely calls Him "My God" (John 14:28; 17:3; 20:17). Yes, the fourth Gospel Consistently indicates that the Trinity doctrine is a product of abstruse reasoning: it is not a product of divine revelation."[447]

Hence, "In its finished form the Trinitarian doctrine went beyond the Biblical materials in both form and content. It was deeply indebted, as indeed was the Christological dogma, to the philosophical and religious thought of Greco-Roman antiquity."[448] Our first weak link is placed in the category of links of lies from demons, deceivingly put forth as truth by men.

Review *of* weak link two

Part II asks the question: 'Who is the only true God?' We verified from scripture the importance of God's name Jehovah. Besides being mentioned in the Bible nearly 7,000 times, God says the following concerning his own name.

- Exodus 3:15[449]   "Jehovah ... this is my name forever."
- Psalm 83:18[450]   "your name: "Yahweh," the one and only High God."
- Psalm 135:13[451]   "O Jehovah, your name endures forever."
- Isaiah 12:4   "Give thanks unto Jehovah, call upon his name."

---

445 *When Jesus Became God*, Rubenstein, 1999, pp. 211–231
446 1 Timothy 4:1, 7; *TM*
447 *Christology and the Trinity An Exploration*, Foster, 1997, p. 6
448 *No Orthodoxy But the Truth*, Dawe, 1969, p. 21
449 *TBLE*
450 *PTM*
451 *TB*

- Isaiah 42:8   "I am Jehovah, that is my name."
- Ezekiel 36:23[452]   "I will vindicate my greatness … they shall know that I am Jehovah."
- Micah 4:5[453]   "we will walk in the name of Jehovah our God."
- Malachi 1:11   "my name will be great among the nations, Jehovah … said."

Jesus Christ also highly valued his Father's holy name.

- Matthew 6:9[454]   "Father of us, O Spiritual One, your name be truly honored."
- John 5:43   "I have come in the name of my Father."
- John 17:6[455]   "I have made thy name known."
- John 17:26[456]   "So have I declared, so will I declare, thy Name."

The importance of restoring God's name Jehovah in his own word prevents confusion and helps sincere Christians to understand the Bible. We clarified this while examining two scriptures with a completely different meaning when God's name Jehovah was restored in its rightful place. They were Psalm 23:1 and Psalm 110:1. Thus, *The Catholic Encyclopedia* Vol. 8, 1910 edition, p. 329 acknowledges: "Jehovah, the proper name of God in the Old Testament."

Bible translator and Baptist Minister Jay P. Green says: "we have chosen to use J, thus Jehovah, rather than Yahweh, because this is established English usage for Biblical Names." Yes, God's name Jehovah was to last forever: "And God said moreover unto Moses, Thus shalt thou say unto the children of Israel, Jehovah, the God of your fathers, the God of Abraham, the God of Isaac, and the God of Jacob, hath sent me unto you: this is my name for ever, and this is my memorial until all generations."[457] "Is this Scripture in harmony with the views of those who claim that God's name should not be used in the New Testament? Is it in harmony with the ones that claim Jesus is God's name in the New Testament or that Lord is his name? This Scripture clearly states that God's name will be Jehovah

---

452 *YLT*
453 *TMB*
454 *CPV*
455 *GHCM*
456 *GHCM*
457 Exodus 3:15

(YHWH) forever.[458] Jehovah will be the memorial (sign to remember God by) to all generations. There is no hint in this Scripture or any other Scripture, that God changed his name or that he commanded it not to be used anymore at some point."[459]

Once we established God's name is Jehovah in English, it became rather obvious who the Father is in John 17:1, 3. "For you are our Father ... you, O Jehovah, are our Father," and "O Jehovah, you are our Father."[460]

Jesus affectionately calls God his Abba (Dad). "He [Jesus] continued to pray, "Father, dear Father.""[461] Of course, the Father Jehovah verifies his love of the Son from the heavens stating: "This is My Son, whom I love so dearly. I am so highly pleased with Him ... This is My Son, whom I love dearly. You must keep on listening to Him."[462]

Loaded with all these unbreakable links of biblical truths, we regress to our introduction. Jesus prayer in behalf of his disciples says: "Father ... you, [are], The one and only true God."[463] This is the second and unquestionably the most important biblically revealed weak link of the trinity chain. How so?

Christendom teaches Jesus Christ to be Jehovah as one in the same. This theological theory would make Jesus the Father as well. This not only contradicts the Bibles clear message, it also contradicts the trinity chain teaching that the Father and Son are "truly distinct one from another."[464] Obviously then, if Jesus Christ calls his Father, Jehovah, the only true God, it is impossible for Jesus to be Jehovah!

Also, whom shall we say Jesus' disciples thought about as Jesus prayed to his Father in the heavens? Were they thinking the first person of God? Certainly not! The disciples' Father was Jesus' Father—Jehovah.

It has been demonstrated in large quantities to us how the name Jehovah is much more acceptable than Yahweh. Why? "Whatever may be said of the dubious pedigree, 'Jehovah' is and should remain the proper English rendering of Yahweh, the God of Israel who revealed his name to Moses in the burning bush."[465]

---

458   Cf. Malachi 3:6
459   *The Lord and the Tetragrammaton,* Mazzaferro, p. 8
460   Isaiah 63:16; 64:8
461   Mark 14:36; *ENT,* brackets mine
462   Matthew 3:17; Luke 9:35; *LDB*
463   John 17:1, 3; *TM,* brackets mine
464   *The Catholic Encyclopedia,* 1912, Vol. XV, p. 47
465   *Introduction to the Old Testament,* Pfeiffer, 1952, p. 94

Yes, Jehovah is the English version of God's proper personal name. For those insisting on God's name Jehovah as improper, will these ones equally insist on the name Jesus as improper? The Hebrew name for Jesus is Yeshu'a or Yehoshu'a. Are critics willing to give up the ever-popular English name of Jesus for its original, Yehoshu'a? To insist on one and not the other is simply showing a particular bias and being hypocritical to the utmost degree. Besides, Jesus name means Jehovah is salvation.

Interestingly, Martin Luther candidly acknowledges: "That they (the Jews) declare the name Jehovah unpronounceable, they do not know what they babble, and since it can be written with quill and ink, why then can it not be pronounced with the mouth which is better than quill and ink? Or, why do they not call it unwritten, unreadable, unthinkable? All in all, it is a rotten thing ... This name Jehovah, Lord, belongs alone to the True God."[466]

In addition, we briefly dealt with a hot topic among scholars today, concerning the name Jehovah within the Christian Greek Scriptures. It was proven that God's name was substituted with surrogates like Kyrios, not the other way around. Why? All manuscripts of the Septuagint[467] available today, contain the divine name right up to the middle of the second century CE.

Under the Greek word Kyrios (Lord), one Greek Lexicon says: "God as the Supreme Lord and sovereign of the universe, usually in Sept [uagint] for Heb [rew] YHWH Jehovah."[468]

In addition, there was substantial opposition to the early Christians written use of God's name within their circulated Gospels. The Talmud Shabbat 13:5 substantiates this. At the very least, in your very own copy of the Bible, God's name is found in the book of Revelation four times. Hallelujah[469] is mentioned at Revelation 19:1, 3, 4, and 6.

It is my personal opinion that if an original copy of the Christian Greek Scriptures were to be unearthed today and found to have God's name Jehovah throughout; Christendom would not restore this holy name in their modern Bible translations. Why? Today, we have ample evidence of Hebrew Scriptures that contain God's name Jehovah throughout. Yet, modern popular Bible translations are bent on removing God's name and replacing it with surrogates to fit their theology. Thus, new findings of the Tetragrammaton would not hinder their purpose to remove it. Remember, "In the Scriptures there is the closest possible

---

466 *Dr. Martin Luther's Complete Writings*, 20th part 1747, 6th part 1741 respectively
467 Greek translation of the Hebrew Scriptures, LXX
468 *A Greek and English Lexicon of the New Testament*, Robinson, 1859
469 Praise Jehovah you people

relationship between a person and his name the two being practically equivalent so that to remove the name is to extinguish the person. To forget God's name is to depart from him."[470]

Truly then, there is only one reasonable and logical conclusion: "Father ... you [are] the only true God."[471] These are neither anyone else's fallible words nor mine. Rather, these are the humble, honest, and infallible words of Jesus Christ; spoken in prayer to his God and Father, Jehovah. Who are we to believe: Jesus, or the uninspired manmade traditional weak links of the trinity chain?

Review of weak link three

Our final weak link was found in part III answering the question: 'Does Almighty God have a God?' Since we rarely encounter the Father Jehovah, and the holy spirit when talking with Trinitarians, the truth is this: Jesus Christ is the Trinitarians God. Thus, to them Jesus is Almighty God. However, what does the Bible really teach?

The only one to ever be called and possess the title Almighty God is the Father Jehovah. Never are Jesus and the holy spirit given this exclusive title. Notice the following.

- Genesis 17:1   "Jehovah said I am God Almighty."
- Exodus 6:3   "I appeared as God Almighty ... my name Jehovah."
- Revelation 4:8[472]   "Holy, holy, holy, is Jehovah God the Almighty."
- Revelation 11:17[473] "We give you thanks, Jehovah God, the Almighty."
- Revelation 21:22[474] "Jehovah God the Almighty."

We reviewed scripture after scripture revealing for us that Jesus has a God and Father. Notice the following verses.

- Matthew 27:46   "My God, my God, why hast thou forsaken me?"
- John 20:17475   "I ascend to my Father and ... my God."

---

470 *Zondervan Pictorial Bible Dictionary*, 1964, p. 571
471 John 17:1, 3; *NWT*, brackets mine
472 *VC*
473 *NSB*
474 *VC*
475 *TLB*

- 1 Corinthians 15:24[476] "He surrenders the Kingdom to his God and Father."
- Hebrews 1:9[477] "Therefore God, even your God, has anointed you."
- Revelation 1:6[478] "He made us to be a kingdom … to his God and Father."
- Revelation 3:2, 12 "my God … my God … my God … my God … my God."

There are in addition prophecies of Jesus Christ, which he acknowledges: "All things must be fulfilled. They are things written in the Law of Moses, and the Prophets, and the Psalms, concerning me."[479] Please notice the following.

- Psalm 40:8[480] "I am pleased to do your will, O my God."
- Isaiah 11:2 "the spirit of Jehovah … the fear of Jehovah."
- Micah 5:4 "shall feed his flock in the strength of Jehovah."
- Micah 5:4 "In the majesty of the name of Jehovah his God."

These Scriptures are indisputable. Jesus has a God and Father whether in heaven or on the earth. Hence, Jesus Christ cannot be Almighty God Jehovah who is the source of all life and power and who has no God above him, thus AL—mighty.[481]

Further proof was provided and revealed to demonstrate Jesus Christ as God's Son, not Almighty God Jehovah. The question was raised: 'who is greater in authority: the one who is sent, or the one sending forth? Also, can Almighty God be given anything he doesn't already possess?

Scriptures give us the answers that Jesus is sent forth and the one given all authority by Almighty God. Jesus is inferior and subordinate to his God and Father, Jehovah. "The Christology of the apologies, like that of the New Testament, is essentially subordinationist. The Son is always subordinate to the Father, who is the one God of the Old Testament … What we find in these early authors, then, is not a doctrine of the Trinity … Before Nicaea, Christian theology was almost universally subordinationist."[482]

---

476 *TCNT*
477 *NSB*
478 *NSB*
479 Luke 24:44; *NSB*
480 *NSB*
481 Hebrew El Shaddai
482 *Gods and the One God*, 1st Ed., Grant, 1986, pp. 109, 156, 160

Emil Brunner makes note of this 'granting' by the Father also, thus subordination of the Son declaring: "In the New Testament the Son, or Jesus Christ, is never called the Creator. This title is given to the Father alone. It is He who 'granted unto the Son to have life in Himself.'"[483] Allow the following verses of God's word to ring true.

- Matthew 28:18 — "All authority hath been given unto me in heaven … earth."
- John 5:26[484] — "He gave also to the Son to have life in himself."
- John 5:27[485] — "he gave him authority to do judging."
- John 12:49[486] — "Father having sent me, he gave me a command."
- John 13:3[487] — "the Father had given everything into His hands."
- John 14:28 — "the Father is greater than I."
- 1 Corinthians 11:3[488] — "God is the Head of Christ."
- Philippians 2:9[489] — "God has highly exalted Him, and given Him the name that is above every other name."
- Revelation 1:1[490] — "The unveiling [Apocalypse] of Jesus Christ which God gave him."

Therefore, if Jesus Christ were Almighty God he would rely on the strength and power of no one. He wouldn't have to be given anything—whether in heaven or on earth. Certainly, no one would dare to send him forth for any reason. "The Omnipotent Jehovah cannot be thus dependant on another. "I live by the Father," Joh 6:57. "My Father is greater than I", Joh 14:28. The connection proves that this refers to his highest nature. His prayer, Joh 17:5, for the glory of his divine nature which he had with the Father "before the world was" proves the dependence of his nature."[491]

We also recognize as Bible students certain verses calling Jesus God, such as John 1:1 and Isaiah 9:6. This is not out of harmony with Jehovah's thoughts and

---

483 *The Christian Doctrine of God. Dogmatics*: Vol. I, 1949
484 *KI*
485 *KI*
486 *HBJS*
487 *HCSB*
488 *TCNT*
489 *TNTBW*
490 *MNT*
491 Henry Grew, 1857

words. Unfortunately, Trinitarians have developed a strict view of monotheism. This is not and never has been God's view. For Isaiah 55:8 states: "My thoughts are not your thoughts, neither are your ways my ways, declares Jehovah."[492] Why?

Although there is certainly only one true God Jehovah, he allows for others to take on the title god if, and only if, he appoints them as his representatives, his agents as it were. All others are to be viewed as false gods such as in 2 Corinthians 4:4 when Satan is called: "the god of this age."[493] For Satan made himself a false god. Jehovah didn't appoint him.

In contrast, we saw in regards to the angels being referenced to as gods at psalm 8:5; for the angels are Jehovah's duly appointed messengers. Jehovah too calls and appoints man as 'god' in certain circumstances. In Exodus 7:1, Jehovah calls Moses a god to Pharaoh.[494] Why? Verse two says: "Thou shalt speak all that I [Jehovah] command thee."[495] Yes, Jehovah appointed Moses as a god to represent him. Moses did not appoint himself. Since Jehovah appointed Moses as god, would it be correct to assume Moses to be a false god? Certainly not! To suggest otherwise would be to label Jehovah a liar.

Other men were appointed as gods because they were sitting in God's seat as judges to the people, his representatives.[496] In other words, these men were Jehovah God's agents. "The main point of the Jewish law of agency is expressed in the dictum, a person's agent is regarded as the person himself. Therefore any act committed by a duly appointed agent is regarded as having been committed by the principal."[497]

If angels and mere imperfect man can and are called gods and act as agents of Jehovah, certainly God's Only-begotten Son, the first born of all creation Jesus Christ, is much more deserving of this title god without usurping Jehovah.[498] For Jesus states: "I am a representative from him, and that One sent me forth."[499] The Bible declares: "God's Son is the brightness of his glory, and the express image of his being."[500]

---

492 *NSB*
493 *EB*
494 Cf. Exodus 4:16
495 *ASV*, brackets mine
496 Cf. Psalm 82:6; John 10:34
497 *The Encyclopedia of the Jewish Religion*, Werblowsky, Wigoder
498 See Colossians 1:15–17
499 John 7:29; *NWT*
500 Hebrews 1:3; *NSB*

For those students of God's Word who enjoy biblical mathematics, Brian Holt provides an interesting find. He asks: "So what does the scholarly community admit? That of the 1, 315 times someone is referred to as God in the New Testament, only a maximum possible number of nine can be attributed to Christ! And if that is not bad enough, six of the nine are hotly disputed among many reputable scholars ... Thus, not only is the ratio of evidence that the Bible calls Jesus *theos* unbelievably small (0.0068, less than 1 percent of the time) ... We are amazed this is what millions of people would rather accept as proof of who Jesus is rather than the hundreds and hundreds of scriptures that show Jesus is not God. And these hundreds and hundreds of scriptures that show he is not God do not hinge on what Bible translation we use!"[501]

The truth will set you free

All throughout history, mankind has been dominated and held captive by chains comprised of links of lies concerning whom the true God of the Bible is. When men were able to possess a personal copy of the Bible and discover for themselves who the true God really is, Christendom would declare these ones heretics and would murder them in the name of their 'Trinitarian God.'

Michael Servetus (1511-53) was one such lover of truth who was put to death at the hands and orders of John Calvin. Why? Because of his disbelief in the trinity. At age twenty Michael Servetus published *Errors of the Trinity*. Concerning the trinity he states in his book: he "will not make use of the word Trinity, which is not to be found in Scripture, and only seems to perpetuate philosophical error." He continues, the trinity "cannot be understood, that is impossible in the nature of things, and that may even be looked on as blasphemous!" He also mentioned "the papistical Trinity, infant baptism, and other sacraments of the Papacy, are the doctrines of demons." Does this not remind us of 1Timothy 4:1? "As time goes on, some are going to give up on the faith and chase after demonic illusions put forth by professional liars ... they've lost their capacity for truth."[502]

There have been countless others who lost their lives for not believing in the trinity chain. Some sources reveal thirty thousand deaths by the Catholic Church in the 16th century alone. Today however, there is ample freedom in most countries to own a copy of the Bible for yourself. This gives each and everyone of us the opportunity to "call out for understanding, raise [our] voice to insight ... seek [wisdom, truth, understanding] as [we] do silver, search for it as for treasure ...

---

501 *Jesus—God or The Son of God?* Holt, 2002, p. 326, emphasis his
502 *TM*

then [we] will understand the revering of Yahweh, you will find the knowledge of God; for Yahweh gives wisdom, from his mouth come knowledge and insight ... then you will understand righteousness and justice ... for wisdom will come into your heart, knowledge will be at home in your breast ... insight will protect you, saving you from the evil way, from the man who speaks falsehoods, from those who have abandoned right paths, to walk in dark ways."[503]

Now we are able to discover truth for ourselves in the word of God, keeping us from men who speak falsehoods. Many have realized in this time of the end the so-called unbreakable trinity chain, actually consists of breakable 'weak links' when compared to Bible truth. One writer truthfully acknowledges: "When the writers of the New Testament speak of God they mean the God and Father of Our Lord Jesus Christ. When they speak of Jesus Christ, they do not speak of him, nor do they think of him as God."[504]

A well known professor, Boobyer, writes: "The fact has to be faced that the New Testament research over, say, the last thirty or forty years has been leading an increasing number of reputable New Testament scholars to the conclusion that Jesus ... certainly never believed himself to be God."[505]

I will briefly discuss two more individuals and their belief of who God really is after their own personal careful research. Their logical conclusions and reasonableness based on Holy Scriptures are admirable and should be duly noted. These learned men are Isaac Newton and Thomas Jefferson.

Most of the world recognizes the great accomplishments of Isaac Newton such as the discovery of gravity and the invention of calculus. However, it is his deep love of the Bible and truth that is of interest to me. Isaac Newton lived between 1642–1727. Like Michael Servetus, Isaac Newton passionately rejected the doctrine of the trinity. An outstanding contribution to the biblical scholarship of the time was his work *An Historical Account of Two Notable Corruptions of Scripture*. This work was produced in 1754, twenty-seven years after his death. What was the reason for such a belated publishing?

According to three books of history, as late as 1698 the act for the Suppression of Blasphemy and Profaneness made it an offense to deny one of the persons of the trinity to be God, punishable with loss of employment, office, and imprisonment for a repetition. Isaac Newton's dear friend who translated the works of Josephus, William Whiston, lost his position at Cambridge for this reason in 1711. In 1693 a pamphlet against the trinity chain was burned and the very next

---

503 Proverbs 2:3–13; *RJC*, brackets mine
504 *The Divinity of Jesus Christ*, Creed, p. 123
505 *Bulletin of the John Rylands Library*, Vol. 50, 1968, pp. 251, 253, 259

year its printer and author were prosecuted. In 1697 an eighteen-year-old student, Thomas Aikenhead, was charged with denying the trinity. He was hanged at Edinburgh, Scotland.[506]

Apparently, Newton was very aware of the animosity to those who loved truth and despised the trinity. At any rate his work reviewed two Bible passages, 1 John 5:7 and 1 Timothy 3:16. In regards to 1 John 5:7 Isaac Newton proved that the words "in heaven, the Father, the Word, and the Holy Ghost; and these three are one," which was used to support the trinity chain, did not appear in the original Greek Scriptures inspired by God. He proved Cardinal Ximenes first took this text into the Greek in 1515. Isaac Newton's conclusion was "Thus is the sense plain and natural, and the argument full and strong; but if you insert the testimony of 'the Three in Heaven' you interrupt and spoil it."[507]

Newton proved concerning 1 Timothy 3:16, the word 'God' was inserted to make the phrase read, "God was manifest in the flesh." This scripture was hotly debated and used in support of the trinity chain for many years. Today however, modern versions have substituted 'he' for 'God' acknowledging the error.[508] Isaac Newton said of these two passages, "If the ancient churches in debating and deciding the greatest mysteries of religion, knew nothing of these two texts, I understand not, why we should be so fond of them now the debates are over."[509]

Notice one conclusion by Newton regarding the trinity chain, "Homoousion[510] is unintelligible. Twas not understood in the Council of Nice, nor ever since. What cannot be understood is no object of belief."[511] In direct dissimilarity Newton says of the apostle John's writings, "I have that honour of him as to believe that he wrote good sense; and therefore take that sense to be his which is the best."[512]

God's word makes sense and is reasonable. Doctrines introduced after the Bible are incomprehensible. Sir Isaac Newton did not accept the doctrine of the trinity on the basis of scripture, reason, and teaching of early Christianity. He states: "We are commanded by the Apostles (2 Timothy 1:13) to hold fast the form of sound words. Contending for a language which was not handed down from the

---

506 Thoughts taken from *Our Unitarian Heritage*, Wilber, 1925, pp. 289–294; *History of English Nonconformity*, Clark, 1913, Vol. II, p. 157; *Religious Opinions of Milton, Locke and Newton*, McLachlan, 1941, pp. 146–147
507 *An Historical Account of Two Notable Corruptions of Scripture*, 1830, p. 60
508 Cf. *JB* with fn
509 *An Historical Account of Two Notable Corruptions of Scripture*, p. 95
510 This theory states the Son is of the same substance as the Father
511 *Sir Isaac Newton Theological Manuscripts*, p. 17
512 *An Historical Account of Two Notable Corruptions of Scripture*, p. 61

Prophets and Apostles is a breach of the command and they that break it are also guilty of the disturbances and schisms occasioned thereby. It is not enough to say that an article of faith may be deduced from scripture. It must be exprest in the very form of sound words in which it was delivered by the Apostles."[513]

Isaac Newton used scriptural logic to find truth. Notice his summary of why the trinity chain should be rejected. "Because God begot the Son at some time, he had not existence from eternity. Proverbs 8:23, 25, Because the Father is greater than the Son. John 14:28, Because the Son did not know his last hour. Mark 13:32, Matt. 24:36, rev. 1:1, 5:3, Because the Son received all things from the Father."[514]

Therefore, because Isaac Newton used sound reasoning and simple scriptural logic, his conclusions regarding the fallibility of the trinity chain merit our respect and consideration.

Thomas Jefferson, the third President of the United States, also rejected the trinity chain. At best, Jefferson was a Unitarian and really had a loathing for the hypocrisy of the clergy. The following is Thomas Jefferson's conclusion concerning the trinity. "No historical fact is better established, than that the doctrine of one God, pure and uncompounded, was that of the early ages of Christianity ... Nor was the unity of the Supreme Being ousted from the Christian creed by the force of reason, but by the sword of civil government, wielded at the will of the Athanasius. The hocus-pocus phantasm of a God like another Cerberus, with one body and three heads, had its birth and growth in the blood of thousands of martyrs ... The Athanasian paradox that one is three, and three but one, is so incomprehensible to the human mind, that no candid man can say he has any idea of it, and how he can believe what presents no idea? He who thinks he does, only deceives himself. He proves, also, that man, once surrendering his reason, has no remaining guard against absurdities the most monstrous, and like a ship without rudder, is the sport of every wind. With such person, gullibility which they call faith, takes the helm from the hand of reason, and the mind becomes a wreck."[515]

Hence, Jefferson recognized the unequivocal importance of reason along with biblical truth. Otherwise, as Jefferson puts it: We are "like a ship without rudder ... the sport of every wind ... gullibility takes the helm from the hand of reason, and the mind becomes a wreck." Very well articulated.

---

513 *The Religion of Isaac Newton*, pp. 54-55, Yahuda Manuscripts 15.1fol.11r.
514 *Isaac Newton, A Biography*, p. 642
515 *Letters to James Smith*, December 8, 1822

Worship what we know

Speaking to Jesus Christ a woman of a different faith said: "You people say that in Jerusalem is the place where persons ought to worship." Jesus replies: "Woman, believe me, the hour is coming when neither on this mountain nor in Jerusalem will you worship the Father. You worship what you do not know; we worship what we know ... now is, when the true worshippers will worship the Father in spirit and truth, for such the Father seeks to worship him. God is spirit, and those who worship him must worship in spirit and truth."[516]

Regrettably, like many in Christendom today this Samaritan woman was convinced her way of worshiping God was the correct way. Yet, Jesus responds with: "You worship what you do not know, we worship what we know." The application of Jesus' words certainly can and should be said of the trinity chain, and those who worship the trinity God. They worship what they do not know. Allow me to explain.

The Trinitarians God consist of 'three persons,' the Father, the Son and the Holy Ghost. The second person of this trinity is Jesus Christ. The first person is the Father, Jehovah. The third person has no name, but is referred to as the holy spirit. All three combine to make up this triune God. My question to all those who are sincere in Christendom is: what is your God's name?

If some respond with Jesus, this would be incorrect seeing as this is the name of the 'second person' of the triune God. The same applies to the name Jehovah, the 'first person.' Thus, the only conclusion then is the Trinitarian God has no name.

Christendom cannot reasonably or logically use a name for God that does not designate the entire trinity 'Godhead.' Hence, their God is a mystery, has no name, and is unknowable. If the trinity God has no name, he is indistinguishable from the many false gods of this world.[517]

Just as well, Trinitarians admit their God is incomprehensible. For a fact the Athanasian Creed states: "The Father is Incomprehensible, the Son Incomprehensible, and the Holy Ghost Incomprehensible ... there are not ... three Incomprehensibles, but one Incomprehensible." According to well-respected dictionaries, incomprehensible means: "beyond understanding," and "Not able to understand."[518] Therefore, if the trinity God has no name, is unknowable,

---

516 John 4:20–24; *TGON*
517 Cf. 1 Corinthians 8:4–6
518 *MSN Encarta and Compact Oxford English Dictionary*

beyond understanding, and a mystery, Trinitarians are worshiping what they do not know.

This fact is extremely distressing, especially when I see sincere ones recognizing the need for a name of their God by erringly calling him Jesus. Through my personal studies of God's name Jehovah, I came to realize an outstanding observation. Literally thousands of churches around the world have some form of God's name YHWH above or on their altars. Norway is one such country.[519] How many in Christendom actually realize this personal name Jehovah/Yahweh belongs to the only true God of the Bible?

On the other hand, Jesus said: "We worship what we know." If we label ourselves as Christians, ones who obey and follow Jesus Christ in every detail, it would stimulate us to reexamine what Jesus knew and who he worshiped. As mentioned earlier in this book, Jesus declares with clarity: "Yahweh our God is the one, the only Yahweh."[520] We notice Jesus reinforces God's name Jehovah/Yahweh and declares God to be not 'three persons of God,' but 'one' God, one Yahweh. Is this the God Trinitarians worship? Jesus says: "It is Jehovah your God you must worship, and it is to him alone you must render sacred service."[521] Are we as Christians worshiping the God Jesus Christ instructed us to? Are we worshiping Jehovah whom Jesus calls his Father and God?[522] If not, we are worshiping an unknown, incomprehensible God, not the God of the Bible, Jehovah.

How much better the simplicity of teaching from scripture. "Addressing his "Father," Joh 17:1-3, he [Jesus] plainly and positively declares THE FATHER TO BE "THE ONLY TRUE GOD." You believe the Father is one person. If then you believe that "the only true God" is three persons, does not your faith stand in the wisdom of men," which denies the testimony of Jesus Christ, that ONE person is "the ONLY true God?"[523]

I declare to all as the Apostle Paul stated to those in Athens who worshiped unknown gods: "What you worship but do not know—this is what I now proclaim."[524] The only true God is not a trinity chain connected by lies consisting of weak links. We know this because we learned through the pages of this book based on the Bible that the trinity is a breakable, fallible and one of many

---

519 See http://www.divinename.no
520 Mark 12:29 *NJB*; Cf. Deuteronomy 6:4
521 Matthew 4:10 *NSB*; Cf. Deuteronomy 5:9
522 Cf. John 20:17; Matthew 27:46; Revelation 1:6; 3:2, 12; Hebrews 1:9; Isaiah 11:1, 2; Micah 5:4
523 Henry Grew, 1857
524 Acts 17:23; *NEB*

manmade "doctrines that come from devils."[525] God's word the Bible is the only anchor of truth our links of faith should be chained to. As a result of adhering ourselves to the only inspired words of God, the Bible, we are able to confidently say as our King and Savior Jesus: "We worship what we know!" (John 4:22)

Let us worship the only true God of the Bible, Jehovah. Love for him must be preeminent under the leadership of his Son, Jesus Christ, along with the help of his holy spirit. How spiritually sweet it is to "learn the truth that will set you free,"[526] from the bondage of demonic, manmade, and uninspired weak links belonging to the trinity chain.

---

525 1 Timothy 4:1; *NJB*
526 John 8:32; *VC*

Part V

Extra biblical exegeses—John 1:1

Test your belief against the whole Bible

Undoubtedly, there has been an enormous amount of debate concerning this scripture, John 1:1. I want to share with you the things I have learned over the years regarding some details of this particular verse. Please, I ask that you search out the scriptures I will be sharing. Test them out and make sure of all things in regards to what you have been taught. I certainly have and continue to do this, along with using my power of reason that God has given to all of us. Carefully take to heart the following scriptures. "God revealed them to us through the Spirit! For the Spirit examines everything—even the depths of God!"[527] "On the other hand, don't be gullible. Check out everything, and keep only what's good. Throw out anything tainted with evil."[528] "And this I pray, that your love may abound yet more and more in knowledge and all discernment; so that ye may approve[529] the things that are excellent; that ye may be sincere and void of offence unto the day of Christ."[530]

I have quoted this scripture throughout this book, but it is significantly worth repeating. "My dear friends, don't believe everything you hear. Carefully weigh and examine what people tell you. Not everyone who talks about God comes from God. There are a lot of lying preachers loose in the world."[531] Just as well is the following scripture in 2 Corinthians 10:4 "We use our powerful God-tools for smashing warped philosophies, tearing down barriers erected against the truth of God."[532]

---

527 1 Corinthians 2:10; *TPNT*
528 1 Thessalonians 5:21; *TM*
529 Fn Or, distinguish the things that differ
530 Philippians 1:9–10; *ASV*
531 1 John 4:1; *TM*
532 *TM*

Jesus and Paul fully reasoned from the scriptures

We have many great examples of those in the Bible that reasoned with others from scripture to prove their case, like the apostle Paul. The greatest example of course was that of our Lord, Jesus Christ. Lets notice Paul first.

"As was Paul's custom, he went there to preach, and for three Sabbaths in a row he opened the Scriptures to the people, explaining the prophecies about the sufferings of the Messiah and his coming back to life, and proving that Jesus is the Messiah"[533] Also, when Paul "arrived at Ephesus ... first he entered the synagogue and reasoned with the Jews."[534]

Now, notice how the great teacher Jesus reasoned. "God's Spirit led Jesus into the desert wilderness. There he was tested by the Devil. He fasted forty days and nights, and was very hungry. Satan, the Tempter, said to him: "If [since] you are the Son of God order these stone to turn into bread." In reply Jesus answered: "It is written; man shall not live on bread alone, but on all (everything) (every word) (every utterance) (every declaration) that proceeds from the mouth of Jehovah,"[535] "Again it is written," Jesus relied, "You must not put Jehovah your God to the test,'"[536] "Go away Satan!" demanded Jesus. "It is written, It is Jehovah your God you must worship, and it is to him alone you must render sacred service."[537]

At John 10:35 Jesus says: "If those to whom God's word was addressed are called gods (and the Scripture cannot be annulled)."[538] Notice that Jesus said scripture couldn't be annulled or broken. According to *Strong's Exhaustive Concordance*, this word annulled means: "break up, destroy, dissolve."[539] I mention this simply because "Every part of Scripture is God-breathed and ... showing us truth ... correcting our mistakes, training us to live God's way,"[540] as by now you are certainly very well aware of. Therefore, Jesus is saying that not one single word of God can be dissolved or destroyed, as men would often like to do according to their own desires and made up theologies.

If scriptures call imperfect men, gods, judges appointed by Jehovah, then certainly Jesus had a right to call himself the Son of God—because he was. This

---

533 Acts 17:2, 3; *TLB*
534 Acts 18:19; *VC*
535 See Deuteronomy 8:3
536 See Deuteronomy 6:16
537 Matthew 4:1-10 *NSB*; see also Deuteronomy 6:13–15
538 *WEY*
539 See G3089
540 2 Timothy 3:16, 17; *TM*

means then if any scripture contradicts what we have been taught, it is up to us to adjust our accepted and inaccurately taught wisdom to align with God's holy and perfect wisdom.

Definition of 'God'

Before I begin with the explanation of John 1:1, I believe it is important to give clarification of the following. To complete a translation in our English, we need to take into consideration the fact that English has both a common noun 'god,' (one used of anything and anyone) and a proper noun 'God,' (used exclusively of the only true God). In English we use and view the proper noun 'God' like a name, without either a definite[541] or indefinite[542] article, even though a name is a definite noun. This has led to much confusion for Bible students. In other words, In English 'God' has an ambiguous meaning. "Moderns are often unaware that Theos [God] had a much broader semantic range than is allowed for G/god in contemporary Western European languages."[543]

Simply stated, when translating from Greek to English, expounding on what type of 'God' is being alluded to is a must for the reader to get the full accurate meaning of what is written in Jehovah's word. For example, in Greek, if you leave off the definite article (The) from Theos (God) in a sentence like the one in John 1:1c, then Greek readers will assume you mean "a god." This must be made clear to the English reader when translated from the Greek. So the lack of the definite article (The) "makes *theos* [God] quite different than the definite *ho theos*, [The God] as different as "a god" is from "God" in English."[544]

Therefore, Bible translators have a Godly responsibility to make this difference evident to their readers. Regrettably, most do not. What could be a possible reason for this? Scholar Jason D. BeDuhn continues: "The culprit appears to be the King James translators ... these translators were much more familiar and comfortable with their Latin Vulgate than they were with the Greek New Testament. They were used to understanding passages based on reading them in Latin, and this worked its way into their reading of the same passages in Greek. *Latin* has no articles, either definite or indefinite. So the definite noun "God" and the indefinite noun "god" look precisely the same in Latin, and in John 1:1-2 one

---

541 The
542 a, an
543 *The Earliest Patristic Interpretations of Psalms 82, Jewish Antecedants and The Origin of Christian Deification*, Mosser, *Journal of Theological Studies* 56, April 2005, p. 22
544 *Truth in Translation*, BeDuhn, p. 115

would see three occurrences of what appeared to be the same word, rather than two distinct forms used in Greek. Whether a Latin noun is definite or indefinite is determined solely by context, and that means it is open to interpretation. The interpretation of John 1:1-2 that is now found in most English translations was well entrenched in the thinking of the King James translators based on a millennium of reading only the Latin, and overpowered their close attention to the more subtle wording of the Greek. After the fact—after the King James translation was the dominant version and etched in the minds of English speaking Bible readers—various arguments were put forward to support the King James translation of John 1:1c as "the Word was God," and to justify its repetition in more recent, and presumably more accurate translations. But none of theses arguments withstands close scrutiny."[545]

Scrutinizing John 1:1

Most translations of John 1:1 read this way: "In the beginning was the Word, and the Word was with God, and the Word was God."[546] The first obvious point I believe needs to be made clear straightaway is only two distinct beings are mentioned in this verse. Hence, there is no mention of the 'third person' of the trinity. Obviously I agree with Trinitarians when they say: 'the word is distinct from God, yet is said to be God.' The only real issue at hand then, is whether John is calling Jesus the only true God or, is Jesus God-like making him a divine being, in the class of God, but not the only true God by nature or essence. In either case then, could Jesus be called a false God? Let us conscientiously observe John 1:1.

In verse 1 & 2 the Word is spoken of as being with God. Literally toward, face to face, active.[547] Since the Bible is man's way of knowing God, the logical question to ask then is this: Am I able to be with, toward, face to face, someone and at the same time be that person? This would be beyond anyone's capability. Are there any other examples of this in the scriptures? By power of reason we have to honestly say there is not.

The book *The Moffatt New Testament Commentary, The Gospel Of John* gives a little more insight and understanding as to the meaning of "with God." Mr. Macgregor writes: "**The Logos was with God:** 'towards God,' 'not absorbed in Him, but standing over against Him as a distinct person' (E.F. Scott). The word **with** (in the Greek), while emphasizing the communion of the Logos with God,

---

545 *Truth in Translation*, p. 116
546 *KJV*
547 Cf. *MNT*

yet safely guards the idea of his individual personality: it expresses *nearness* combined with the since of *movement towards* God, and so indicates an active relationship."[548]

If being "with God" expresses nearness and movement towards God, this poses a very difficult position for hard-core Trinitarians. Is it possible for an individual to move towards himself? Logic, reason, and Bible sense shows the need for two ontologically separate individuals to attain movement towards one another. One expressive English translation by R. Frederick Harrison captures this understanding and true meaning of being "with God." It reads: "At first, there was the Word, and the Word grew closer and closer to God until it reflected all of his qualities." Indeed, the trinity chain becomes weaker and weaker upon close examination of each link. Let's look at this verse, John 1:1, even closer now and base the understanding of this verse on scripture alone.

The b&c clauses of this verse read this way in the Greek: "and the Word was with the God, and a god was the Word."[549] In the original Greek there are what is called the definite article.[550] This definite article was used in the Greek to point to an Identity, or specific individual. This was especially done to distinguish the true living God from his false counterparts.[551] This is clearly seen in the b portion of the verse one where it reads, "the Word was with the (definite article), God." I am sure we would agree that John is identifying the only true God, the Father Jehovah, whom the Word was with.

Now, notice in the c part that god precedes the verb (*was*), and has no definite article (the), in front of it. When this occurs in the Greek it points to a quality about someone, it is descriptive, not identifying someone. It should also be noted here that there are no indefinite articles (a, an), in Greek. Hence, when translating into English to give quality to someone, the indefinite article (a, an) is often used. Many have been quick to reply that when translations render verse one as "a god," the translators are wrong because they are adding the word "a", which is not in the Greek translation.

Some scholars have even gone so far as to give what they consider to be 'scriptural examples' that would have to employ 'a' if there is to be consistency. A few of these so-called proof texts are John 1:6 "There was a man sent from a god," John 1:12 "To all who received Him ... He gave power to become children of a god," and finally John 1:18 "No one has ever seen a god." I am completely

---

548 Macgregor, 1928, p. 4, emphasis his
549 *DBW*
550 The
551 This of course is not to indicate Jesus as a false god.

surprised that any Bible scholar would even dare to use these examples. For they must know that these verses—used to defend their position—are nowhere near the same grammatical structure as John 1:1. If this scholar is trying to advocate the non-use of the word 'a' in scripture, then again he is sorely mistaken and misleading his audience. We will see examples of this shortly. These scholars must also be acquainted with the fact—as was pointed out earlier—that Greek language does not have the indefinite articles 'a' and 'an.' This is not the case in the English language. Thus, when translating from Greek to English, the translator has the responsibility to employ proper English grammar for the reader to grasp the appropriate understanding. Jason BeDuhn, professor of religious studies at Northern Arizona University captures this thought well. He says: "We are not 'adding a word' when we translate Greek nouns that do not have the indefinite article as English nouns with the indefinite article. We are simply obeying the rules of English grammar that tell us that we cannot say "Snoopy is dog," but must say "Snoopy is a dog." For example, in John 1:1c, the clause that we are investigating, ho logos is "the word," as all translations have it. If it is simply written logos, without the definite article ho, we would have to translate it as "a word."[552]

Evangelical scholar F. F. Bruce agrees: "Had theos as well as logos been preceded by the article [The] the meaning would have been that the Word was completely identical with God, which is impossible if the Word was also 'with God.'"[553] Even Trinitarian Robert Bowman recognizes the absurdity of this: "The usual translation of John 1:1 can be misunderstood to imply that the Word was the same person as the person with whom he existed in the beginning, which would of course be nonsense."[554]

Therefore, John's statement that the Word or Logos was "a god," "God-like," "Divine," does not mean at all that Jesus was "the God" whom he was with. "[A] Peculiarity of Greek is that the article is often used for defining individual identity and is thus absent for the purpose of ascribing quality or character."[555] Again, Robert Bowman—although a devout Trinitarian—candidly observes: "The significance of *theon* [God] being definite in Clause B, then, is to identify the One spoken of there as a specific person—God the Father. If, then, *theos* in Clause C were to be 'definite' in the same way that theon is in Clause B, it would then be saying that the Word was God the Father. Such a statement would contra-

---

552 *Truth in Translation*, p. 114
553 *The Gospel of John, Introduction, Exposition and Notes*, 1983, p. 31
554 *Jesus Christ and the Gospel of John*, p. 27
555 *Complete Guide to Bible Verses*, Comfort, p. 109

dict Clause B and imply some sort of modalistic view of God, which of course Trinitarians oppose."[556]

For this reason, Catholic Jesuit scholar, John L. McKenzie observes: "John 1:1 should rigorously be translated 'the word was with the God [= the Father], and the word was a divine being.'"[557] The Bible has many examples of this same sentence structure. Please notice a few of them:

- (Mark 6:49) "It was a ghost."
- (Mark 11:32) "All verily held John to be a prophet."
- John 4:19) "thou art a prophet."
- (John 8:34)[558] "whoever commits sin is a slave of sin"
- (John 8:44)[559] "He was a murderer from the beginning."
- (John 8:48) "thou art a Samaritan and hast a demon?"
- (John 9:17) "He is a prophet."
- (John 9:24) "this man is a sinner."
- (John 10:1)[560] "the same is a thief and a robber."
- (John 10:13) "he is a hireling."
- (John 10:33)[561] "For a good work ... You, being a man."
- (John 18:35–37) "Am I a Jew ... Art thou a king then?"

Let's investigate one more. Notice John 6:70 "Did not I choose you—the Twelve?" said Jesus, "and even of you one is a devil."[562] Here the Greek literally says: "one a devil is."[563] Here the noun (devil), is not preceded by the definite article, the. This means that the noun can act more like an adjective or quality, rather than a identification of someone. To reflect this most translations place the indefinite article (a) in front of devil, because, even though the indefinite article (a) is not in the Greek, it is implied from the Greek language.

Thus, in this example Jesus was not identifying Judas as 'THE Devil,' (as if Judas was Satan himself); rather he was saying that Judas had the qualities or

---

556 *Jesus Christ and the Gospel of John*, p. 40
557 *McKenzie Dictionary of the Bible*, p. 317
558 NKJVI
559 NIVI
560 KJV
561 NASB
562 WNT
563 NIVI

character of the devil. He was acting, or becoming like the devil; so he was a devil though not 'THE Devil.'

This really is an excellent example to help us understand how the lack of the definite article (the), can cause a noun (in this case devil), to become qualitative rather than to identify a specific individual.

John 1:1 really then should be translated in a way for the reader of God's Word to obtain the clearest understanding. Translating John 1:1 as "a god" or "divine being" is certainly acceptable and makes the most intelligent sense. William Loader, a Bible scholar readily admits this: "It is true, on the most natural reading of the text, that there are two beings here: God and a second who was theos but this second is related to God in a manner which shows that God is the absolute over against which the second is defined. They are not presented as two equal gods."[564]

Many Scholars agree Jesus is 'a' god.

Notice what Bible Scholar William Barclay—who is a Trinitarian writes: "When in Greek two nouns are joined by the verb to be and when both have the definite article, then the one is fully identified with the other; but when one of them is without the article, it becomes more an adjective than a noun, and describes rather the class or the sphere to which the other belongs ... John has no definite article before Theos, God. The Logos, therefore, is not identified as God or with God; the word Theos has become adjectival and describes the sphere to which the Logos belongs ... This passage then (John 1:1) does not identify the Logos and God; It does not say that Jesus was God, nor does it call him God; but it does say that in his nature and being he belongs to the same class as God."[565]

Another source remarks: "another reason to omit the article is if the noun is functioning as a predicate adjective, giving a quality of the subject. That is probably John's main reason for not including it here ... That is John is quite aware that the Word was not all of God. The Father still existed separately after the Word became flesh (Jn 1:14). Thus, 'The Word was God' could be misleading: it could imply that all of God had become incarnate in Jesus. The omission of the article makes this verse mean 'The Word was divine' or 'What God was the Word was.' In other words, the text is indicating that the Word had all of the qualities of God. But this text is also indicating that not all of God was in the Word."[566]

---

564 *The Christology of the Fourth Gospel-Structures and Issues*, p. 155
565 *Jesus as they saw him*, 1962, pp. 21–22
566 *Hard Sayings of the Bible*, Keiser Jr., Davids, Bruce, Brauch, 1996, p. 491

Marianne Thompson, whom we quoted from earlier, points out: "'God' does not connote a 'divine essence' that can be shared by a number of beings, even though there may be a number of beings who are called 'god.' In this sense, *theos* functions slightly differently than does the English term 'deity.' Although we use 'deity' to refer both to God ('the Deity') and to a property (as in the 'deity of Christ'), 'god' does not refer to a characteristic or property the possession of which renders one 'divine.' Rather, 'God' in biblical texts and Jewish thought either refers to the one and only God or, when use of a human figure, relates that figure to God by the exercise of some divine prerogative that is further exercised by God's authority."[567]

Murray Harris notes the translation of John 1:1 needs careful explaining: "The Word was God' suggest that 'the Word' and 'God' are convertible terms, that the proposition is reciprocating. But the Word is neither the Father nor the Trinity. Therefore few will doubt that this time-honored translation needs careful exegesis, since it places a distinctive sense upon a common English word. The rendering cannot stand without explanation."[568]

There are many scholars that agree with Mr. Barclay. Interestingly, most of them are Trinitarians. The New World Translation is certainly not the first to translate John 1:1 as "a god", and certainly will not be the last to do so. I have included for your benefit a collection of translators that have worded John 1:1 other than "and the Word was God."[569] This list consist of over seventy different Bible scholars, most are Trinitarians. They certainly saw something in the Greek that moved them to refrain from the traditional saying. Translating John 1:1 as "a god," "a Divine being" or "God-like," gives the reader a much clearer understanding and is grammatically correct and acceptable when translating from the original Greek to our English.

Just a brief reminder that there are a few scriptures that refer to Jesus as God. Some are Isaiah 9:6 "For a Child hath been born to us, A Son hath been given to us, And the princely power is on his shoulder, And He doth call his name Wonderful, Counsellor, Mighty God, Father of Eternity, Prince of Peace."[570] John 20:28 "And Thomas answered and said to him, 'My Lord and my God.'"[571]

Keep in mind; in these scriptures and others, Jesus is never called Almighty God. This is always reserved for Jehovah, the only true God, as was explained

---

567 *The God of the Gospel of John*, p. 46
568 *Jesus as God*, p. 69
569 List at end of this section
570 YLT
571 YLT

earlier. The following makes this abundantly clear. Genesis 17:1 "And it came to be when Abram was ninety-nine years old, that [Jehovah] appeared to Abram and said to him, "I am El Shaddai [God Almighty]—walk before me and be perfect."[572] Exodus 6:3 "and I appear unto Abraham, unto Isaac, and unto Jacob, as God Almighty; as to My name Jehovah, I have not been known to them."[573]

Lets evaluate even further if Jesus could be considered a false god since Jehovah is the only true God.

Is Jesus Christ a false God?

As has been thoroughly explained, Jehovah alone is referred to as the only true God. Does this mean then that Jesus must be a false God since there is no God but Jehovah? Let us answer this most vital question from the scriptures. It is well known that many teach from the Bible that Jesus is the created Son of God and is subordinate to his Father.[574] Still, as a powerful one who serves as God's spokesman, or Logos, he may well be designated "a god." A number of Bible versions render John 1:1 as saying that the Logos was "a god." For example, *Das Evangelium nach Johannes*, 1979 by Jürgen Becker reads: "und der Logos war bei dem Gott, und ein Gott war der Logos." English translation: "and the Logos was with the God, and a god the Logos was."

Does this conflict with Isaiah 43:10, 11, which says: "YOU ARE MY WITNESSES," DECLARES JEHOVAH! "I have chosen you as my servant so that you can know and believe in me and understand that I am the one who did this. No god was formed before me, and there will be none after me. "I ALONE AM JEHOVAH, AND THERE IS NO SAVIOR BESIDES ME."[575] Noting carefully the context of those words helps a sincere honest hearted Bible student to reach the right conclusion.

The Almighty God Jehovah was contrasting himself with the man-made idols in nations surrounding Israel. Jehovah asks: "To whom, then, will you compare God? What image will you compare him to?"[576] Certainly not an image made by a metalworker or one carved from a tree. Such "gods" could not "stretch out

---

572   *TS*, brackets mine
573   *YLT*
574   Cf. John 14:28; 1 Corinthians 11:3
575   *NSB*, caps his
576   Isaiah 40:18–20 *NSB*; 41:7

the heavens like a canopy, and spread them out like a tent to live in" as Jehovah did.[577]

Further, Jehovah is able to predict the future; surely the idols of the nations cannot "Tell us what the future holds, so we may know that they are gods."[578] This thought is repeated at Isaiah 43:9, where Jehovah states: "All nations have gathered together ... Who among them could have revealed this ... foretold this to us? They should bring their witnesses to prove that they were right."[579]

Rightly, the Almighty says: "I ALONE AM JEHOVAH. THAT IS MY NAME. I WILL NOT GIVE MY GLORY TO ANOTHER! I will not let idols share my praise."[580] Take note it is to graven images and idols that are created and worshipped as gods by man, which is being contrasted with the only true God Jehovah.

So the context establishes that the Almighty is hurling a challenge at the so-called man-made gods of the nations, not at ones that Jehovah has placed via himself as gods by divine agency. Being mere man-made idols with no divine power, they positively are not gods to be worshiped; they are in reality, nothings. These are false gods from the Bible's standpoint.

Brian Holt points out for us: "Jehovah was talking about how there were no man-made gods that could rival Him or equal His power. The Israelites often looked to other gods for help and Jehovah was letting them know there were not others gods that could help them. They were figments of their imagination, manifested in man-made idols."[581] Jehovah continues: "Does there exist a God besides me? No, there is no Rock. I have recognized none. The formers of the carved image are all of them an unreality, and their darlings[582] will be of no benefit."[583] Therefore, the context of Isaiah 43:10 makes it clear that Jesus is not being considered. The "gods" under consideration are the powerless man-made idols of the nations.

---

577 Isaiah 40:21–26; *NSB*
578 Isaiah 41:23; *NSB*
579 *NSB*
580 Isaiah 42:8; *NSB,* caps his
581 *Jesus—God or Son of God?* p. 53
582 These man-made images carved from wood and stone
583 Isaiah 44:8-17

Ones correctly called G/god in the Bible

The word 'God' or 'god' is commonly used regarding a superhuman object of veneration. Recall that in the minds of many people, 'God' means either the supreme being, the Almighty, or a false god, such as an idol. The Bible allows for other usage of the term 'god' that is not restrictive reasoning as is so prevalent in today's religious circle. "There is ample evidence to show that [the OT] conception of monotheism was held in conjunction with a belief in a spiritual world peopled with supernatural and superhuman beings who, in some ways, shared the nature, though not the being, of God."[584]

"The unique character of Yahweh is the answer to the question about monotheism of early Israel. Monotheism as a speculative affirmation is simply not found in the early books of the Bible; the affirmation presupposes a pattern of philosophical thinking which was foreign to the Israelite mind. Nor is there a clear and unambiguous denial of the reality of other Elohim [Gods] before Second Isaiah in the 6th century. This does not mean that early Israel was polytheistic or uncertain about the exclusive character of Yahweh. They perhaps would have said that there are many Elohim but only one Yahweh, and would have denied to any Elohim the unique character which they affirmed of Yahweh."[585]

We can verify this from Psalm 82:1, 2. There the Divine One (Jehovah God) is distinguished from human judges whom the psalmist terms "gods." Jesus himself later referred to this passage. For the reason that Jesus had spoken of Jehovah God as being his Father, some Jews wanted to stone him. To their accusation that he was "making himself a god," Jesus responded: "Has it not been written in your Law, 'I SAID, YOU ARE GODS'? If he called them gods, to whom the word of God came (and the Scripture cannot be broken), do you say of Him, whom the Father sanctified and sent into the world, 'You are blaspheming,' because I said, 'I am the Son of God'?"[586] "The psalmist envisioned God presiding over an assembly of judges. The word gods (elohim) is used here for authorities in Israel, mere men. (Cf. Ps. 45:6; Ex. 21:6; 22:8–9) Some have thought this refers to angels (e.g., the Syriac trans.) in Gods heavenly court. However, the remainder of the psalm clarifies that these are God's representatives who are in authority on earth."[587]

---

584 *The Method and Message of Jewish Apocalyptic*, Russell, p. 235
585 *The Dictionary of the Bible*, McKenzie, p. 317
586 John 10:33–36; *NASB*
587 *The Bible Knowledge Commentary: An Exposition of The Scriptures*, Walvoord, Zuck

Psalm 45:6 reads: "Thy throne, O God,[588] is forever and ever." Here we notice King Solomon being called God. Obviously, the Psalmist is not referring to the King as Almighty God Jehovah. The *NIV Study Bible* remarks on this verse in a footnote: "O God. Possibly the king's throne is called God's throne because he is God's appointed regent. But it is also possible that the king himself is addressed as "god." ... in this Psalm, which praises the king and especially extols his "splendor and majesty" (v. 3), it is not unthinkable that he was called "god" as a title of honor."[589] Others read similarly. "The king in courtly language, is called 'god,' i.e., more than human, representing God to the people."[590]

"Vs. 6a begins lit. "Your throne, O God." Although the Israelite monarch was never regarded as an incarnate god, as were the pharaohs of Egypt, he could be given a divine title because at his coronation he became the son of God by adoption."[591] "In the ancient world kings were commonly accorded divine titles as viceregents of deity or as belonging to a superhuman class."[592]

The Anchor Bible candidly declares: "Psalm 45 was a poem addressed to a king, not to God ... In the Psalm the king was also addressed with reference to his throne and his scepter, but the words could be understood as addressed to God." Then, referring to Hebrews that quotes Psalm 45, it states: "Then, in reference to the Son he spoke of God's throne and the Son's kingdom. Next, in the following verse, he continued to deal with the Son in direct address as indicated by the Psalm quotation ... for the author, the Son was the first-born, the apostle of God, the reflection of God's glory, and the stamp of his nature (1:3, 6), but he was not God himself."[593] Unmistakably, the Bible refers to man and angels as gods, ones appointed to act as agents in Jehovah's behalf.

Conclusively there is only one true Almighty God, even as the apostle Paul wrote: "For even if there are so-called gods whether in heaven or on earth, as indeed there are many gods and many lords, yet for us there is *but* one God, the Father, from whom are all things and we *exist* for Him; and one Lord, Jesus Christ, by whom are all things, and we *exist* through Him."[594] The Lord Jesus Christ is no false god, and no mere man-made idol. "He is the image of the invisible God," and "the radiance of His glory and the exact representation of His

---

588 Referring to King Solomon
589 1995 ed., p. 824
590 *NAB*, 1995 fn, p. 676
591 *The Interpreter's One-Volume Commentary on the Bible*, 1971, p. 276
592 *The Interpreter's Bible*
593 pp. 20-21
594 1 Corinthians 8:5, 6; emphasis theirs

nature."[595] Thus it is fitting for John 1:1 to acknowledge Jesus as "a god," "god-like," or "a Divine Being."

"We notice John's use of the article in three instances. He does not write without care and respect, nor is he unfamiliar with the niceties of the Greek tongue. In some cases he uses the article, and in some he omits it. He adds the article to the Logos, but to the name of God he adds it sometimes only. He uses the article, when the name of God refers to the uncreated cause of all things, and omits it when the Logos is named God ... God on the one hand is Very God (Autotheos, God of Himself); and so the Savior says in His prayer to the Father, 'That they may know Thee the only true God;' but that all beyond the Very God is made God by participation in His divinity, and is not to be called simply God (with the article), but rather God (without the article). And thus the first-born of all creation, who is the first to be with God, and to attract to Himself divinity, is a being of more exalted rank than the other gods beside Him, of whom God is the God, as it is written, 'The God of gods, the Lord, hath spoken and called the earth.' The true God, then, is 'The God,' and those who are formed after Him are gods, images, as it were of Him the prototype."[596]

- Exodus 7:1[597]   "THEN the Lord spoke to Moses saying, Behold I have made thee a god to Pharao, and Aaron thy brother shall be thy prophet."
- Exodus 7:1[598]   "And the Lord spoke to Moses, saying, Behold, I have made thee a god to Pharao ..."
- Exodus 4:16[599] "You will be as God to him"
- Psalm 8:5[600]   "Yet we've so narrowly missed being gods."
- Psalm 97:7[601]   "On your knees, all you gods—worship him!"
- Psalm 138:1   "Before the gods will I sing praises unto thee."
- Psalm 82:1[602]   "He pronounces judgment on the god-like ones."

---

595 Colossians 1:15; Hebrews 1:3; *NASB*
596 *Origen's Commentary on John, Ante-Nicene Fathers*, Vol. 9, 1994, p. 365
597 *LXX*
598 *LXX2*
599 *NASB*
600 *PTM*
601 *PTM*
602 *NSB*

The Sahidic Coptic translation of John 1:1c

I have recently discovered more evidence to support the rendering of John 1:1c as "a god." This evidence is supported by the early second century Sahidic Coptic translation of John 1:1c. Unfortunately I have not, as of yet, been able to give much study and attention to this subject. Nonetheless, what I have found and learned is impressive, and I will share this with you.

Coptic was a language spoken by Christians in Upper Egypt, in the Sahidic dialect. This Coptic, Egyptian language was written using all Greek letters supplemented by seven Egyptian hieroglyphs. The Coptic Gospel of John was translated in 1911 by the hands of Reverend George William Horner. An interesting fact is the Coptic language is similar to English insofar as it contains the definite article (the), as well as the indefinite articles (a, an). This should be of great interest to students of the Bible because the Greek language only supplies the definite article, (the).

I was very interested in how over seventeen hundred years ago, these early Coptic translators understood the meaning of John 1:1c. Their translation literally is: "and was a god the Word." George Horner translated the Coptic Gospel of John in English this way: "In the beginning was being the Word, and the Word was being with God, and [a] God was the Word."[603] There have been several English translations since.

Sadly, but not so surprising, is the fact that this Sahidic Coptic translation of John 1:1c is rarely talked about in debates and seems to be hidden in the Religious world. Despite the foregoing, I was able to locate a couple of comments on this significant subject. "The Coptic New Testament is among the primary resources for the history of the New Testament text. Important as the Latin and Syriac versions may be, it is of far greater importance to know precisely how the text developed in Egypt."[604] Bruce Metzger states in his book: it "is usually considered to be the best text and the most faithful in preserving the original."[605]

"Sahidic was the earlier dialect in Egypt, possibly even the official language of Alexandria long before the spread of Christianity; the Bible was probably translated into this language as early as the middle of the third century ... As regards the New Testament Coptic versions, they are a primary translation of a pure Alexandrian text and thus are quite valuable for text-critical purposes."[606]

---

603 *The Coptic Version of the New Testament in the southern dialect*, 1911
604 *The Text of the New Testament*, Aland, 1987, p. 200
605 *A Textual Commentary on the Greek New Testament*, 2nd ed., 1994, p. 5
606 *The Journey from Texts to Translations*, Wegner, 1999, pp. 247, 248

I would encourage all serious Bible students to inquire more information concerning this subject. Remember, well over seventeen hundred years ago, John 1:1c was translated as many Greek scholars have it today: "the Word was a god."

Final thoughts

A final thought on this is John never gives any indication that he believed Jesus to be the only true God. Rather he writes: "No man hath seen God at any time; the only begotten Son, which is in the bosom of the Father, he hath declared him."[607] "No man hath seen God at any time. If we love one another, God dwelleth in us, and his love is perfected in us."[608] "Not that any man hath seen the Father, save he which is of God, he hath seen the Father."[609]

These harmonize with: "And he said, Thou canst not see my face: for there shall no man see me, and live."[610] This is simply because God is a Spirit Being and invisible, and too superlative to behold with our eyes. "God is a Spirit: and they that worship him must worship him in spirit and in truth."[611] Regarding Moses the Bible states: "By faith he forsook Egypt, not fearing the wrath of the king: for he endured, as seeing him who is invisible."[612]

Ask yourself this question. Has anyone ever seen Jesus Christ? Of course, even his enemies testify that he was real. Then Jesus Christ could not have been the only true God who as scripture testifies to, is invisible and no man has ever seen. To say otherwise would be going beyond God's Word, the Bible, which the trinity chain unquestionably does. The only conclusion can be: "Thank the God of all gods, His love never quits."[613] For "Jehovah is God! Jehovah is God!"[614]

---

607 John 1:18; *KJV*
608 1 John 4:12; *KJV*
609 John 6:46; *KJV*
610 Exodus 33:20; *KJV*
611 John 4:24; *KJV*
612 Hebrews 11:27; *KJV*
613 Psalm 136:2; *PTM*
614 1 Kings 18:39; *NSB*

List of translations regarding John 1:1

JOHN 1:1 RENDERING	TRANSLATOR & AUTHOR	DATE
1- and a God was the Word	The Coptic Version of the Gospel of John in the Sahidic Language. 2nd/3rd century CE (translated in 1911)	2nd cent.
2- The Word of Speech was a God	John Crellius, Latin form of German, The 2 Books of John Crellius Francus, *Touching One God the Father*	1631
3- and the Word was a God	Reijner Rooleeuw, M.D.—*The NT of Our Lord Jesus Christ*, translated from the Greek	1694
4- and was himself a divine person	Edward Harwood, *The NT*, collated with the most approved manuscripts.	1768
5- a God	Joseph Priestly, LL.D., F.R.S.	1794
6- and the Word was a god	*The NT, in an improved version*, upon the basis of Archbishop Newsome's New Translation: with a Corrected text, London	1808
7- the Word was a god	Belsham NT	1809
8- a God	Lant Carpenter, LL.D., in *Unitarianism in the Gospels* London: C. Stower, 156	1809
9- The Word was a God	Abner Kneeland—*The NT in Greek & English*	1822
10- the Logos was a god	John Samuel Thompson, *The Montessoran; or The Gospel History according to the Four Evangelist*, Baltimore; published by the translator	1829
11- a god	Andrews Norton, D.D. in a *Statement of Reasons for Not Believing the Doctrines of Trinitarians*, Cambridge: Brown, Shattuck, and Company, 74	1833

12- [A]s a god the command was	Herman Heinfetter, *A Literal Translation of the NT*	1863
13- and a god was the Word	*The Emphatic Diaglott*, Benjamin Wilson, NY and London, (J21, Interlinear reading)	1864
14- And the logos was a god	Leicester Ambrose Sawyer, *The Final Theology*, Vol. I, NY, NY; M.B. Sawyer and Company	1879
15- [A]nd a God (i.e. a Divine Being) was the Word	Robert Young, LL. D., *Concise Commentary on the Holy Bible*, Grand Rapids: Baker, n.d., 54	1885
16- the Word was Deistic [=The Word was Godly]	Charles A.L. Totten, *The Gospel of History*	1900
17- [A]nd was a god	J.N. Jannaris, *Zeitschrift fur die Newtestameutlich Wissencraft*, (German Periodical)	1901
18- a God	Paul Wernle, Professor Extraordinary of Modern Church History at the University of Basil, *In The Beginnings of Christianity*, Vol. I, *The Rise of Religion*, 16	1903
19- The Word/word was itself a divine Being/being	Curt Stage, The NT	1907
20- it was strongly linked to God, yes itself divine Being/being	Bohmer	1910
21- [A]nd (a) God was the word	*The Coptic Version of the NT*, George W. Horner	1911
22- God of Kind/kind was the Word/word	*Das Neue Testament*, Ludwig Thimme	1919
23- God (of Kind/kind) was the Logos/logos	Baumgarten et al	1920

24- the Word was with *the* God, and the Word was God	*A Plain Translation*, by a student; published by McCarron, Bird & Co., Melbourne	1921
25- the logos was divine	*The NT A Translation* by James Moffatt	1922
26- was face to face with God	*A Centenary Translation*, Helen B. Montgomery	1924
27- [a God/god was the Thought/thought	Holzmann	1926
28- the Word was with Jehovah	*The Christian's Bible*, George LeFevre	1928
29- and the Word was a divine being	La Bible du Centenaire, L'Evangile selon Jean, Maurice Goguel	1928
30- and the Logos was divine (a divine being)	Robert Harvey, D.D., Prof. of NT Language and Literature, Westminster College, Cambridge, in the *Historic Jesus in the NT*, London, Student Movement Christian Press	1931
31- [A]nd the Word was of divine nature	Ernest Findlay Scott, *The Literature of the NT*, NY, Columbia University Press	1932
32- the Word was god	Charles Cutler Torrey	1933
33- and the Word was divine	William Temple, Archbishop of York, *Readings in St. John's Gospel*, London, Macmillin & Co.	1933
34- and the Word was Divine	*The Bible, An American Translation*, J.M. Powis Smith and Edgar J. Goodspeed, Chicago, IL	1935
35- itself a God/god was the Word/word	Friedriche Rittelmeyer	1938

36- And the Word was Divine Ftn reads: "<u>Divine.</u> In the Greek this word is the same As the word translated "God" In verse 1, except the definite article is lacking in this manner the Word is not identified with God."	Ervin Edward Strinfellow (Prof. of NT Language and Literature/Drake University)	1943
37- the Word was of divine kind	Lyder Brun, Norw. Prof. of NT Theology	1945
38- was of divine Kind/kind	Fredrich Pfaefflin, The NT	1949
39- and the Word was a god	*New World Translation of the Christian Greek Scriptures*, Brooklyn, NY	1950
40- godlike Being/being had the Word/word	Albrecht	1957
41- and the Word was a God	*The NT in English*, James Tomaneck	1958
42- When the creation began the Word was already there, and the Word was with God, and the Word was Divine	T.W. Manson, The Beginning of the Gospel	1958
43- the word of the world was a divine being	Smit	1960
44- God (=godlike Being/being) was the Word/word	Menge	1961
45- what God was, the Word was	*New English Bible*	1961
46- and what God was, the Word was	*The New English Bible with the Apocrypha*, Oxford	1961

47- In the beginning was the creative purpose of God. It was with God and was fully Expressive of God [just as wisdom Was with God before creation]	Dymond, E.C. NT, original manuscript	1962
48- the word was a divine being	Jesuit John L. McKenzie wrote in his *Dictionary of the Bible*: "John 1:1 should rigorously be translated …"	1965
49- and the nature of the Word was the same as the nature of God	*The NT Vol. I, The Gospels and the Acts of Apostles A New Translation*, William Barclay	1968
50- and the Word was a god	The Kingdom Interlinear Translation of the Greek Scriptures; based on Westcott and Hort, 1881	1969
51- The Word was with God and shared his nature	*Translator's NT*	1973
52- The Word had the same nature as God	Philip Harner, JBL, Vol. 92	1974
53- The Word was divine	Maximilian Zerwich S.J./Mary Grosvenor	1974
54- and a god (or, of Divine Kind) was the Word	Das Evangelium Nach Johannes, Siefried Shulz Gottangen, Germany	1975
55- and a godlike sort was the Logos	Das Evangelium Nach Johannes, Johannes Schneider Berlin, Germany	1978
56- and a god was the Logos	Das Evangelium Nach Johannes, Jurgen Becker Wurzburg, Germany	1979
57- God (of Kind/kind) was the Logos/logos	As mentioned in William Loader's *The Christology of the Fourth Gospel*, p. 155, cf. p. 260	1980

58- In the beginning there was the Message. The Message was with God. The Message was deity.	*International Bible Translators NT*	1981
59- He was with God and in all like God	Die Bibel in Heutigem Deutsch	1982
60- divine (of the category divinity) was the Logos	Haenchen, Translated by R. Funk	1984
61- In (the) beginning was the Word, and the Word was continually with the (only) God, and the Word was God (the same Character as God).	C. Howard Matheny, Good News From God	1984
62- so the Word was Divine	*The Original NT*, Hugh J. Schonfield	1985
63- a God/god (or: God/god of Kind/kind) was the Word/word	Johannes Schulz, as mentioned in William Loader's *The Christology of The Fourth Gospel*, p. 155, cf. p. 260	1987
64- what God was, the Word was	*Revised English Bible*	1989
65- The divine Word and Wisdom was there with God, and it was what God was	*The Complete Gospels*, Robert W. Funk	1991
66- the Word was face to face with God, and the Word represented God	*The Christian Bible*, an anonymous committee	1991
67- was active with God	*The Pioneer's NT*, Ruth Martin	1992
68- The Divine word and Wisdom was there with God, and it was what God was	*Scholar's Version, The Five Gospels*	1993

69- the Word was a divine Being	J. Madsen, *NT a Rendering*	1994
70- and the Logos was a god	*NT*, a version by Roy Koeblitz	1995
71- and the Word was God***	Footnote reads: Was God: Lack of definite article with "God" in Greek signifies predication rather than identification, *The Catholic Bible/New American Bible*	1995
72- and the Word represented God	*The Christian Bible*, Christian Bible Society	1995
73- the Word was what God was	*NT and Understanding Version*, William Paul	1995
74- and the Word was God***	Footnote reads: or, Deity, Divine (which is actually a better translation, because the Greek definite article is not present before this Greek word.), *Extreme NT*, Tommy Tenney	2001
75- Prior to the world's existence, the Word already existed. The Logos dwelled with God and the Logos was a divine being	*Jesus of the Four Gospels*, Walter Schenck	2001
76- and god[-ly/like] was the Word	Catholic Jesuit Prof. Felix Just, Loyola Marymount University	2001
77- the Word was like God (Greek: Theos: a deity, a god, magistrate, supreme God, God-like)	*New Simplified Bible*, Jim Madsen	2005
78- the Word was a god	*Revised Version, Improved and Corrected*	

79- At first, there was the Word, and the Word grew closer and closer to God until it reflected all of his qualities

An Expressive English Translation, R. Frederick Harrison   nd

Part VI

Extra biblical exegeses: knowledge—John 17:3

Salvation through literature?

There have been many who have suggested to me in my ministry that I do not believe in Jesus Christ. In not so many words they have said: 'Salvation is found in knowing Christ personally, it isn't found in taking in knowledge through literature.' I agree whole-heartedly and sincerely that salvation does not come from literature outside of God's word the Bible. Even knowing the contents of God's word will not give us everlasting life. It is the obeying of God and his Son, even unto death, that would offer each and every one of us that chance of this free gift. John 3:36 clearly declares: "He who believes in the Son has eternal life; but he who does not obey the Son will not see life, but the wrath of God abides on him."[615]

The opposite of disobedience is of course to obey or to listen and walk faithfully with God, no matter what. Works or deeds by themselves will not guarantee life everlasting for anyone. It is faith by works together that is needed to please God well.[616] Of course, all of this is mute if we do not "endure until the end."[617] Never forget dear reader, as explained in this book by Gods word, everlasting life means knowing Christ personally and the only true God Jehovah, Jesus' Father.[618]

John 17:3 mistranslated?

Many have said the *NWT* mistranslates John 17:3 which is: "This means everlasting life, their taking in knowledge of you, the only true God, and of the one whom you sent forth, Jesus Christ." Of course, sincere individuals are focusing in on the words: "Taking in knowledge." First of all, if anyone would hold a critical view of this translation of this verse, please be aware that the 1984 *NWT*

---

615 *NASB*
616 Cf. James 2:18–26
617 Matthew 24:13; *NSB*
618 See John 17:3

Reference Edition renders "ginosko" in a footnote, "to know." This footnote allows the reader the choice. It should also be noted that the first edition of the *NWT*, 1950, also brings out openly in a footnote: "Or, their knowing you." So this brings forth the question: Is Ginosko simply a basic meaning of knowing or does it imply more? Notice the following.

R.F. Weymouth, The NT in Modern Speech reads this way: "And in this consists the Life of the Ages–*in knowing Thee* the only true God and Jesus Christ whom Thou hast sent." But notice Weymouth's footnote to this scripture. "Knowing Or, as the tense implies, 'an ever-enlarging knowledge of.'" Is Weymouth the only translation to say this? Notice what others say about "knowing."

The Emphasized NT, under "Know," p. 270: "Important shades of meaning are; "get to know (John Xvii.3, 7,8,25), "understand"(1Jn. Ii.3, 13; iv 16; v.20) and "approve," "acknowledge,"(Ps. I.6; Mt. vii.23; Ro.vii.29; 2 Tim.ii.19)

Marvin R. Vincent Word studies in the NT, 2 Vol. set by Mcdonald Publishing Company, Mclean, Virginia, p. 495 says: "This is striking that eternal life consists in knowledge, or rather the pursuit of knowledge, since the present tense marks a continuance, a progressive perception of God in Christ. That they may learn to know."

Vines's Expository Dictionary says under 'know': "Ginosko ... signifies to be taking in knowledge, to come to know, recognize, understand, or to understand completely."

The Companion Bible says in it's Appendix 132: "ginnosko=to know (by experience or effort); to acquire knowledge, become acquainted with; hence to come or get to know, learn, perceive."

The Interpreters Bible says: "Eternal life (vs.3), the summon bonum in the Gospel, as the Kingdom of God is in the Synoptics, consist in the knowledge of God yet not the static knowledge of the Gnostics, but a progressive knowledge, "*learning to know thee*"(note the force of the present tense, [in-order-that you-may-be-knowing you])."

The International Critical Commentary, St John, Vol. II, J.H.Bernard, Edinburgh, T&T Clark, 1928, p. 561 says: "The present tense (GINWSKWSIN) marking that continual growth in the knowledge of God which is characteristic of spiritual life, as physical growth is a character of bodily life."

Robertson's Word Pictures of the NT states: "Should know (ginwskwsin). Present active subjunction within a (subject clause), "should keep on knowing."

Raymond Brown—The Gospel according to John, The Anchor Bible, Vol. 29A states: "[John 17:3] 3 ... they know you. Although some witnesses have a future indicative, the best witnesses have a present subjunctive; this implies that the knowledge is a continuing action."

The Complete Bible in Modern English, 1922, *by* Ferrar Fenton reads: "And the eternal life is this: to obtain a knowledge of you the only true God, and the Messiah Whom You have sent."

Although there are many more to quote, you should be able to make out by now that a critical view of the NWT—which would also include the above scholars—of this scripture is not warranted. The basic meaning of ginosko is 'to know,' but this Greek word has various shades of meaning as has been proven. I have never believed that Jesus meant by "taking in knowledge"—with the subjects being God and his Son Jesus Christ—as being a matter of head knowledge only. This would apply to all professing Christians.

The truth is I agree with those on the following expression. Such "knowing" of God and his Son is not just a matter of academic learning, or acquired information. It actually means to recognize the authority of God and his Son, submit to their authority, and live by their authority. I agree wholeheartedly with the following.

Vol.36 of the *World Biblical Commentary Series, John,* 2nd Edition by George R. Beasley-Murry admits: "[John 17:3] As a definition of eternal life it reads remarkably like a confession of faith: the eternal life, of which the gospel speaks, consists in the knowledge of God and of Jesus the Son, the Christ he has sent … the utterance reflects more closely the gospel tradition of Jesus' teaching, above all expressed in Matthew 11:27 … Such knowledge advances beyond the intellect to include relationship and communion," (p. 297). Beautifully stated.

I want to recount one final reminder on this passage. I feel most persons choose to ignore, as has been pointed out consistently in this book, this is a prayer by Jesus to his Father in the heavens. He addresses his Father as the only true God. Hence, there isn't only a need to acknowledge Jesus Christ, but as Jesus himself confesses concerning everlasting life: "knowing you [Father Jehovah], the only true God, and your son Jesus Christ." As true Christians, we stress the need for intimate and personal knowledge of both the Father and his Son. Philippians 2:11 says: "And every tongue should confess that Jesus Christ is Lord, to the glory of God [Jehovah] the Father."[619]

Christians are witnesses of Jesus & Jehovah

It is true that genuine Christians must be witnesses of Jesus Christ. Just before ascending to heaven Jesus said to his disciples: "You are witnesses of these

---

619 *NSB*, brackets mine

things,"[620] and "You will witness about me in Jerusalem and the whole of Judea, in Samaria, and on until you reach the furthermost part of the earth."[621] And in the last book of the Bible it speaks of true Christians as those: "Who keep God's commands and hold firm to the witness of Jesus."[622] Only one group amid the religions of the world, Jehovah's Witnesses, has continued to bear witness to Jesus and Jehovah. This they do because they willingly out of love observe the commandments of God.

However, in the last book of the Bible, its writer the apostle John says concerning himself as a Christian: "John, who bare witness of the word of God, and of the testimony of Jesus Christ."[623] A true Christian has to bear witness of both God and of his Christ or messiah. Let no one forget or hide the fact that the title Christ or messiah means 'anointed one.' To be an anointed one there has to be an anointer or one who anoints. So, in order to bear full witness concerning Jesus Christ, we also have to bear witness to the one who anointed Jesus and made him the Christ. We have to bear witness to the anointer as well as the anointed one.

Who anointed Jesus and with what? Jesus himself tells us who anointed him. When, in the Jewish synagogue, the book of Isaiah was handed to him—more than likely a copy of the Septuagint version—he turned to chapter sixty-one, verses one and two, and read them as follows: "The Spirit of the Lord Jehovah is upon me; because Jehovah hath anointed me to preach good tidings unto the meek; he hath sent me ... to proclaim the year of Jehovah's favor."[624] After reading those words, in which the Hebrew name of God occurs as YHWH, Jesus opened up his sermon to the Jews, saying: "To-day hath this scripture been fulfilled in your ears." Thus Jesus publicly said that the Lord Jehovah had anointed him with holy spirit.

Jesus—while living on the earth—did not anoint himself with holy spirit from heaven. This is where his: "God and Father" resided.[625] Three and a half years later Jesus baptized his disciples with holy spirit from heaven at Pentecost 33CE; but Jesus did not baptize himself with spirit. The Lord Jehovah did this and Jesus said that the Lord Jehovah was the one who sent him to preach as well as to "proclaim the year of Jehovah's favor." So Jesus and Jehovah are not the same indi-

---

620 Luke 24:48; *NSB*
621 Acts 1:8; *VC*
622 Revelation 12:17 *TM*; cf. Revelation 1:9, 10; 19:10; 20:4
623 Revelation 1:1–2
624 Cf. Luke 4:17–19
625 Cf. John 20:17

vidual. Jehovah is the sender and Jesus is the sent one. Jehovah is the anointer and Jesus is the anointed one; the messiah.

Jesus was all the time bearing witness of his anointer; who is the Lord Jehovah. Jesus was born under the obligation to be a witness of Jehovah, for by the Jewish virgin girl Mary, Jesus was born into the very nation to whom God by his prophet Isaiah said: "Ye are my witnesses, saith Jehovah, and my servant whom I have chosen."[626] On trial for his life before the Roman Governor Pontius Pilate, Jesus said: "To this end have I been born, and to this end am I come into the world, that I should bear witness unto the truth."[627] (John 18:37, *AS*) Bear witness to whose truth? In his last prayer with his apostles Jesus said to God in heaven: "Sanctify them in the truth: thy word is truth." It was the truth of his God and Father Jehovah.

There was every reason why the apostle John—in the last book of the Bible—should call Jesus Christ: "The faithful witness, the firstborn of the dead, and the ruler of the kings of the earth … and he made us to be a kingdom, to be priests unto his God and Father."[628] And the apostle John adds: "These things saith the Amen, the faithful and true witness, the beginning of the creation of God."[629]

Of who was Jesus Christ: "The faithful and true witness?" As a result of his birth into the nation—to whom the words of Isaiah 43:10-12 were directed—Jesus Christ was obligated to be a witness of Jehovah. He lived up to this obligation, for all the written record as to what he said and as to all the Hebrew Scriptures that he quoted, proves that Jesus was a witness of his Father. If the question were today directed to Jesus Christ, of which God are you a witness? He would reply: 'Of Jehovah.' He was—and still is in heaven—the: "Faithful and true witness" of "his God and Father."[630] The answer to the above title question should now be obvious. True Christians are to be witnesses of Jehovah and Jesus Christ as the first century Christians were.

---

[626] Isaiah 43:10
[627] John 18:37
[628] Revelation 1:5–6
[629] Revelation 3:14; see also *KJV*
[630] Revelation 1:5–6

Part VII

Extra biblical exegeses: The cross—a Christian symbol?

Spiritually trained mind must lead us

When I discuss the background of the cross, I want you to recognize my awareness of many individuals having great emotional attachment to this seemingly Christian symbol. I at one time for years wore a cross necklace as a symbol of my faith. However, we need to in addition, heed God's counsel found at Jeremiah 17:9 "The heart is more deceitful than all else,"[631] and "he who trusts in his own heart is a fool."[632] Therefore, we must be careful that our emotional allegorical heart does not lead our spiritually taught mind in what is acceptable worship to God.

I certainly do not have any intention to offend anyone by the information I present in this section. Unfortunately, not offending someone today would seem to be an impracticable task. I only wish to promote truth and facts as I have found through my research for accurate knowledge of God's word. Please keep in mind that according to scripture we are to: "Worship the Father in spirit and in truth anywhere."[633]

God pronounces with clarity that any who love and practice lies will experience everlasting cutting off.[634] We are also admonished: "Don't believe everything you hear. Carefully weigh and examine what people tell you. Not everyone who talks about God comes from God. There are a lot of lying preachers loose in the world."[635] Why? 1 Timothy 4:1 affirms: "The Spirit explicitly says that some will fall away from the faith (truth) in later times. Spirits and doctrines of demons will seduce them."[636] Every Christian has a responsibility to adhere to truth; especially when it relates to pure worship of the true God. Many pagan practices—not just

---

631 *NASB*
632 Proverbs 28:26; *NASB*
633 John 4:23–24 *VC*; cf. John 8:31–32; Joshua 24:14; 1 Samuel 12:24; Psalm 25:5; 43:3; 86:11; Isaiah 38:3; Mark 7:7–8; Colossians 2:8
634 Cf. Revelation 21:8, 27; 22:15
635 1 John 4:1–2 *TM*; cf. 2 Corinthians 13:5
636 *NSB*; cf. 2 Timothy 4:3–4

the trinity chain—have filtered their way through the centuries to become manmade traditions, which are not biblical teachings.[637]

I will provide sufficient facts to verify why many believe the cross is one such practice and teaching that should be avoided by anyone claiming to be Christian. I ask with my whole heart to please listen, meditate, and pray about the information I present. Ask yourself as you read through: 'is the 'cross' in harmony with all scripture?' 'Does God approve of it and it's origin?' 'Is what I have been taught through my faith in harmony with God's thoughts on the 'cross'?'[638] Indeed, these are questions that demand an answer. Of course, the answers must be taken from the Bible. Please consider the following.

Meaning of the word cross

Most Bible translations say Christ was 'crucified' rather than 'impaled'. This is because of the common belief that the torture instrument which he was hung and died upon was a 'cross'—made of two pieces of wood—instead of a single pale, tree, or stake.

The Bible does not use any form of the word 'cross', (Latin crux, made of two pieces of wood rather than one). If the two beam cross were used, God certainly would have made sure it was included in his inspired word. It is of great interest that we find the Bible uses only two words to describe the instrument that Christ died on. Most translators choose to replace these two words with the Latin word crux, cross. The only two words the Bible uses are *STAUROS and XYLON*, (Stauros is used 27 times and xylon is used 5 times).

What are the definitions of these words used to describe Christ instrument of death? Notice what *W.E. Vines Complete Expository Dictionary of Old and New Testament Words* has to say: "denotes, primarily, an upright pale or stake. On such malefactors were nailed for execution. Both the noun and verb stauroo, to fasten to a stake or pale, are originally to be distinguished from the ecclesiastical form of a two beamed cross."[639]

Another source, *Douglas' New Bible Dictionary*, 1985, under cross, p. 253 states: "The Greek word for cross (stauros; verb stauroo ...) means primarily an upright stake or beam and secondarily a stake used as an instrument for punishment and execution."

---

637 Cf. Matthew 15:3; Mark 7:13; Colossians 2:8
638 Cf. Isaiah 55:8–9; Galatians 1:8
639 P. 138, under cross

The book: *Dual Heritage—The Bible and The British Museum* states: "It may come as a shock to know there is no word such as cross in the Greek of the New Testament. The word translated cross is always the Greek word [Stauros'] meaning a stake or upright pale. The cross was not originally a Christian symbol; it is derived from Egypt and Constantine."[640]

Although A.E. Knoch uses "cross" in the text of the *Concordant Literal Version*, in the Keyword Concordance under "cross" he says: "An upright stake or pale, without any crosspiece, now, popularly, cross." Under "crucify" he adds: "Drive a stake into the ground, fasten on a stake, impale, now popular usage, crucify, though there was no crosspiece."

The Imperial Bible Dictionary acknowledges: "The Greek word for cross is, [stauros], properly signified a stake, an upright pole, or piece of paling, on which anything might be hung, or which might be used in impaling, [fencing in], a piece of ground ... Even amongst the Romans the crux, [from which our cross is derived], appears to have been originally an upright pole."[641]

The book: *Come Out of Her My People* by C.J. Koster, pp. 29–30, 34 says: "Another "later rendering," a tradition of the Church which our fathers have inherited, was the adoption of the word "cross" and "crucify." These words are nowhere to be found in the Greek of the New Testament. These words are mistranslations, a "later rendering," of the Greek word stauros and stauroo ... In spite of this strong evidence and proof that the word stauros should have been translated "stake", and the verb stauroo to have been translated "impale", almost all the common versions of the scriptures persist with the Latin Vulgate's crux (cross), a fallacious "later" rendering of the Greek stauros ... Let us rather use the true rendering of the scriptural words stauros and stauroo, namely "stake" and "impale", and eliminate the un-scriptural "cross" and "crucify.""

The synonym for stauros is xylon meaning: "Wood, a piece of wood, anything made of wood, is used with the rendering tree ... (b) of the cross, the tree being the stauros, the upright pale or stake to which Romans nailed those who were thus to be executed."[642]

The Non-Christian Cross by John Denham Parsons, 1896, pp. 15, 17 states: "Now the Greek word which in Latin versions of the New Testament is translated as crux, and in English versions is rendered as cross, i.e., the word stauros, seems to have, at the beginning of our era, no more meant a cross than the English word stick means a crutch ... this last named kind of stauros, which was admittedly that

---

640   See also *Strong's* and *Young's Analytical Concordance*
641   Edited by P. Fairbairn, 1874, Vol. I, p. 376
642   W.E. Vine's *Expository Dictionary of Old and New Testament Words*, p. 642

to which Jesus was affixed, had in every case a cross-bar attached, is untrue; that it had in most cases, is unlikely; that it had in the case of Jesus, is unproven."

A Greek-English Lexicon by Liddell and Scott, 1968, pp. 1191, 1192 says: "Wood cut and ready for use, firewood, timber, etc ... piece of wood, log, beam, post ... cudgel, club, ... stake on which criminals were impaled ... of live wood, tree."

History of The Cross by Henry Dana Ward, p. 14 says regarding Zulon [xylon]: "Zulon and stauros are alike the single stick, the pale, or the stake, neither more nor less, on which Jesus was impaled, or crucified ... Neither stauros nor zulon ever mean two sticks joining each other at any angle, either in the New Testament or in any other book."

I would like to make a special note here concerning the fact that Luke, Peter, and Paul also used xylon as a synonym for stauros which gives added evidence that Jesus was impaled on an upright stake without a cross beam of any kind; for that is what xylon means.[643] As a side point, xylon appears in the Greek Septuagint at Ezra 6:11 where it speaks of a single beam or timber; on which a lawbreaker was to be impaled.

"It should be noted, however, that these five references of the Bible to the execution of Jesus as having been carried out by his suspension upon either a tree or a piece of timber set in the ground, in no wise convey the impression that two pieces of wood nailed together in the form of a cross is what is referred to. Moreover, there is not, even in the Greek text of the Gospels, a single intimation in the Bible to the effect that the instrument actually used in the case of Jesus was cross-shaped. Had there been any such intimation in the twenty-seven Greek works referring to Jesus, which our Church selected out of a very large number and called the "New Testament," the Greek letter chi, which was cross-shaped, would in the ordinary course would have been referred to."[644] Please pay careful attention to the following.

The book: *The Non-Christian Cross* by J.D. Parsons, 1896, says: "There is not a single sentence in any of the numerous writings forming the New Testament, which, in the original Greek, bears even indirect evidence to the effect that Stauros used in the case of Jesus was other than an ordinary Stauros; much less to the effect that it consisted, not of one piece of timber, but of two pieces nailed together in the form of a cross ... It is not a little misleading upon the part of our teachers to translate the word Stauros as cross when rendering the Greek documents of the Church into our native tongue, and to support that action by putting cross in our

---

643   Cf. Acts 5:30; 10:39; 13:29; Galatians 3:13; 1 Peter 2:24
644   *The Non-Christian Cross*, Parsons, 1896, pp. 19–20

lexicons as the meaning of Stauros without carefully explaining that that was at any rate not the primary meaning of the word in the days of the Apostles, did not become it's primary signification till long afterwards, and became so then, if at all, only because, despite the absence of corroborative evidence, it was for some reason or other assumed that the particular Stauros upon which Jesus was executed had that particular shape."[645] He continues saying: "no less than four different Greek words are translated in our Bibles as meaning "crucify" or "Crucified," and that not one of the four meant "Crucify" or "crucified."[646]

Paul Wilhelm Schmidt—who was a professor at the University of Basel—in his work *Die Geschichte Jesu* (The History of Jesus),[647] made a detailed study of the Greek word stauros. On p. 386 of his work he said: "[Stauros] means every upright standing pale or tree trunk."

The Latin Dictionary by Lewis and Short gives as the basic meaning of crux: "a tree, frame, or other wooden instruments of execution, on which criminals were impaled or hanged."

The Companion Bible,[648] in the appendixes says: "Homer uses the Stauros of an ordinary pole or stake, or a single piece of timber. And this is the meaning and usage of the word throughout the Greek classics. It never means two pieces of timber placed across one another at any angle, but always of one piece alone. Hence the use of the word Xylon [which means a timber] in connection with the manner of our Lord's death, and rendered tree in Acts 5:30, 10:39, 13:29; Gal. 3:13; 1 Peter 2:24 ... There is nothing in the Greek New Testament even to imply two pieces of timber ... The evidence is thus complete, that the Lord was put to death upon an upright stake, and not on two pieces of timber placed at any angle."

The Encyclopedia Britannica, 11th edition says: "Lipsius and other writers speak of the single upright stake to which criminals were bound as a cross, and to such a stake the name crux simplex has been applied." Yes, it was this simple stake that Jesus was suspended on with his hands nailed above his head.

Daz Kreuz und die Kreuzigung (The Cross and the Crucifixion)[649] says: "Trees were not everywhere available at the places chosen for public execution. So a simple beam was sunk into the ground. On this the outlaws, with hands raised upward and often also with their feet, were bound or nailed.' After submitting

---

645 PP. 23–24
646 P. 24
647 Vol. II, 1904, pp. 386–394
648 P. 186
649 Fulda, Breslau, 1878, p. 109

much proof, Fulda concludes on pp. 219, 220: 'Jesus died on a simple death-stake: In support of this there speak (a) the then customary usage of this means of execution in the Orient, (b) Indirectly the history itself of Jesus' sufferings and (c) many expressions of the early church fathers." Fulda also points out that some of the oldest illustrations of Jesus impaled depict him on a simple pole.

P.W. Schmidt wrote on pp. 387–389 concerning the execution of punishment of Jesus: "Besides scourging, according to the Gospel accounts, only the simplest form of Roman crucifixion comes into consideration for the infliction of punishment upon Jesus, the hanging of the unclad body on a stake, which, by the way, Jesus had to carry or drag to the execution place to intensify this disgraceful punishment ... Anything other than a simple hanging is ruled out by the wholesale manner in which this execution was often carried out: 2000 at once by Varus (Jos. Ant. XVII 10.10), by Quadratus (Jewish Wars II 12.6), by the Procurator Felix (Jewish Wars II 15.2), by Titus (Jewish Wars VII.1)."

Again, *History of The Cross-by Henry Dana Ward* [650] says the following in regards to the way in which criminals were executed and why: "Crosses must have been commonly of the simplest form, "because they were used in such marvelous numbers. Of Jews alone, Alexander Jannaeus crucified 800, Varus, 2000, Hadrian, 500 a day; and the gentle Titus so many that there was no room for the crosses, nor crosses for the bodies.".-Smith's Dict. of the Bible. Alexander the Great crucified 2000 Tyrians, and both the Sogdian king and people, for their brave defence of their several countries. And Augustus crucified 600 Sicilians. Under such circumstances, men could not be particular about the form of the stauros, or the manner of applying it. Some were nailed, others were tied hand and foot and lifted up on the stauros; others on the tree. Others, also, were spiked to the earth with the stauros driven through their body, and others were spitted on it. Thus the crucifying or impaling was executed in the cruelest manner, and the sufferers were left to rot unburied, or to be devoured by the birds and beasts. In difference to the Mosaic law, the bodies in Judea were removed and buried, and the crosses were burned, to avoid legal defilement by the accursed thing, as it was written: "His body shall not remain all night upon the tree, but in any wise thou shalt bury him that day (for he that is hanged is accursed of God); that the land might not be defiled" (Duet. XXI. 23)."

The Anchor Bible Dictionary [651] says: "Under the Roman Empire, crucifixion normally included a flogging beforehand. At times the cross was only one vertical stake."

---

650 Pp. 16–17
651 1997 under cross

The Erdman's Bible Dictionary[652] says: "Use of an upright stake as an instrument of torture and execution attained particular significance as the culmination of Christ's persecution and thus as a symbol of atonement for mankind."

I consider it apparent by now the scriptures and many historical references demonstrate Jesus to have been impaled on a single stake, tree, or pale—without a cross beam at any angle. Of course this being in the Greek word form of stauros, xylon. Obviously many scholars acknowledge this also. How sad it is that the ruler and god of this world, Satan, as well as his "ministers," have blinded the majority of mankind to the light of this truth.[653]

---

652 1989 under cross, crucifixion
653 Cf. 2 Corinthians 4:4; 11:14–15; Luke 4:5–6; John 12:31; 14:30; 16:11; Ephesians 2:2; 1 John 5:19; Revelation 12:9; Acts 26:17–18

Origin of the cross

The very next logical question we must ask ourselves then is: 'where did the cross originate?' Please, again let us take a close look at what *W.E. Vines Expository Dictionary* has to say on p. 138 under cross: "The shape of the latter [cross], had its origin in ancient Chaldea, and was used as the symbol of the god Tammuz [being in the shape of the mystic Tau, the initial of his name], in that country and in adjacent lands, including Egypt. By the middle of the 3rd cent. A.D. the Churches had either departed from, or had travestied, certain doctrines of the Christian faith. In order to increase the prestige of the apostate ecclesiastical system pagans were received into the Churches apart from regeneration by faith, and were permitted largely to retain their pagan signs and symbols. Hence the Tau or T, in its most frequent form, with the cross-piece lowered, was adopted to stand for the "cross" of Christ. As for the Chi, or X, which Constantine declared he had seen in a vision leading him to champion the Christian faith, that letter was the initial of the word "Christ" and had nothing to do with "The Cross [for xulon, "a timber beam, a tree," as used for the stauros, see under TREE]."

In regards to this 'vision' that Constantine supposedly saw: "According to Voltaire, some authors pretend that Constantine saw this vision at Besancon, others at Cologne, some at Treves, and others at Troyes. Cardinal Newman is silent on the matter, but he allows that there were disputes among early Christian writers whether the apparition was that of the monogram without the cross, or the cross without the monogram. But more serious difficulties remain. Constantine's "vision" is not mentioned by a single Father of the fourth and fifth centuries, none of whom appears to have been acquainted with the work in which Eusebius relates it. Eusebius himself says nothing about it in his *Ecclesiastical History*, written twelve years after the event. Why did Eusebius first hear of it in a private conversation with Constantine twenty-five years after it occurred, when it was seen by the whole army as well as by the emperor? And what necessity was there for Constantine to "confirm with an oath" a fact of such publicity?"[654]

We must also remember the cross was adopted as a 'Christian' symbol[655] after it was adopted by Emperor Constantine—who continued to be a sun worshipper—and the cross was the symbol of the sun-god Sol. "Not till after Constantine and his Gaulish warriors planted what Eusebius the Bishop of Caesarea and other Christians of the century in question describe as a cross, within the walls of the

---

654 *Crimes of Christianity: Christ to Constantine*, Foote, Wheeler, 1887, Vol. I
655 312CE

162   The Trinity's Weak Links Revealed

Eternal City as the symbol of their victory, did Christians ever set on high a cross-shaped trophy of any description."[656]

The New Catholic Encyclopedia[657] says: "The representation of Christ's redemptive death on Golgotha does not occur in the symbolic art of the first centuries. The early Christians, influenced by the Old Testament prohibition of graven images, were reluctant to depict even the instrument of the Lord's Passion."

It is interesting to note here the similarities between the Catholic Pope parading down the street holding the old crucifix of his on a stick and what the Egyptian priest did. Notice what the book *The Worship of the Dead* [658] had to say on this: "The cross in the form of the 'Crux Anasta' ... was carried in the hands of the Egyptian priests and Pontiff kings as the symbol of their authority as priest of the Sun god and was called 'the Sign of Life.'"

The Ante-Nicene Fathers[659] says at the beginning of the third century Minucius Felix[660] wrote to the pagans on Octavius and revealed the attitude that early Christians had toward the cross up to that time. He said: "Crosses, moreover, we neither worship nor wish for. You, indeed, who consecrate gods of wood, adore wooden crosses perhaps as parts of your gods ... Your victorious trophies not only imitate the appearance of a simple cross, but also that of a man affixed to it."

History of The Cross[661] says: "Only fifty years after Cyprian, the custom of introducing symbols of man's invention into the sanctuaries of worship prevailed so far as to cause the council of Eliberis, Spain (A.D. 305), in their canon 38, to declare, "That pictures or likenesses ought not to be allowed in the churches, lest the object adored and worshipped should be represented on the walls."[662]

AntePacem-Archaeological Evidence of Church Life Before Constantine[663] has this to say: "The sign of the cross has been a symbol of great antiquity, present in every known culture. It's meaning has eluded anthropologist, though its use in funerary art could well point to a defense against evil. On the other hand, the famous crux anasta of Egypt, depicted coming from the mouth, must refer to life or breath. The universal use of the sign of the cross makes more poignant the

---

656   *The Non-Christian Cross*, Parsons, p. 28
657   1967,Vol. IV, p. 486
658   Garnier, 1904, p. 226
659   Vol. 4, p. 191
660   An early Church Father
661   Ward, p. 38
662   Rock's Heir, p. 374
663   Snyder, 1985, p. 27

striking lack of crosses in early Christian remains, especially any specific reference to the passion event, cannot be found prior to the time of Constantine."

The Cross-In Ritual, Architecture, and Art[664] states: "It is strange, yet unquestionably a fact, that in ages long before the birth of Christ, and since then in lands untouched by the teaching of the Church, the Cross has been used as a sacred symbol ... The Greek Bacchus, the Tyrian Tammuz, the Chaldean Bel, and the Norse Odin, were all symbolized to their coteries by a cruciform device."

The Ancient Church[665] remarks: "From the most remote antiquity the cross was venerated in Egypt and Syria; it was held in equal honor by the Buddhist of the East; and, what is still more extraordinary, when the Spaniards first visited America, the well-known sign was found among the objects of worship in the idol temples of Anahuac. It is also remarkable that, about the commencement of our era, the pagans were wont to make the sign of a cross upon the forehead in the celebration of some of their sacred mysteries."

Rev. Alexander Hislop in his book *The Two Babylons*,[666] frankly calls the cross: "This pagan symbol ... the Tau, the sign of the cross, the indisputable sign of Tammuz, the false messiah ... the mystic Tau of the Chaldeans [Babylonians] and Egyptians-the true original form of the letter T—the initial of the name Tammuz ... the Babylonian cross was the recognized emblem of Tammuz."

The Encyclopedia Britannica says: "In the Egyptian Churches, the cross was a pagan symbol of life borrowed by the Christians and interpreted in the pagan manner."

Art and Architecture (Early Christian Art), The Anchor Bible Dictionary[667] says: "One critical scene (the crucifixion of Jesus) and its accompanying symbol (the cross) did not occur in early Christian art. Probably the first scene of Jesus' suffering occurs on the Vatican's Passion sarcophagus, carved ca. mid-4th century."

The book *Come Out of Her My People*[668] says: "Why then was the "cross' [crux] brought into messianic worship? Again, historical evidence points to Constantine as the one who had the major share in uniting Sun-worship and the Messianic Belief. Constantine's famous vision of "the cross superimposed on the sun," in the year 312, is usually cited. Writers, ignorant of the fact that the cross was not to be found in the New Testament Scriptures, put much emphasis on this vision as the onset of the so-called "conversion" of Constantine. But, unless Constantine had

---

664 Tyack, 1900, p. 1
665 Killen, p. 316
666 Pp. 197–205
667 Vol. 1, p. 461
668 Koster, pp. 30–33

been misguided by the Gnostic Manichean half-Christians, who indeed used the cross in their hybrid religion, this version of the cross superimposed on the sun could only be the same old solar cross, the symbol of the Sun-deity, the center of cosmic religion, the astrological religion of Babylon. The fact remains: that which Constantine saw, is nowhere to be found in scripture. We read in the book of Johannes Geffcken, The Last Days of Greco-Roman Paganism, p. 319, "that even after 319 A.D. the coins of Constantine show an even-armed cross as a symbol for the Sun-god." Many scholars have doubted the "conversion" of Constantine because of the wicked deeds that he did afterwards, and because of the fact that he only requested to be baptized on his death-bed many years later, in the year 337. So, if the vision of the cross impressed him, and was used as a rallying symbol, it could not have been used in honour of our Saviour, because Constantine continued paying homage to the Sun-deity and to one of the Sun-deity's symbols, the cross. This continuation of Sun worship by Constantine is attested of by his persistent use of images of the Sun-deity on his coins that were issued by him up to the year 323. Secondly, the fact of his motivation to issue his Sunday-keeping edict in the year 321, which was not done in honour of our Saviour, but was done because of the "venerable day of the Sun," as the edict read, is proof of his continued allegiance to Sol Invictus. Further proof of its pagan origin is the recorded evidence of the Vestal Virgins of pagan Rome having the cross hanging on a necklace, and the Egyptians doing it too, as early as the 15th century B.C.E. The Buddhist, and numerous other sects of India, also used the sign of the cross as a mark on their followers' heads. The cross thus widely worshipped, or regarded as a 'sacred symbol,' was the unequivocal symbol of Bacchus, the Babylonian Messiah, for he was represented with a head-band covered with crosses."

One translation of the Bible, *The 21st Century New Testament*[669] says: "The Greek term signifies an upright stake on which criminals were executed, with no suggestion of a cross-beam. In the Latin versions the term 'crux' was used, but according to Livy of the 1st century B.C., the word meant no more than an upright stake; it was only later that the crux came to mean a cross. Josephus relates how 2,000 were crucified at one time [Antiquities book 17; 10:10] hardly practicable if crosses had to be made for each one. There are Greek words, which denote a cross, but none of these appear in any of the four gospel accounts of Jesus' execution. At Galatians 3:13 Paul refers to the instrument as 'a timber' [A.V. a tree] a reference to the upright stake on which bodies of criminals were hanged under the Mosaic Law [Duet. 21:22], and which Jesus fulfilled by his death. Some have contended that the Romans did use crosses for execution at

---

669 *VC*, under appendix

that time although Livy refutes this. Even if this were so, the Romans were also careful to observe local customs as far as possible to avoid unnecessarily upsetting the populace, and so likely would have modified their method to conform to the Jewish practice. A rough upright stake would be in any case less trouble to produce than a hewn cross with a joint strong enough to bear the weight of a man. Christians are sometimes disturbed to learn that the cross, considered for centuries as a Christian symbol, had its origin long before Christ and was actually used in pagan mythology. It was the symbol of the god Tammuz, and Bacchus, and the Egyptian Osiris. It was worshipped by the Celtic druids and worn on necklaces by the Vestal Virgins of Rome ... As the Greek text shows, Christ was not executed on a Cross, that symbol can be regarded for what it is, a pagan corruption of Christian worship introduced in the early centuries of our common era. Thus in harmony with 2 Corinthians 6:15 although long cherished, it is something that Christians should shun."

Adoration and worship of the cross

The next point that must not be overlooked is the adoration, and worship of this symbol, the cross. I'm sure you will agree with me that many peoples and faiths use the figure of the cross as an object of worship; and where that happens we can honestly say we are no better than the pagans, for these did the very same things. Let's take a look at a biblical account, which, I feel really drives home the point of our not having anything to do with the pagan cross.

The account is found in the book of Ezekiel 8:1-17. As we briefly review this we should notice God's thought and feelings on the matter. Ezekiel is having a spiritual dream where Jehovah takes him to his very own place of what is suppose to be the place of pure worship. What does he show Ezekiel? Among other disgusting things, he finds Israelite women sitting and weeping over the god Tammuz.

You may recall from the above information that the symbol for this god was the cross! According to *World Mythology and Legend*[670] agrees saying: "In Canaan Tammuz was called Adoni (my lord), and a great festival, celebrating his death and resurrection, was observed.... wailing women tore their hair and lacerated their breast during the seven days of the festival." He also adds this: "The Hebrew Prophet Ezekiel tells how in the year 592 B.C., in a mystic vision he saw the iniquity of the Jewish inhabitants of Jerusalem. In particular, he relates how he was brought to the north gate of the house of the Lord; and behold, there sat

---

670 Mercatante, 1988, p. 607

women weeping for the god Tammuz (8.14). The prophet thus, unintentionally, witnesses to the wide spread influence of the cult of the Mesopotamian god Tammuz and to a notable feature of that cult. The Jewish women were performing a ritual lamentation for the death of Tammuz, which was annually mourned at the summer solstice when the year begins to wane." This was in direct violation of God's law at Leviticus 19:28, which reads: "Never slash your body to mourn the dead … I am Jehovah."[671]

God feels disgusted by this[672] and he says they have offended him.[673] We really need to ask ourselves: 'Does God truly approve of the use of this pagan cross in true worship today?' In Malachi 3:6 we read: "For I, the LORD, do not change."[674] Since God has not changed the answer is obviously no.

Recall please, the words of Jesus at Mark 12:30: "You should love Jehovah your God with all your heart, and with all your being (with every breath you take) (your life), with your entire mind and with all your strength. (Deuteronomy 6:4)."[675] Now think of this, if we are involving in our worship to God a practice that is of pagan origin; do we truly love him with our whole heart, strength, and mind? Are we worshipping him with "spirit and truth?"[676] These are vital questions that deserve serious meditation and prayer.[677]

In his book, *The History of The Cross*, Henry Dana Ward mentions a few groups of Christians in the Middle Ages that recognized the contempt of using the cross in worship. "The Bogomils clearly considered the cross not as an item to be worshipped, but one to be despised. They posed the problem in the form of a rhetorical question, asking, "If someone killed the king's son with a piece of wood, do you think the king would regard that weapon as holy?" It was what killed the savior Christ, so there was certainly no need to worship it. They called it the "adversary of God" and considered it of the devil. In fact, all icons were taboo to the Bogomils, as they were to early Christians … The Waldenses had similar beliefs. The Cathars also rejected the cross as a symbol of worship. They felt it should inspire horror, not veneration. They argued that if a roof beam falls

---

671 Cf. Deuteronomy 14:1; Jeremiah 16:6; 41:5
672 See verses 13–14
673 See verse 17
674 *NASB*; cf. Hebrews 1:17
675 *NSB*
676 John 4:23–24
677 Cf. Proverbs 3:5–6; 1 Timothy 4:1; 1 John 4:1

and crushes the son of a household, the beam is not set up in a place of honor and worshipped."[678]

Mr. Ward makes another interesting observation on pp. 20, 21: "For though Aaron and all Israel made of their ornaments the golden calf, and danced, feasted, and shouted before it, "Behold, these be thy gods, O Israel, which brought thee up out of the land of Egypt;" and though the chief Pontiff and all Christendom make an ornament of the image of the cross, and lift it in reverence and worship, on their person, on the church spire, and on the communion-table in the house of God, and say, "Behold the cross of thy Lord and Saviour! Behold, these be thy Saviour, O Israel, which redeemed thee from the bondage of corruption!" the images alike are idols—the image of the calf and the image of the cross, both are a pretence and an abomination."

The Two Babylons[679] says: "In the Papal system, it is well known the sign of the cross and the image of the cross are all in all. No prayer can be said; no worship engaged in, no step almost can be taken, without the frequent use of the sign of the cross. The cross is looked upon as the grand charm, as the great refuge in every time of danger, in every hour of temptation, as the infallible preservative from al the powers of darkness. The cross is adored with all homage only due to the Most High,—and for anyone to call it, in the hearing of a genuine Romanist, by the scriptural term, 'the accursed tree,' is a mortal offense.... The same sign of the cross that Rome now worships, was used in the Babylonian mysteries, was applied by paganism to the same magic purposes, was honored with the same honors. That which is now called the Christian cross was originally no Christian emblem at all, but was the mystic Tau of the Chaldeans and Egyptians. That mystic Tau was marked in baptism on the foreheads of those initiated in the mysteries, and was used in every variety of way, as a most sacred symbol.... The vestal virgins of Rome wore it suspended from their necklaces, as the nuns do now. The Egyptians did the same, and many of the barbarous nations also ... There is hardly a pagan tribe where the cross has not been found. The pagan Celts worshiped the cross long before the incarnation and death of Christ (*Crabb's Mythology*, p. 193). Though not an object of worship among Buddhists, the cross is a favorite emblem and device among them ... Compare this language with the language of Rome applied to the cross, and it will be seen how exact is the coincidence."

"The first form of that which is called the Christian cross, found there on Christian monuments, is the unequivocal pagan Tau, or Egyptian 'sign of life.'

---

678 The foreword, p. 3, pars. 3, 4
679 Hislop, pp. 288–294

The design of it's first employment on their sepulchers, therefore, could have no reference to the crucifixion, but was simply the result of the attachment to old and long-cherished pagan symbols, still strong in those who adopt the Christian name, while largely pagan in heart and feeling. This, and this only, is the origin of the worship of the cross."[680]

Be determined to worship God in truth

In conclusion, I certainly hope and pray you recognize the evidence against the use of this traditional cross is overwhelming. The historical facts demonstrate that the apostles and early Christians did not regard the impalement of Christ to be on a two-beamed cross, but rather on what the Bible truly says: an upright stake, tree, or pale.[681] These facts also illuminate that the cross was of pagan origins and adopted into the Christian congregations in the 4th century by Constantine—who at the same time—worshipped his pagan sun god, Sol Invictus.

"Only one such question need to be stated, and it is this: Is it likely that the Infinite Ruler of the universe, either at mid-day or at mid-night, went out of his way to induce a Sun-God worshipper who would not enter the Christian Church till a quarter of a century later and ere then was to become a murderer of innocent persons like the boy-Caesar Licinius, to adopt a symbol which he warranted would enable Constantine to lead on the Gauls to victory?"[682]

Using the cross in any element of our worship or even as an emblem of our affection for Jesus is simply not required; nor does Jehovah accept it. God through the Apostle Paul said: "We walk by faith, not by sight."[683] God also says at 2 Corinthians 6:14–16 "Do not form an unequal partnership with unbelievers, for what does virtue and lawlessness have in common? and how could light and darkness share anything together? What harmony do you think there could be between Christ and the Devil? So what partnership could there be between a believer and an unbeliever? What could the Most Holy room of the temple have in common with idols?"[684]

---

680 Wilkinson, Vol. 5, pp. 283, 284
681 Stauros, xylon
682 *The Non-Christian Cross*, Parsons, 1896, p. 72
683 2 Corinthians 5:7 *NSB*; cf. 4:18
684 *VC*

Certainly, the cross is something to be avoided simply because it is a lie. We must also keep in mind that those practicing and loving lies will not be a part of God's Kingdom; they will be destroyed forever.[685]

Let us not escape the following truth. When we "do not become involved with anything unclean"—this pagan practice of the cross along with other false ideas such as the trinity—then and only then; will God "accept you. I will be like a father to you, and you will be like sons and daughters to me, says Jehovah the Almighty."[686] Clearly then, each individual is accountable for himself to God.[687]

Having said all the above let us never fail to recognize this most important detail. It was the sacrificed life of Christ Jesus, his shed blood for you and me that all Christians should be focused on. It is not the stake or pale that died for us. It was God's "only begotten God-like one," Jesus Christ.[688]

The words of E.E. Cunnington are straight to the point: "There may, or may not, have been a second horizontal piece. To say that our Lord was 'crucified' on a single upright beam, the hands being brought together over the head, would be in perfect harmony with the gospel narrative; and does not affect in the least degree any article of faith."[689]

I have revealed truth to you in regards the real meaning of the unscriptural traditional cross. Now it is up to you to decide. Yet, my dear reader, I ask you to never forget one last scripture if you already are not aware of it. James 4:17 says: "Anyone, then, who knows the right thing to do and fails to do it, commits sin."[690]

Please, consider these biblical essentials by prayer and supplication to God, and he will make all matters straight for us. May all Christians continue to "Grow up in all *aspects* into Him who is the head, *even* Christ"[691] and "Increase in the knowledge (Greek: epignosis: full discernment, recognition) of God."[692]

---

685 Cf. Revelation 21:8, 27; 22:15; Psalm 5:6; Proverbs 6:16–19; John 8:44
686 2 Corinthians 6:17–18 *VC*; see also Revelation 18:2, 4 and 5
687 Cf. Galatians 6:4–5; Romans 14:4, 12; 2 Corinthians 5:10; Matthew 12:36
688 John 1:18 *NSB*; cf. 1 Peter 2:24; Isaiah 53:5, 12; Titus 2:13, 14; 2 Corinthians 5:14, 15, 21; Hebrews 9:28
689 *The New Testament (or Covenant) of Our Lord and Saviour Jesus Christ*, 1935, Appendix 12, p. 523
690 *NRSV*; cf. Luke 12:47; John 9:40, 41; James 1:22; Proverbs 26:12
691 Ephesians 4:15; *NASB*, emphasis theirs
692 Colossians 1:10; *NSB*, cf. 2 Timothy 3:16–17

978-0-595-44288-1
0-595-44288-9

Printed in the United States
105925LV00004B/91/A